Praises for *Ezekiel: The Watchman*

Jim Thompson's commentary on Ezekiel will strengthen, encourage, and fortify the faith of its readers. It is written from a dispensational perspective with a reverent view of Scripture as God's Word. It contains many sound, practical insights and applications, and it is written in an easy-to-understand style with a shepherd's heart that is concerned for his readers' sanctification and the glory of God. This commentary is suitable either for daily devotional reading, personal study, or interactive group study.

Dr. Thomas Stegall
Grace Gospel Press

A number of years ago, in a pastors' fellowship meeting, we were discussing our favorite books in the Bible. Jim Thompson surprised all of us when he said his favorite was the book of Ezekiel. I'd never heard anyone say that before. This commentary on Ezekiel represents the author's labor of love that has lasted many years. I highly recommend you purchase this book. You will be informed, inspired, and challenged—and who knows? Maybe Ezekiel will even become one of your favorite books in the Bible.

Les Lofquist, D.D.
Professor of Practical Theology
Shepherds Theological Seminary

Ezekiel's prophecy contributes so much to the Biblical narrative, injecting key ideas at a critical time in Israel's history. While commentaries handling Ezekiel's material can often make it difficult to connect with today's reader, Jim Thompson's approach shows the importance of Ezekiel's prophecies for every generation, by providing an accessible and practical engagement with Ezekiel. Thompson walks carefully through the text, but not in so technical a way as to confuse his readers. Thompson' direct connection with the reader helps encourage the reader that Ezekiel's prophecy is not beyond one's understanding, and that what God revealed through Ezekiel provides both motivation and strength for our daily lives.

Christopher Cone, Th.D, Ph.D, Ph.D
President and Research Professor
Vyrsity and Colorado Biblical University

Jim's heart for God, passion for ministry, and commitment to truth more than qualify him to write this powerful commentary on Ezekiel. This is a wonderful resource for any teacher or student who has a genuine appetite for the Word of God! I most admire Jim's Biblical fidelity and therefore I highly recommend this work because it will bless you greatly!

Timothy Q. Prewitt
General Director
World Reach, Inc.

Thompson's *Ezekiel the Watchman* provides a helpful tool for studying what for many is a confusing book of the Bible. While one may not agree with or not understand some of the details, overall, the exposition points the reader in the right direction, especially in its belief in a future for national Israel and the memorial nature of the millennial sacrifices. It is a Bible study resource worth having on the believer's bookshelf.

Dr. Mike Stallard,
Director of International Ministries
Friends of Israel

Dr. Jim Thompson's work on Ezekiel has inspired me to preach and teach this great Old Testament book very soon. Like many, I have never understood many of the types, symbols, and visions of this book. Dr. Thompson uses a literal, grammatical, contextual, and historical exegesis of this prophetic book to help the reader understand the point of each chapter. Not only did I learn much, but also was encouraged to literally interpret the Scripture unless it does not make sense. In the author's words, "If the literal sense makes sense, then seek no other sense."

Dr. Thompson handled chapter 38 of Ezekiel in a way that clarified many questions regarding the nations which would attack Israel and when this would take place. This book also serves to confirm that God is not finished with Israel as a nation, which gives great security to believers today. This commentary is not just about prophecy; it's about a believer's relationship and fellowship with the Lord today.

Dr. Jay Jackson
Pastor
McCalla Bible Church, AL

Ezekiel
The Watchman

Jim Thompson
Foreword by Gary Gilley

Grace Acres Press
Lee's Summit, Missouri

Grace Acres Press
Lee's Summit, MO 64082

© 2021 by Grace Acres Press. All rights reserved.

No part of this publication may be reproduced, stored in a retrieval system, or transmitted in any form or by any means, electronic, mechanical, photocopying, recording, scanning, or otherwise, except as permitted by law, without the prior written permission of the Publisher.

Grace Acres Press also publishes books in a variety of electronic formats. Some content that appears in print may not be available in electronic books.

Note: Unless otherwise indicated, all Bible quotations are from the *New King James Version* (NKJV).

Print ISBN: 978-1-60265-078-7

Library of Congress Control Number: 2020950609

Printed in United States of America
25 24 23 22 21   01 02 03 04 05 06 07 08

Foreword

When my friend Jim Thompson told me he was completing work on a commentary on Ezekiel, my first reaction was surprise. Of all the Old Testament books Ezekiel is arguably the most complicated, complex, and controversial and, in places, depressing. To write a useful commentary on this prophetic book would be time-consuming, labor-intensive and difficult. How could a busy pastor produce more than a cursory overview of such biblical literature? Then Pastor Thompson asked me if I would read his extensive manuscript, looking for biblical consistency and providing feedback regarding the theologically debated sections, of which there are more than a few. Having completed my assignment I was so impressed that I decided to study through the biblical book myself using *Ezekiel, the Watchman* as my guide. As I did so I realized just how thorough and valuable this commentary actually is.

It would be easy for students of Scripture to read through Ezekiel and gain little in the process. They most likely would be mystified by the visions (especially chapter one), bored and distressed by the many pronouncements of judgment, confused by the teaching of the New Covenant, perplexed by the many dramas and prophecies, and totally overwhelmed in their attempt to understand the closing chapters regarding the Messianic Temple, and the accompanying sacrificial system in the Millennial Kingdom age. Many, when they had completed their reading of Ezekiel, might scratch their heads, check the book off their tasks to be completed list, and vow not to return for many years. But this volume invites us to slow down, to look more closely and deeply, to appreciate and even enjoy the riches permeating every nook and cranny of this incredible Old Testament book.

Thompson writes both as a scholar and as a pastor, and this combination provides uniqueness and value to the work. As a scholar, Thompson leaves no stone unturned as he systematically analyzes the text verse by verse. He does not shy away from the difficult sections, yet is not overly dogmatic where the meaning of the passage is unclear. Using a grammatical-historical hermeneutic, Thompson interprets the prophecies literally, resisting allegorical meanings. He often states that "when the plain sense makes good sense, seek no other sense." This is wise advice. But Thompson is also a pastor and that shines through and enhances his exegesis. He is not detached from real people living normal lives, therefore he knows how to apply the biblical text to God's saints. This gives *Ezekiel, the Watchman* a personal touch that readers will appreciate. Thompson exemplifies well the pastor-scholar that the church of Christ most desperately needs today.

Few Christians would claim that Ezekiel is their favorite Old Testament book, but Jim Thompson's wonderful commentary just might change a few minds.

Gary E. Gilley,
Pastor, Southern View Chapel, Springfield, Illinois

Preface

No prophet of the Old Testament has had a greater impact on my life than Ezekiel. Writing this commentary is one of the most rewarding things I have yet accomplished in my ministry. I first began studying Ezekiel some thirty years ago and continue to learn more and more each time I read this prophet. I have taught this book in both women's and men's Bible studies and have preached sermons using insights and passages from Ezekiel. It was during those times that I realized not much has been written to help the average "person in the pew," especially from a dispensational point of view. Ezekiel is a complicated book, so I write this to aid the Sunday-school teacher or Bible study leader of the local church.

We can all find hope in the book of Ezekiel. Many times we are misunderstood by others, and in some cases are poorly treated. Ezekiel was asked to do some strange things, to give some very pointed messages, and to sacrifice his personal desires and pleasures so that the message of God could be given. No one today has had to humble himself to the degree that Ezekiel did. Ezekiel's very name, which means "God strengthens," should also encourage us.

I want to express my thanks to the people of Portage Bible Church in Indiana as well as Wilton Bible Baptist in Alabama for their patience as I wrote this commentary. Also, to my wife I give deep thanks for her support and understanding during the many hours I spent locked up in my study, and away from home. She is the one who encouraged me to write this commentary and prodded me to keep on keeping on.

If I have learned anything from Ezekiel (and I have learned much), it can be summarized in one statement: A teacher is only as effective as the people are teachable. This becomes the encouragement for all of us not to grow faint and give up. Remember the words of the apostle Paul to the Corinthians' church, *I planted, Apollos watered, but it is God who gives the increase* (1 Corinthians 3:6). If we are faithful to do what God has called us to do, He will be faithful to do what He has promised to do.

May God grant you His peace and grace as you study the book of Ezekiel and may you be strengthened in your walk and ministry.

Jim Thompson
Keep Looking Up
Colossians 3:1–4

Table Of Contents

Introduction 1
Ezekiel 1:1–28
      The Vision 3
Ezekiel 2:1–8
      The Messenger 9
Ezekiel 2:9–3:11
      The Message 13
Ezekiel 3:12–15
      The Motivation 17
Ezekiel 3:16–27
      The Watchman 19
Ezekiel 4:1–5:4
      Four Signs of Judgment 23
Ezekiel 5:5–17
      God's Judgment 31
Ezekiel 6:1–14
      God's Fury Against Idolatry 35
Ezekiel 7:1–27
      God's Fury is Complete 41
Ezekiel 8:1–11:25
      A Trip Back to Jerusalem 47
Ezekiel 12:1–28
      Acting Out the Exile 67
Ezekiel 13:1–23
      Warning Against False Prophets 75
Ezekiel 14:1–23
      Warning Addressed to the Elders 83
Ezekiel 15:1–17:24

    Parables Spoken Against Israel 91
Ezekiel 18:1–32
    Personal Responsibility 101
Ezekiel 19:1–14
    Lamentation for Judah.. 105
Ezekiel 20:1–24:27
    History of Corruption.. 109
Ezekiel 25:1–7
    Ammon 123
Ezekiel 25:8–11
    Moab 127
Ezekiel 25:12–14
    Edom 129
Ezekiel 25:15–17
    Philistia 131
Ezekiel 26:1–28:19
    Tyre 133
Ezekiel 28:20–24
    Sidon 161
Ezekiel 29:1–32:32
    Egypt 165
Ezekiel 33:1–34:31
    Blessings on Israel.. 193
Ezekiel 35:1–15
    The Destruction of Edom 217
Ezekiel 36:1–38
    The Restoration of Israel 223
Ezekiel 37:1–28
    The Regathering of Israel 235

Ezekiel 38:1–39:29
   The Northern Invasion 245
Ezekiel 40:1–43:27
   The Millennial Temple 263
Ezekiel 44:1–46:24
   Worship in the Millennial Temple 293
Ezekiel 47:1–12
   Waters of the Millennial Temple 315
Ezekiel 47:13–48:35
   The Land of the Millennial Temple........................319
Bibliography..327

Introduction

EZEKIEL: THE MAN

Ezekiel was a prophet of God during the time of the Babylonian captivity (Ezekiel 1:1). His name means "God strengthens." Some ninety-three times in this book God calls him *son of man*, which was the title Jesus used for Himself throughout the Gospels. Ezekiel was a priest (Ezekiel 1:3) but never served in that capacity, probably due to the captivity. From this, we can be assured that the reference to the *thirtieth year* found in Ezekiel 1:1 is a reference to Ezekiel's age.[1]

We know that his father's name was Buzi (Ezekiel 1:3) but we know very little of this man, since this verse is the only reference there is to him. Ezekiel was a contemporary of Jeremiah and Daniel; in fact, Daniel is mentioned as one of the righteous men in Ezekiel chapter 14. When Daniel was taken captive, he was taken to the court of the king (Daniel 1), whereas when Ezekiel was taken captive, he was taken to the rivers of Babylon (Ezekiel 1:3).

EZEKIEL: THE MINISTRY

Ezekiel has been called by some the most spiritual of all the prophets, simply because he dealt particularly with the Person of God.[2] As already noted, Ezekiel began his ministry at the age of thirty, which was the fifth year of King Jehoiachin's captivity. Jehoiachin came to the throne in December 597 BC, but after

---
[1] Read Numbers 4:3 for a clearer understanding of the age of a priest.
[2] J. Vernon McGee, *Ezekiel* (Nashville, TN: Thomas Nelson, 1991), viii.

three months he was taken captive by Nebuchadnezzar and deported to Babylon.

Ezekiel ministered to the captives during a time when many false prophets were proclaiming a quick return to Jerusalem. He had to counter both the false hope given by these prophets and the indifference and despondency that were prevalent in those days of sin and disaster. Among many discouragements that existed is that the people would not listen. Ezekiel resorted to new methods of teaching: instead of straightforward preaching, he would "act out" his sermons.[3]

Many have said that Ezekiel is the most difficult book to understand. John Calvin said: "If anyone asks whether the vision is lucid, I confess its obscurity, and that I can scarcely understand it."[4] Perhaps this is why, as H. A. Ironside states: "Of ALL the prophetic books, Ezekiel is the one that has been neglected most."[5]

EZEKIEL: THE MESSAGE

The message in the book of Ezekiel is of God's judgment upon the nation of Israel for their sins. The purpose was to bring them to repentance. We learn from Ezekiel that God's truth does not depend upon results. As you read this wonderful book, search your own heart, and ask God to reveal any unconfessed sin that would hinder you from fully serving the Lord with all the blessings God has to offer.

---

[3] Read Ezekiel 4 and 5 for an example of this.
[4] McGee, *Ezekiel*, 13.
[5] H. A. Ironside, *Ezekiel the Prophet* (Neptune, NJ: Loizeaux Brothers, 1949), xi.

Ezekiel 1:1–28

The Vision

Verses 1–3
Psalm 137:1 reads: *By the rivers of Babylon, there we sat down, yea, we wept when we remembered Zion.* The river Chebar was a branch off the Euphrates River that flowed to the east of Babylon. It was there that the heavens were opened, and Ezekiel saw visions of God. Two things should be especially noted in these verses. First is that the vision came from God (verse 1c); second is that Ezekiel was in the frame of mind to receive the message (compare Psalm 137:1).

Verse 4
We read of an approaching storm from the north. What is the significance of the north? Psalm 48:2, *Beautiful in elevation, the joy of the whole earth, is Mount Zion on the sides of the north, the city of the great King.* Isaiah 14:13, *For you have said in your heart: "I will ascend into heaven, I will exalt my throne above the stars of God; I will also sit on the mount of the congregation on the farthest sides of the north."* Psalm 75:6, *For exaltation comes neither from the east nor from the west nor from the south.*

The north seems to be the direction from which the throne comes. This storm, then, would represent a tremendous movement of the throne of God, especially as He comes to administer judgment upon the earth. In this storm we find a "great cloud" (mist) and fire within this cloud (flashing light). Hebrews 12:29 states that *our God is a consuming fire.* Remember Paul's conversion and the light that he saw (Acts 9)?

Feinberg states: "In this inaugural vision the prophet is seeking to picture something which far surpasses the power of any human language to express." His picturesque representation can be compared with Isaiah's vision (Isaiah 6) because it expresses the absolute sovereignty of God. The wind, cloud, and fire (verse 4) are all symbols of God's glory (Psalm 18:8–13; Habakkuk 3; Jeremiah 4:11–13).[6]

Verse 5a

In the fire come four living creatures. These creatures are identified in Ezekiel 10:15. From what we know about cherubs, they have special access to the throne. We know from Genesis 3:24 that God *placed cherubim at the east of the garden of Eden, and a flaming sword which turned every way, to guard the way to the tree of life.* Also, from Ezekiel 28:14, we can conclude that Satan was the *anointed cherub who covers.* One thing is for certain: These are not fictional characters that Ezekiel made up to scare Israel. This is a real vision, and these creatures are real creatures.

Verses 5b–21

Here we find a complete description of these four creatures. Their general appearance was that of the likeness of a man; however, we know that they were not human, as we have previously determined.

In verses 5 through 10, we read of Four Faces. Many have tried to figure out an exact meaning for these, or at least explain what the significance of these four faces is. Some suggest that they represent Christ as He is portrayed in the Gospels: His

---

[6] Charles Lee Feinberg, *The Prophecy of Ezekiel* (Chicago: Moody Press, 1969), 18.

kingship (Matthew and the lion), His servanthood (Mark and the ox), His humanity (Luke and the man), and finally, His deity (John and the eagle). Although this makes for good reading, it is probably not the case. It is more accurate to see these creatures as a representation of the highest form of God's creation, in that humankind represents the first or priority of all creatures, the lion represents the first or priority of the wild animals, the ox represents the strongest of all animals, and the eagle represents the first or priority of all birds.

Their movement is found in verses 11 through 14. They had wings that stretched upward, touched each other, and were used to cover their bodies. We are told that when they moved, they went straight, in either a forward or backward motion, but they did not make turns. They moved like lightning. The appearance was that of *torches going back and forth among the living creatures.* They must have moved very swiftly and precisely.

The wheels are found in verses 15–21. Again, we find it helpful to quote Feinberg: "Wheels, it has been suggested, mean primarily and naturally the revolution of time. The wheels connect the chariot with the earth. Nothing is stationary in God's universe; all is in motion and progression." [7] The implication from these verses is that the wheels were the creatures' means of transportation. *When the living creatures went, the wheels went beside them; and when the living creatures were lifted up from the earth, the wheels were lifted up* (v. 19).

---

[7] Feinberg, 19.

Verses 22–28

Strong's defines the firmament in verses 22 through 25 as "an expanse, i.e. the firmament or (apparently) visible arch of the sky."[8] We know from the text that this firmament is above the four living creatures and that a voice, probably that of the Lord God Himself, came from above the firmament, indicating that the firmament separated the chariot from the throne. Ironside refers to this firmament as a "heavenly dome."[9]

We see the throne in verses 26 through 28. It should be noted that five times the word *likeness* is used. It is hard to describe that which is indescribable, and the best Ezekiel could do was come up with similarities or metaphors. Ezekiel then notices what he describes as a likeness with the appearance of a man high above it. He goes on to describe this man as best he can. "As Ezekiel looked up, he saw the likeness of a Man upon that throne. This is a clear intimation that the Man of God's counsels, the Lord Jesus Christ, is ever to occupy that place of power and majesty. It was the preincarnate Christ that the prophet beheld, 'the likeness of a Man.'"[10]

APPLICATION

Many have avoided this great chapter in Ezekiel as much as they avoid the book of Revelation. Some ask, "What does any of this have to do with me?" As God commanded Ezekiel to warn Israel of impending judgment, we have the sole responsibility to warn people of God's judgment and wrath to come. This chapter

---

[8] *Biblesoft's New Exhaustive Strong's Numbers and Concordance* (1994/2003).
[9] Ironside, 12.
[10] Ironside, 13.

pictures for us an awesome, mighty, and majestic God and this is the same message we need for people to hear today. *Knowing, therefore, the terror of the Lord, we persuade men* (2 Corinthians 5:11).

Study Questions
1. Who do you know that needs to hear the Gospel message?
2. Do you share the bad news as well as the good news of the Gospel?

Ezekiel 2:1–8

The Messenger

EZEKIEL'S ATTENTION

Verses 1–2

The term *son of man* is a recurring title given to Ezekiel throughout this book. It is used almost 100 times, thereby emphasizing the humanity of Ezekiel and thus his total and utter dependence upon the Lord. He is commanded to stand before the Lord. Standing indicates a readiness to action, a willingness to obey and a desire to "get going." It was the Lord who set Ezekiel on his feet, again indicating the frailty of his humanity. Remember, when God calls one to do a specific task, He will give you the power to accomplish that task. The best way to accomplish that which God desires is first to realize we cannot accomplish anything with just our own strength. This is Ezekiel's calling. Maybe the reason for such a high dropout rate among full-time Christian workers is that they have never been called of God to the ministry.

EZEKIEL'S ASSIGNMENT

Verses 3–5

For most, this marching order would be extremely discouraging. Ezekiel is told to go to a people who are rebellious and come from a heritage of rebellious fathers. God describes them as *impudent* (hard of face) and *stubborn* (obstinate). In fact, the theme of rebellion occurs some eight times in chapters 2 and 3. They refused to admit their sin, they saw their captivity as a temporary setback, and they would not admit the truth about why they were in captivity. It is very difficult to reach a people who think they are okay and refuse to admit or even recognize that there is a problem. Ezekiel has his work cut out for him. The one thing they would know for certain is that a prophet has been among them.

EZEKIEL'S ASSURANCE

Verses 6–8
It is obvious from this text that Ezekiel was fearful of going to these people. Three times the Lord told him not to be afraid. The Lord also cautions Ezekiel not to be like those people. It is true that the messenger can kill the message: if Ezekiel were to be rebellious and refuse to obey, not only would Israel not hear the Word of the Lord, but Ezekiel would be guilty of being just like them.

APPLICATION

A great principle is to be learned here. We are to obey the Lord's command, no matter how much it may hurt and no matter who listens, because there is greater joy in obedience and serving the Lord. Results are not the reason we do what we do: it is faithfulness that God wants. 1 Corinthians 4:2: *Moreover it is required in stewards that one be found faithful.*

Study Questions
1. Do you pick and choose which biblical commands to obey?

2. Do you find some commands harder to obey than others? Name them.

Ezekiel 2:9–3:11

The Message

THE SCROLL

Verses 2:9–3:4

A scroll was given to Ezekiel. The Lord Himself unrolls the scroll, which contains words of lamentation, mourning, and woe. Ezekiel is told to "eat" the scroll. We see the same command given to the apostle John in the book of Revelation. Eating implies consumption and Ezekiel is commanded to consume the scroll. The scroll contained God's message of judgment and the fact that it was God's Word made it sweet in the mouth of Ezekiel. Sweetness comes from the source, not the content. According to Brownlee, "The prophet is told to gorge himself on the scroll in order that he may devour the whole of it. The indication that he must fill his stomach and intestines with it shows that this scroll is not to be thought of as a small, token-size manuscript. The total consumption of the roll also indicates his complete submission to the will of God."[11]

God then commands Ezekiel again to go and tell the house of Israel. But the emphasis must be placed upon the text *speak with My words to them*. Our message should never be our own message, but instead God's message spoken through us.

---

[11] William H. Brownlee, "Ezekiel 1–19," in *Word Biblical Commentary* vol. 28 (Waco, TX: Word Books, 1986), 32.

THE SPEECH

Verses 3:5–7
Ezekiel did not have to learn a new language; there was no barrier to overcome concerning the language. He is being sent to his own people, who should be familiar with him as he would be with them. The Lord makes it very plain that had He sent Ezekiel to a people of unfamiliar tongue, then his ministry would have been accepted, and they would have listened. But as it stands, Israel will not listen to Ezekiel because they will not listen to the Lord. Again, the reason is hard-heartedness and stubbornness. One cannot help but recall the words of our Lord in Mark 6:4: —*A prophet is not without honor except in his own country, among his own relatives, and in his own house.*

THE STRENGTH

Verses 3:8–11
Now is a good time to remember that Ezekiel's name means "God strengthens." Every time he heard his name, he must have been reminded of this great promise; God said He would make Ezekiel as hard-hearted toward not turning back as Israel was in turning away from their sins. God is telling Ezekiel not to let the rebellion or stubbornness of the house of Israel cause him to weaken or be afraid. This is not a time of discouragement but a time of determination. Flint represents the hardest stone in Israel. It was from this stone that they made their weapons (compare Joshua 5:2–3). It is not a matter of *if* Israel will be rebellious, it is a matter of *when* they will be rebellious, and Ezekiel needs to hunker down to do his God-assigned work. Ezekiel was to be obedient no matter what the results.

APPLICATION

Many today are results-oriented: if there are no results, we get discouraged and quit. The Lord is telling Ezekiel: do not look to results, look to obeying Me and you will be found faithful.

Study Questions
1. Are you willing to obey the Lord without ever seeing results?
2. Do you ever get discouraged if you do not see fruit from your labors?

Ezekiel 3:12–15

The Motivation

GOD'S SPIRIT

Verse 3:12
Ezekiel's motivation is the Spirit of the Lord and the throne-chariot. He is to take great courage in knowing that the Lord is with him.

ANGELIC SPIRITS

Verses 3:13–14a
Ezekiel is being transported by the throne-chariot described in chapter 1.

EZEKIEL'S SPIRIT

Verses 3:14b–15
Ezekiel went in anguish (*bitterness*) and anger (*heat*). Ezekiel, to be sure, had mixed emotions concerning the ministry that he was about to enter. This was not going to be easy. More than likely, he knew some of what had happened to Jeremiah and he might have been concerned; it is even more likely that he was angry and in anguish that God would even waste his time by sending him to these people. After all, why not just destroy them if they are that evil? The lesson here is that we should always obey the Lord, no matter how we feel about what the Lord has

called us to do. Our feelings should have nothing to do with our obedience.

This section ends with Ezekiel dwelling among the captives near Tel-Abib, which is by the River Chebar; he stayed there for seven days. The seven days indicate a period of mourning, for Ezekiel knew what was to befall the nation of Israel. They were not returning home soon; they must face tough times and Ezekiel was the one commissioned to relay God's message of judgment to them. Compare Genesis 50:10; 1 Samuel 31:13; Job 2:13.

Ezekiel 3:16–27

The Watchman

THE APPOINTMENT

Verses 3:16–17
When one studies any great battle of history, you find that it is the captain who fights until the bitter end. While others may retreat, the captain is the one who holds the front line and fights to the death. Like any great captain, Ezekiel is committed to standing firm for the truth of the Word of God and is holding the front lines.

In the days of Ezekiel, the cities were protected by great walls. Watchmen were posted on these walls to watch for approaching danger and to warn both those who were outside the protection of those walls as well as those who were inside. According to Isaiah 56:10–11, a watchman was a leader or shepherd. Jeremiah 6:17 tells us their purpose was to warn. Psalm 127:1 states: *Unless the LORD builds the house, they labor in vain who build it; unless the LORD guards the city, the watchman stays awake in vain.* To get a clear illustration of the work of a watchman, read 2 Samuel 18:24.

It was seven days after the initial vision that the Lord appointed Ezekiel to be the watchman over Israel. God had appointed Ezekiel to be a watchman for the purpose of warning Israel of their sin and their need to repent. "His function as a watchman over the city was preeminently to warn of impending disaster; the prophet as a watchman was to call to repentance and faith."[12]

THE ANNOUNCEMENT

Verses 3:18–19
We are given the details of Ezekiel's responsibilities to the unrighteous, here called the *wicked*. To refuse to warn not only meant their death, but also that Ezekiel would suffer a consequence as well. This speaks volumes to any pastor or church leader: they have a responsibility to warn those who are unsaved of the eternal damnation they face. It should be noted that the exhortation given here is to warn, not to achieve results. It is comparable to Christians today who are commanded to *preach the Gospel to every creature* (Mark 16:15)—but we are not commanded to focus on results, only the doing. The results are the Lord's work, not ours (1 Corinthians 3:6). The watchman who neglects this responsibility will be held accountable and, in a sense, be considered a manslayer.[13] On a positive note, verse 19 states that when a watchman delivers the message God has given him, the listener will still be held accountable, but the prophet will have delivered his own soul.

There is great responsibility upon the one who delivers the message of God. In 1 Corinthians 4:2 Paul tells us that it is required that a steward be found faithful. Ezekiel reminds us all too clearly of the consequences we face if we are not faithful to proclaim the message of hope and love from God. It was Robert

---

[12] Feinberg, 29.
[13] Feinberg, 29.

Murray McCheyne who said, "I preach as never to preach again; as a dying man to dying men."[14]

Verses 20–21
We are reminded that the righteous man also needs to be warned of his sin. These verses have been misinterpreted as referring to one who loses his salvation. Feinberg believes the man spoken of in Ezekiel to be one who is an unbeliever and only displaying acts of righteousness.[15] This may be hard to prove, as the text clearly draws a distinction between the unrighteous and the righteous. The Lord is teaching Ezekiel that no matter who is in sin, whether they belong to the family of God or not, Ezekiel is responsible to warn them and there is a consequence for those being warned as well as for those doing the warning. Hebrews 13:7 clearly states that preachers today are held accountable for what they do with the Word of God. They are clearly to warn the unsaved of eternal damnation (Romans 6:23) and the saved of future judgment (2 Corinthians 5:10).

THE ACTING OUT

Verses 3:22–23
Ezekiel is told to go into the plain and wait for the Lord to talk with him. Ezekiel, wasting no time, went immediately and there saw the glory of the Lord, just as he witnessed in chapter 1. His response was the same as that of everyone else when confronted with the glory of the Lord: he fell on his face.

---

[14] Quoted in Mark Rooker, "Ezekiel," in *Holman Old Testament Commentary* (Nashville, TN: Broadman & Holman, 2005), 55.

[15] Feinberg, 29-30.

Verses 24–25
Ezekiel is directed to shut himself inside his house and be bound by robes so that he could not move. He was to have no contact with his fellow man.

Verses 26–27
Ezekiel is speechless. He was to speak only when given permission by the Lord and he was to speak only the words of the Lord. God caused his tongue to cling to the roof of his mouth. Thus Ezekiel was to make sure it was God's message that he proclaimed. Bible teachers and preachers today are not free to say what they will, to embellish or add to the Word of God, but they are free to proclaim all that God has spoken. We are to preach the Word as Paul told Timothy in 2 Timothy 4:2.

Verse 27
This section ends by telling Ezekiel that whoever hears will hear and whoever refuses will refuse. While Ezekiel was tasked with speaking, the implication is that a person's reception or rejection of Ezekiel's message will be determined by that person's openness—or lack of it—to God. This message is similar to words found at the close of each of the letters to the seven churches in Revelation 2 and 3.

Ezekiel 4:1–5:4

Four Signs of Judgment

In this section, we find four signs given as a warning of judgment to the nation of Israel: the Brick Sign (4:1–3), the Bed Sign (4:4–8), the Bread Sign (4:9–17), and the Barber Sign (5:1–4). It is obvious from these verses that Israel has been a disappointment to the Lord, and that they have fallen into grave sin. God is using Ezekiel and his acting out of these judgments to get Israel's attention.

SIGN 1: THE BRICK SIGN

Verses 4:1–3
The *clay tablet* mentioned in verse 1 could be translated "tile" and would better be considered a brick. Ezekiel was to draw a picture of Jerusalem on this brick, so clearly this tablet represented Jerusalem, God's holy city.

Ezekiel is then told to *lay siege* to the tablet. To lay siege against a city was to stop the flow of supplies in and out of the city for the purpose of wearing down the inhabitants therein. The supplies would include not only food and water, but also the weapons necessary to fight the enemy.

Next, he was to *build a siege wall* or fort against the brick. This may have represented the walls around Jerusalem (compare 2 Kings 25:1).

Next, he was to *heap up a mound* or build a ramp (mount). This was a tactic of the enemy to approach a city. With every usual means of access denied, a ramp was built and used to get to the wall.

To *set camps* referred to the enemy surrounding the city and watching that nothing went in or out. Battering rams were used to beat the walls and break holes to gain access.

Next, Ezekiel is told to set an *iron plate* between him and the tablet. This was to represent a wall between God's people and God's prophet. This iron plate would have been like a griddle that was used to bake bread. Isaiah 59:2 states: *But your iniquities have separated you from your God; and your sins have hidden His face from you, so that He will not hear.* As the siege against Jerusalem continued, God's people would cry out for deliverance, but because of their unrepentant hearts, God would neither listen nor answer their prayers. God makes it perfectly clear to Ezekiel that this was to be a sign of coming things.

SIGN 2: THE BED SIGN

Verses 4:4–6
As if playing with bricks in the middle of the road in front of all Israel was not enough to humiliate the prophet, God now instructs him to lie on his side. First, he is to lie on his left side. It is unclear exactly how he was to lay the iniquity of the house of Israel upon himself. By lying on his left side with his head pointed to the west, the direction of Israel, he would have been facing north. The kingdom of Israel was north and the number of days he was to lie on his left side represented the number of years of Israel's sin, that being 390 days.

After the 390 days, Ezekiel was to turn over and lie on his right side. This time, with his head pointing to the west, his face would be looking to the south. The southern kingdom was Judah, so 40 days would represent the number of years of the iniquity of the house of Judah.

In both cases, the days represent the number of years of sin, a day each for a year of sin. Rooker writes: "There is no consensus among scholars as to the meaning of these numbers. The combination of these numbers equals 430, the number of years the Israelites were in captivity in Egypt (Exodus 12:40). This association may be of significance since the future deliverance from Babylon (Ezekiel 20:35) is compared to the exodus from Egypt."[16]

Verse 4:7

Ezekiel is told to uncover his arm. Undoubtedly, this was to represent preparation for battle. This would be equivalent to a common phrase used today, "Let's roll up our sleeves and get to work." Compare Isaiah 52:10.

Verse 4:8

This speaks of the confinement of the siege. Given that the first sign, the Brick Sign, visualized the coming siege and the last two signs represent the result of the siege, this sign—the Bed Sign—represents the siege itself. Feinberg writes: "In order to show the restricting and confining nature of the exile, the Lord was said to lay bands on the prophet to hinder this movement from one side to the other until he had completed the allotted time for each part of the nation."[17]

---

[16] Rooker, 56-57.
[17] Feinberg, 34.

SIGN 3: THE BREAD SIGN

Verses 4:9–10
The third sign is referred to as the Bread Sign. Here, Ezekiel was told to make bread. Feinberg writes: "It is not necessary to assume that Ezekiel was in the prone position day and night. It was doubtless part of each day, if he were to prepare his food as stated later in this chapter."[18]

The ingredients for making this bread were grains available in Ezekiel's day (compare 2 Samuel 17:27–29). Barley was considered a poor man's grain. Lentils, a member of the pea family, were edible seeds, normally boiled to produce red pottage (compare Genesis 25:31–34). Millet was a cultivated grass, a small grain that was used like cereal. Spelt, sometimes called fitches, is considered by many to be what we know as rye. It was like wheat with grain that did not thresh free of the chaff. These were not common ingredients for making bread. In fact, some have called this bread "polluted bread." Ezekiel's use and mixing together of these grains probably represents famine or a condition of scarcity of food, which was the condition of Judah.

Ezekiel was to ration the bread by weight. He could eat twenty shekels of bread a day. Since there were large and small shekels, it is hard to be dogmatic as to the exact amounts, but if you use the common measure, in which one shekel equals about half an ounce, then Ezekiel's portion would have been approximately ten ounces of bread a day.

---

[18] Feinberg, 34.

Verse 4:11

Ezekiel could drink water, but again only in limited portions. He was only allowed to drink the *sixth part of a hin.* A hin equaled approximately 1.7 gallons, so one-sixth of that is close to one quart of water. Ezekiel is then instructed to cook and eat this bread in the sight of all the people. Worse yet, he is to use human waste to fuel the fire used to cook the bread. This seems rather disgusting, but verse 13 makes the point of all this very clear: the purpose is to show the defilement of Israel and their impurities. God's disgust for sin and the people who indulge themselves in sin is clear. "The horrors of the siege and exile could not be more vividly depicted. The state of exile itself was defiling, as seen in Amos 7:17. God wanted to impress them with the pollution and uncleanness of idolatrous worship and practices. Idolatry is so vile to God's sight that nothing could be too polluted to portray its essential nature before a thrice holy God."[19]

Verses 4:12–14

We now have, for the first time, Ezekiel objecting to one of God's instructions. He has been asked to play with bricks in the middle of the road, he has been asked to lie on either side for a period of time and then to bake bread out of a strange mixture, and he was to do this in the sight of all the people. He has not refused to do any of these things. But here we find him objecting.

His objection does not come from performing humiliating acts, but from his own personal desire to stay holy and pure before the Lord. His reasoning is found in verse 14, and clearly he is concerned only with his relationship with the Lord. He is

---

[19] Feinberg, 35.

not refusing to do this out of rebellion, but out of a desire to remain pure. He was a priest and had never eaten anything unclean (compare Leviticus 22:8 and Deuteronomy 23:12–14).

Verses 4:15–17
The Lord graciously conceded to Ezekiel's concerns: God allows him to use cow dung instead of human waste for fuel. The food and water were to be rationed out as in a famine condition and verse 17 makes it perfectly clear that all of this was done because of (and to illustrate) Israel's sin. Scriptures are clear that God hates sin (compare Proverbs 6:16–19), and when sin is present, God will chasten his children as a father chastens his own son (Hebrews 12:5–11).

SIGN 4: THE BARBER SIGN

Verse 5:1
Of all the signs Ezekiel was to perform, this may be the most humiliating. He is told to shave his hair and his beard, weigh the hair, and then divide it. Think for a moment about the people watching this. They must have been thinking that this man had gone mad. Who does this? This puts new meaning to drama in our churches.

It should be noted at this point that Ezekiel was told to do this with a sword, not a knife. The sword represented the enemy that would come and take Israel captive. Rooker writes: "If the sign of the tablet represented the fact of the siege, the sign of lying on the side represented the duration, and the sign of the siege diet represented the severity, this sign probably focused on the results of the siege."[20]

Verses 5:2–4
Ezekiel was to divide his shaven hair into three parts. One-third was to be burned amid the city, representing those who died by fire within the city walls. One-third was to be cut to shreds, representing those who died by the sword. One-third was to be scattered in the wind, representing the dispersion of the nation.

There was a ray of hope in all of this, in that Ezekiel was to take a few strands of his hair and bind them in the edge of his garment. Although even some of these strands were to be burned, not all were to be destroyed. This is God being faithful to His promise that He would always preserve a remnant (compare Zechariah 13:8–9). Having some of these preserved strands perish in the fire reminds Ezekiel that even the remnant was to undergo further trials and sufferings. Thus, performing these things to his hair was symbolic of what God would do to the inhabitants of Jerusalem and Judah.

APPLICATION

Again, we need to be reminded of the great truth found in Hebrews 12:29, *For our God is a consuming fire.*

It is obvious to all who read chapters 4 and 5 that service to God may require the extraordinary. There may be times when God calls upon us to do seemingly strange things, but regardless of what God asks, we are to be faithful and obedient at all costs.

---

[20] Rooker, 58.

There is nothing that God requires from us that we should not be willing to do.

Study Questions
1. Is there anything you are not willing to do for the Lord?
2. Are you more concerned about your reputation before God or your reputation before man?

Ezekiel 5:5–17

God's Judgment

ISRAEL'S PLACE AMONG THE NATIONS

Verse 5
Jerusalem was God's chosen city and His special presence resided there. She held an exalted position among the nations. Some think this may refer to its geographically central position in the Middle East.

ISRAEL'S PLEASURE IN SINNING

Verses 6–7
Here wickedness is described as rebellious against the judgments of God and as more than that of the pagan nations around her. The reason for this strict judgment is found in the reality that at least the pagan nations have been faithful and loyal to their gods, which is something that Israel cannot say of herself. Israel may in fact be worse: they are the recipient of God's law, the dwelling place of God's glory, and the object of His great love, and still they rebelled and sinned. Their sin is described as multiplied disobedience: they have not observed God's statutes, they have not kept God's judgments, and in fact, they could not even obey the judgments of the nations that surrounded them. They were, in every sense of the word, a pathetic people, facing discipline from God. She was to have been

the envy of her neighbors but has become a nation to be pitied. "How those with high and ample privilege in spiritual matters need to take these words to heart! Israel, endowed with position and privilege, became turbulent; they raged in their opposition against God. God's honor must be and will be vindicated throughout."[21]

GOD'S PROMISE OF JUDGMENT EXPLAINED

Verse 8
God's judgment is to be public. Israel will be set up as an example to all who desire to sin against God.

Verse 9
God's judgment is to be personal. God's judgment will be unique to Israel and affect only Israel. The promise is that God will not do to another what He is about to do to His special people.

Verse 10
The nation of Israel had become pathetic. Israel would resort to cannibalism: fathers would eat their sons and sons would eat their fathers. One cannot imagine the depths of their sin and the detestable acts in which they were involved (compare Lamentations 4:10 and Jeremiah 19:9).

Verse 11
The nation of Israel had become pitiless. It is a horrible thing to lose the pity of God. Here is the first reference to the defilement of the temple. Some consider this the greatest sin that Israel will

---

[21] Feinberg, 39.

have committed. Refer to chapter 8 for a detailed description of how Israel defiled God's temple.

Verse 12
God's judgment is painful. One needs to refer to chapter 4 and read again about the Barber Sign. This verse further explains the details of that sign. The four well-known judgments are mentioned: pestilence, famine, sword, and scattering; these would be the ultimate judgments from God.

Verse 13
God's judgment is passionate. A reference is made to God's zeal, calling it *My anger* and *My fury.* Here, a stated purpose for His judgments is given: *and they shall know that I, the LORD, have spoken it.*

Verses 14–15
The nation is a portrait on display and the pagan nations will stand amazed as they watch God judge His people. As a consequence, Israel will be lessened in the sight of all those who witness her destruction. A nation once to be feared is now a nation to be pitied. God will make her a waste and bring upon her disgrace and revilement among the other nations. The Lord makes it perfectly clear that this judgment comes from His anger. Hebrews 10:31 states, *It is a fearful thing to fall into the hands of the living God.*

Verses 16–17
God's judgment is perilous. It is swift and complete, leaving no stone unturned. This chapter ends with the daunting words: *I, the LORD, have spoken.* We have seen this phrase three times

now, which indicates the Lord's desire for us to know that these really are His words and not something that Ezekiel invented. The message to Israel is that Ezekiel is just relaying God's message—and that when God speaks, they would do well to humble themselves in the sight of God. 2 Chronicles 7:14 states: *If My people who are called by My name will humble themselves, and pray and seek My face, and turn from their wicked ways, then I will hear from heaven, and will forgive their sin and heal their land.*

APPLICATION

The lessons of chapter 5 are clear, precise, and to the point. God will judge his people if they remain disobedient. There are obvious consequences to our sin, and obedience to God requires a complete commitment to His Word. God will warn us, but after so doing, if we refuse to heed that warning, God will judge. Be careful in your walk with God to do all He requires and to be holy as He is holy (compare 1 Peter 1:15–16).

Study Questions
1. Do you believe that seeking forgiveness for your sin always removes the consequences?
2. Explain in your own words 2 Corinthians 5:10.

Ezekiel 6:1–14

God's Fury Against Idolatry

"The prophecies of chapters six and seven are related in that they elaborate on the symbolism of chapter five. However, each chapter has its distinct message and emphasis. With denunciation after denunciation Ezekiel strove to move the heart of the nation to the Lord. Whether they would hear or refuse, they had to know there was a prophet in Israel as the mouthpiece of the Lord."[22]

THE COMMAND TO PROPHESY

Verses 1–2

Verse 1 of chapter 6 is the same as verse 1 of chapter 7. Again, these words clearly explain that Ezekiel is not making this stuff up, but that in truth, God is speaking.

Ezekiel is told here to speak out against Israel. To *set your face* is an expression that means to move toward with determination, or to have a purpose. Do not back down is the implication. Ezekiel is fully aware of Israel's history in treating former prophets. There is good cause for God to remind Ezekiel that regardless of what happened previously, he must stay true, stay bold, and speak with firm conviction. Psalm 118:6 states: *The LORD is on my side; I will not fear. What can man do to me?*

---

[22] Feinberg, 40.

Bible teachers today would do well to heed this warning. We have too many who are merely "tickling ears" because they fear rejection or want a large church; they are willing to say or do anything to accomplish these worldly goals.

THE CONTENT OF THE PROPHECY

Verse 3
Four specific areas that God will destroy are mentioned. God says He will destroy the *high places:* places of worship that were generally up on a mountain, so as to bring worshippers closer to God or to their people's other gods. High places were primarily associated with pagan worship, and it was in these high places where Israel would worship the idols of the pagan nations. The Old Testament Scriptures are replete with commands to destroy high places. Compare Numbers 33:52, Deuteronomy 12:2–14, 2 Kings 18:4, and 2 Kings 21:10–15.

Verse 4
God says He will destroy the *altars*. These were the places where animals would be sacrificed to the gods. There were also incense altars, used for offering incense to the gods. God's promise is to make these *desolate* (to devastate or make waste) and to *destroy* (crush) them. When God slays the men who worship at these altars, their bodies will lie before the images.

Verse 5
God says He will destroy the worshippers and *scatter their bones*. This is reminiscent of God's words in Psalm 53:5, *There they are in great fear where no fear was, for God has scattered the bones of him who encamps against you; you have put them to shame,*

because God has despised them. Their place of sin will become their place of death and burial.

Verses 6–7
God says He will destroy the *cities*. Much is repeated here from the preceding verses, but this reiteration emphasizes the destruction of the sinner and his place of worship. God does not tolerate sin in His people. Notice that even their works will be abolished. When God destroys the altars, the images, the cities, and the worshippers, there is nothing left that can be done.

Yet all of this is for one purpose and one purpose only: *you shall know that I am the Lord*. This is all God wants, to be acknowledge as God and worshipped as God. Jesus told the woman at the well in John 4 that God seeks such to worship Him. In giving the Ten Commandments to Moses, God said that He was a jealous God and that we are to worship no one or thing but Him. Some eleven times in the Old Testament God refers to Himself as a jealous God, and sixty-five times the phrase *they shall know that I am God* is used.

Israel had a hard time learning this lesson, yet even today, some 2,500-plus years later, we still struggle with this very thing. Many today have their idols and God is still crying out to be worshipped. He is not willing to share His glory with anyone else. He must be acknowledged as the only true and living God!

Verses 8–10
Even in all of this, during God's anger against idolatry, His mercy is still evident. God promises to leave a remnant. Feinberg puts it best, "Those who complain loudly of the severity of the dealings of God in the Old Testament period fail to take into sufficient account how the doctrine of the remnant

underlines the mercy of God in spite of man's failure."[23] God has always promised to preserve Israel, and no matter how evil or sinful the nation has been or is presently, God has promised to never bring them to complete destruction or end.

Verses 11–12

In these verses we find some interesting instructions to Ezekiel. As if it were not enough to play with bricks, lie on his side, make bread, or shave his head, now he is instructed to go into a rage. God commands Ezekiel to *pound* (strike) his fists, *stamp his feet*, and to cry out against the sin of Israel. The punishment will manifest itself in the forms of the *sword, famine,* and *pestilence*. Rooker suggests that this trilogy resulted from violating God's law and may be representative of all the punishments listed in the curse sections of the Mosaic Law. He also writes that these three suggest the comprehensive nature of God's judgment.[24]

Verses 13–14

The remaining verses in this chapter show the absolute completion of God's destruction. Once again, we are told that all of this serves only one purpose: so that all will know that God is the LORD. The main concern here is the vindication of God and His name. It was Ezekiel's love for God and for His truth that motivated him to serve and to be so bold in proclaiming such a damning message.

The judgment of God will be severe upon the land in that the land will become more *desolate* (devastated or wasted) than that of the *Diblah*. It is unclear just exactly what location is referred to by this name. Some have suggested that it is a

---

[23] Feinberg, 41.
[24] Rooker, 72.

reference to Diblathaim, mentioned in Numbers 33:46–47, which is located on the eastern border of Moab. Still others suggest that the name is not Diblah but Riblah; if this is correct, then it could be a reference to a place just north, at the entrance to Hamath on the Orontes River, as found in 2 Kings 23:33 and Jeremiah 52:9. Regardless of the name, Ezekiel is making a reference to all the wilderness from the south to the north, a distance equivalent to the distance from Dan to Beersheba. The point is that God's judgment will be devastating and cause the land to become a wasteland.

Again, the emphasis remains on the purpose of God's judgment: *they shall know that I am the LORD.*

Ezekiel 7:1–27

God's Fury is Complete

Verses 1–2
At the beginning of chapter 7 we have God's declaration that the end has come. The term *end* is used five times in this section (compare Amos 8:2). *End* is defined as extremity or borders and is a reference to limits. One gets the sense that God's patience has reached its limits and the entire land of Israel is about to experience God's swift judgment. In referencing the *four corners of the land*, it is understood that no part of the land will be left untouched.

Verses 3–5
God's wrath is in direct proportion to sin. The punishment will fit the crime. These verses are basically repeated in verses 8 and 9. The repetition is given for emphasis. God's pity is now gone, His mercy is limited, and His justice has come into action. Anyone reading this cannot come away believing that our God is all love with no justice. The love of God is but one of His characteristics, and His justice is not something that can be overlooked or put aside. If fact, it is His love that drives His justice. He only desires His people to know Him for who He really is. But make no mistake, His wrath will spare no one who is in sin.

Verses 6–7

God's judgment against sin as well as against the sinner will be total, complete, and devastating. This judgment is pictured as if it were asleep and suddenly awakened. The King James version translates this as *it watcheth for thee*, which has the meaning of lying in wait. This speaks of the certainty of the judgment. Ezekiel describes this as a time of *doom*, better translated as *destruction*. This is a day when the cry of rejoicing will turn into a cry of distress and agony. A state of panic will set in and there will be much sorrow.

Verses 8–9

God promises accomplishment. Notice the absolute language in the text: *I will soon pour out My fury, I will judge you, I will repay, My eye will not spare, nor will I have pity.* I think the point is clear. There is no question here in this text: judgment is coming and there is nothing that can be done to stop it, short of repentance. When God strikes, they will know it is God (compare 2 Corinthians 5:11 and Hebrews 12:28–29).

Verses 10–13

The coming judgment is compared to a budding tree. Two things come to mind: Numbers 17 and the budding of Aaron's rod, and Jeremiah 1:11–12 with the almond tree in blossom. This suggests an interpretation that would refer to the leadership of Israel as being responsible. Although this is a distinct possibility, John MacArthur believes that verse 11 explains verse 10 and that the phrase *violence had grown up into a rod of wickedness* likely refers to Nebuchadnezzar, the "instrument of God's vengeance" (compare Isaiah 10:5; Jeremiah 51:20).[25] It seems, at least to this author, that it is best to accept the latter view, as it would make sense considering what we know of history. By referencing pride, the meaning appears to be that Israel, especially her leadership, had become so arrogant in their sin, they thought they were beyond God's judgment. As a result of this judgment, commercial trade will suffer. The buyer as well as the seller will be affected. All property rights will vanish. There will be no reason to have joy. According to Leviticus 25:10; 13–17, in the year of jubilee, ownership of real property would revert to the original owners, but because of sin, things will not be normal. There will be no year of jubilee.

Verses 14–16
Israel will be unable to stand and fight for what is right. God's wrath will cause the Jews to be unable to defend themselves. No one will escape the wrath of God. They will be forced to flee to the mountains and become as the *doves of the valleys.* "The pitiful wail of those hiding in the mountains, who were weeping over their sins, and material losses, would sound like mourning doves."[26]

Verses 17–23
Israel's helplessness is described. *Horror* or terror will so grip them that they will be utterly defenseless. Verse 18 describes the signs of mourning that were associated with the pagans. *Sackcloth, horror, shame,* and *baldness* all were outward

---

[25] John MacArthur, *The MacArthur Study Bible* (Nashville, TN: Word Bibles, 1997), 1160.
[26] Charles Dyer, "Ezekiel," in *The Bible Knowledge Commentary* (Wheaton: Victor Books, 1986), 1241.

expressions of grief and pain (compare Deuteronomy 14:1–2). What is described here is a life of misery. Nothing will be of use to them or satisfy them. Comfort and fulfillment will be far away. Their money will be useless, and they will not have the food to sate their hunger—all because of their sin and refusal to repent. Silver and gold will not have the purchasing power they once enjoyed. One gets the impression that they may be trying to "buy off" God. Even the Temple will be destroyed, which surprises many. This place has always been precious to God and many thought He would not destroy it, but even this does not escape His judgment. Their sin has become so deep that they took the articles from the temple and fashioned idols from them. Is it any wonder that God therefore chooses to destroy this Temple? It has lost its importance and is no longer sacred to the people of God. "God has no desire to keep mere outward worship in operation as long as such worship is accompanied with and encrusted over by idolatries that profane the very essence of that worship. Therefore, we read repeatedly that all would be profaned."[27]

Verses 24–26

A reference to Babylon and King Nebuchadnezzar can be found in the phrase *the worst of the Gentiles.* This is an obvious reference to the invasion and captivity by the Babylonians. King Nebuchadnezzar will be ruthless, swift, and unmerciful to Israel. Peace will be sought but will not be found. Israel felt like she was invincible, but when sin goes unchecked and multiplies out of control, there is no telling what will happen. Israel will be in a desperate situation; they will not even be able to find an

---

[27] Feinberg, 47.

answer from God's spokesmen, *the prophets, the priest, or the elders.*

Verse 27

Some seem to think that the *prince* is a reference to Zedekiah, who was still in Jerusalem at that point, and that the *king* is a reference to Jehoiachin, who was in Babylon with the captives. Zedekiah was a pawn of Nebuchadnezzar and would eventually betray the King of Babylon, only to have his eyes put out and sent to Babylon into exile. Zedekiah is discussed in more detail in chapter 12.

One gets a sense of the Jews' deep despair from the phrase *and the hands of the common people will tremble.* But God makes it perfectly clear that He will only judge them according to what they deserve. The problem is that they are so deeply entrenched in sin that God's judgment will be extremely destructive and devastate the nation. Again, God reminds them that He only accomplishes what He accomplishes so that they may know He is God.

How do we avoid being on the wrong end of God's anger? Psalm 81:13–16 is a great reminder of God's mercy: *Oh, that My people would listen to Me, that Israel would walk in My ways! I would soon subdue their enemies and turn My hand against their adversaries. The haters of the LORD would pretend submission to Him, but their fate would endure forever. He would have fed them also with the finest of wheat; and with honey from the rock I would have satisfied you.*

APPLICATION

Chapter 7 is a great reminder that sin is a personal affront to God. The Scriptures are clear in that pride is the root of all sin. *Pride goes before destruction, and a haughty spirit before a fall* (Proverbs 16:18). When there is no repentance, God's judgment is a certainty. He will never punish us for what we do not deserve, but his judgment will always fit the "crime." We should not allow our sin to drag us deep into despair and to the wrong side of God: repent and restore your relationship with God.

Study Questions
1. Do you allow your past sin to affect your future ministry?
2. Do you attempt to justify your sin?

Ezekiel 8:1–11:25

A Trip Back to Jerusalem

Chapters 8 through 11 should be considered as one section. In yet another vision received by the Lord, Ezekiel is transported back to Jerusalem where he is shown some horrific details of the depth of Israel's idolatry. In chapter 8 we see the sin of the people; chapter 9 shows the slaughter of the people; chapter 10 gives us a glimpse of the glory of God; and finally, in chapter 11, we hear the sentence pronounced upon the leaders of Israel.

SIN OF THE PEOPLE
EZEKIEL 8

Verses 1–2
One cannot come away from studying the Word of God without understanding that our relationship with God is truly the only relationship that matters and that all other relationships hinge upon this. The first of the Ten Commandments expresses this great truth: *You shall have no other gods before me* (Exodus 20:3). Obedience to this one commandment alone causes everything else to fall into place spiritually, and the neglect or violation of it brings on the judgment of God's wrath. The sin of Israel was idolatry and this sin affected everything else that Israel was or did.

Ezekiel chapter 8 opens with the statement: *sixth year, in the sixth month, on the fifth day of the month.* This date gives us fourteen months from the first vision of chapter 1. We find Ezekiel sitting in his house with the leadership of Judah when he receives this vision. We are not told why they are meeting, but the discussion was probably concerning the condition of Israel and what solutions, if any, there were. Brownlee may have the best observation: "[T]hese elders have come to report concerning the apostate ceremonies about to be performed in the temple and are thus antithetical in character to the elders of Israel, who are represented as apostate (8:10)."[28] It is at this time that Ezekiel sees the appearance of a man expressed in the same manner as describing the glory of the Lord; compare Ezekiel 1:26–28.

Verses 3–4

We are given the details of Ezekiel's transportation back to Jerusalem. How Ezekiel was transported will probably continue to be debated for years to come, but the phrases *brought me in visions of God* and *like the vision that I saw* give us a clear understanding that this was more of a vision than an actual physical transportation (compare Ezekiel 11:24). Nowhere else in Scriptures do we read *took me by a lock of my hair*. Rather than getting caught up with trying to identify this as a physical or spiritual transportation, it is best to focus upon what Ezekiel saw: after all, this is the point of the text. "What follows in the chapter is not a description of deeds done sometime in Israel's past but a retrospective survey of Israel's spiritual condition. Ezekiel saw conditions as they existed in his day at that very hour."[29]

---

[28] Brownlee, 128.
[29] Feinberg, 50.

There is a progression as to the places he is taken. Ezekiel is taken from Babylon to Jerusalem, *to the door of the north gate of the inner court.* Here is where he sees the *image of jealousy*, a reference to an idol set within the temple confines. The word translated *image* (Hebrew "semel") occurs in only two other Old Testament passages, (Deuteronomy 4:16 and 2 Chronicles 33:7, 15) and in all cases refers to the image or likeness of a pagan god. The text in Ezekiel makes it very clear that this image provoked the Lord to jealousy. God has made it known that He is a jealous God and anything in our lives that replaces the preeminence the Lord deserves amounts to nothing less than an idol and for that God is jealous. Compare Exodus 20:5, 34:14; Deuteronomy 4:24, 5:9, 6:15; Nahum 1:2.

Verses 5–6
Ezekiel is told to look toward the north, observe the *Altar Gate* and notice the *great abominations* that are being committed by the house of Israel. Ezekiel is being told to watch these things as they are happening. These abominations were of such great nature that they were driving away the very presence of God. It is hard to imagine that even greater abominations could occur, but that is exactly the case.

Verses 7–12
What we read next is even more unimaginable. We not only find more idol worship, but also that the very leaders of Israel are ones guilty of it. We have now progressed from the Altar Gate to the Door of the Court. In the wall was a hole and Ezekiel was instructed to begin digging at the hole; upon doing so, he discovered the door. This door gave him access into the temple and what he saw must have shocked him tremendously. Upon

the walls of the temple were portrayed images of all the pagan gods, described as *every sort of creeping thing, abominable beasts, and all the idols of the house of Israel.* What would have to have been even more disturbing was that Ezekiel then witnessed the seventy elders paying homage to these gods. Feinberg observes: "There is no question that such practices were carried on by more than one nation of antiquity, but the consensus of interpreters is that these were the animal cults of Egypt." [30] Specifically mentioned is *Jaazaniah, the son of Shaphan* (compare 2 Kings 25:23). He is mentioned as the probable leader of the seventy elders and even more interesting is the fact that his name means "The Lord hears," which casts the whole scene in an ironic light.

These seventy elders knew their deeds were in direct disobedience to God, for we see them worshipping these gods in the dark, obviously so as to hide their actions. The phrase *every man in the room of his idols* could indicate that not only had they carved out the gods on the walls of the temple, but they also had these images in their own private homes. This would only compound the depth of the sin of these men.

Verses 13–14
Ezekiel is instructed to progress even further. He moves toward *the door of the north gate* and there he finds that the women are also involved in idol worship. They are *weeping for Tammuz,* a Sumerian fertility god. This is the only passage we have that gives evidence that Israel was practicing this custom.

---

[30] Feinberg, 50.

Verses 15–18

At this point one might think that it could not get any worse, but God informs Ezekiel that he is about to witness even greater abominations. As if portraying the idols on the walls of the temple; the seventy elders leading the people in idol worship, even to the point where they had altars set up in their own homes; and the women being emotionally involved were not bad or evil enough, now he sees people who have actually turned their backs on God. They are not just worshipping these pagan gods, but literally turning their backs by facing east to worship.

We now find Ezekiel at the *inner court of the LORD's house.* The exact location is at *the door of the temple of the LORD, between the porch and the altar.* Here he finds twenty-five men worshipping the sun. This is an act of contempt to a holy, almighty majestic God. Only the priest had access to this location. Joel 2:17 reads: *Let the priests, who minister to the Lord, weep between the porch and the altar.*

In addition to all of this, they had *filled the land with violence and provoked the Lord to anger.* An interesting phrase is found in verse 17: *they put the branch to their nose.* This phrase indicates their contempt. The Septuagint (Greek translation of the Old Testament) gives us a clear meaning of this phrase: *and behold, these are as scorners.* By doing these abominations, they were mocking the very God Who provided for them and Who truly loved them.

APPLICATION

Chapter 8 gives us a more comprehensive picture of the depth of the idolatry into which Israel had fallen than any other chapter in the Bible. No matter what one may think, these were horrific acts that constitute a slap in very face of God. One can only imagine how a nation that has been so cared for, so loved, and so protected could turn their backs on the only One Who truly knew them. What must the other nations think? If we learn anything from this account (and there is much to learn), it is that our actions reveal the true nature of our relationship with God. Proverbs 4:23 states this very clearly: *Keep your heart with all diligence, for out of it spring the issues of life.* Oh, how hideous to have a heart so evil that it causes God to become pitiless toward us and no longer listen to our cries!

Study Questions
1. Can you name some idols that exist today?
2. Can you name the idols of your heart?

EZEKIEL 9
SLAUGHTER OF THE PEOPLE

Verses 1–2
Chapter 8 ends with a promise which we see fulfilled in chapter 9. These opening verses introduce us to six men, each holding a *battle-axe*, and another man described as *clothed with linen* with a *writer's inkhorn* at his side. Other translations use "slaughter weapon" or "shattering weapon" rather than battle-axe. Many agree that the one calling out these men, who is further described at the end of verse 2, is the Lord Himself. These men come from the *direction of the upper gate,* which is the place where the *image of jealousy* was found in chapter 8. Rooker believes the six to be guards of the city and the one to be a divine messenger. He writes, "Linen, which was worn by divine messengers (Daniel 10:5; Revelation 15:6) and priests (Exodus

28:42), is symbolic of God's character and holiness and contrasts with the behavior of the Israelites in Ezekiel 8."[31] It is obvious from this text that the one man is superior to the other six men, so the question begs to be asked: who is this one man? Some think this could be a reference to Gabriel; as noted earlier, Rooker holds this view. Still others believe this to be the preincarnate Christ, that is, Christ Himself appearing as a man before His incarnation. This would be the view of Feinberg: "From His clothing and the nature of the work He is seen to accomplish later, it is to be inferred that the Chief of the company was the Angel of the Lord, the pre-incarnate Christ."[32] These seven figures are found standing by the *bronze altar* which represents God's righteous requirements on the earth. It seems they are poised and waiting for the command to go and execute judgment: all is ready, and it is time for God's judgment to begin.

Verses 3–7

The details of the slaughter that was to take place are given. We find the glory of the Lord departing the *cherub, where it had been* and moving to the *threshold of the temple.* God's departing from the place that is precious to Him can only show His absolute and total disgust for the events that were taking place. The man in linen was given instructions to mark those who *weep over the abominations* done within the city. The ones to be marked would be those who were not involved in the sins of the people, and the mark would be a sign of protection, very similar to what we saw with the Passover in Exodus 12 and with the scarlet cord of Rahab's window in Joshua 2:18–21. What follows

---

[31] Rooker, 86.
[32] Feinberg, 55.

is a thorough description of the slaughter that was to take place. *Old and young men, maidens and little children and women,* no one was exempt from God's judgment and all were to be killed except for those who had the mark. The statement, *begin at My sanctuary* brings to mind 1 Peter 4:17: *For the time has come for judgment to begin at the house of God; and if it begins with us first, what will be the end of those who do not obey the gospel of God?* And so it begins; there will be no escape. Many today believe they are just living their lives, without any inference or recognition of God, but the day will come when they will face the long arm of God's justice. No one will be exempt, and no one will be forgotten.

Verses 8–11
The chapter finishes with Ezekiel feeling alone and becoming emotional at the events that were unfolding. After all, these were his brothers, his family, and his people, and to see them slaughtered before his very eyes was a devastating and traumatic experience. The question is asked and the Lord answers, *My eye will neither spare nor will I have pity, but I will recompense their deeds on their own hand.* No amount of intercession would be helpful at this point; in fact, one could say that Israel had reached the point of no return. Because God is a holy God and a just God, He cannot grant Ezekiel's request. How this must have ripped at Ezekiel's heart when he heard the words from the man in linen, *I have done as You commanded me.* Even through his objections, Ezekiel knew in his heart of hearts that God was right in what He was doing.

APPLICATION

As one reads chapter 9 and sees the complete annihilation of the people because they had forsaken the Lord and turned to idols, one must wonder what the Lord is planning for our society today. If He dealt that harshly with sin then, for a nation whom He called out to be His people, what will be His response to the sins of people today, those for whom He paid a dear price and redeemed at the cost of His Son? Compare Acts 20:28. Oh, that we would repent and fall on our faces before a holy and just God before we become the recipients of this wrath!

Study Questions
1. Read Romans 8:1 and explain it in your own words.
2. Do you truly understand the high cost God paid to forgive your sins?

EZEKIEL 10:1–22
GLORY OF GOD

Chapter 10 must be the most heart-wrenching chapter in the entire Bible. It is in this chapter that we see the glory of God depart the temple. Presently His glory is at the threshold (chapter 8), but when we arrive at the end of chapter 10, His glory has departed altogether. This chapter closely parallels chapter 1, and a complete description of the chariot throne can be found in my earlier discussion of Ezekiel's vision (1:4–28).

Verses 1–2
God gives the command to purge the nations. Isaiah 6:6–7 gives us a description of the coals and their purpose. God is in

complete control here, as He is the One giving the orders. *Coals of fire* were used for the purging of sin in Isaiah 6, but here they are used for the destruction of wickedness. Both are acts of purging, the former for purging the individual and the latter for purging the city. Both accomplish the same purpose: cleansing, whether of the individual or the city. Throughout all of Scripture, fire represents God's judgment and here is no exception; compare Genesis 19:24, 1 Corinthians 3:15, and Hebrews 12:29.

Verses 3–5
We see the moving of the glory of God. The glory of God *moves up from the cherub and pauses over the threshold of the temple.* This represents the beginning of the departure from the temple. What a sad day this is for Israel ... and they are so entrenched in sin, they have no idea what is happening.

Verses 6–8
The purging process now begins. The city was to be burned, but a complete description is not given. Feinberg explains: "The prophet did not describe the burning of the city, because his attention was drawn rather to the cherubim."[33] 2 Kings 25:8–10 gives us the details: *And in the fifth month, on the seventh day of the month (which was the nineteenth year of King Nebuchadnezzar king of Babylon), Nebuzaradan the captain of the guard, a servant of the king of Babylon, came to Jerusalem. He burned the house of the LORD and the king's house; all the houses of Jerusalem, that is, all the houses of the great, he burned with fire. And all the army of the Chaldeans who were*

---

[33] Feinberg, 60.

with the captain of the guard broke down the walls of Jerusalem all around.

Verses 9–15
Ezekiel is probably getting a closer look at the chariot throne, which would explain the differences in descriptions. Here we find an even more detailed description, which when added to what we already know from chapter 1 helps us to understand these cherubs even better. Verse 15 makes it clear that what is described here is the same thing Ezekiel saw earlier.

Block explains: "Whereas 1:10 had ascribed four different faces to each of the cherubim, the plain reading of the Hebrew here points to four identical faces for each cherub, with each cherub having a different set. The contradiction at least in the order of faces is more apparent than real. Since the inaugural vision came to the prophet from the north, the frontal view (south) would have had a human face. If the faces in 10:14 are also listed in clockwise order, the sequence is identical, and the cherub's are identified with the bull."[34]

Another difference is that in chapter 1 the eyes covered only the wheels, whereas here, they now cover their whole bodies. This would correlate with what John saw in Revelation 4. The eyes probably represent the omniscient nature of God.

Verses 16–22
We read of the connection of the movement of this chariot with the wheels. Here we see the purpose of the cherubim as transporters of the throne. As the glory of the Lord departs, the indication is clear that the cherubim are responsible for

---

[34] Daniel Block, *The Book of Ezekiel, Chapters 1-24* (Grand Rapids, MI: Eerdmans, 1994), 324-325.

transporting the glory away from the temple. We saw the removal to the threshold of the temple in Ezekiel 9:3, to over the threshold (10:4), to the east gate of the Lord's house (10:19), and eventually the total departure from the city (11:23). The glory does not return until 43:2.

Deuteronomy 31:17–18 states, *Then My anger shall be aroused against them in that day, and I will forsake them, and I will hide My face from them, and they shall be devoured. And many evils and troubles shall befall them, so that they will say in that day, "Have not these evils come upon us because our God is not among us?" And I will surely hide My face in that day because of all the evil which they have done, in that they have turned to other gods.* Again, God said in Hosea 9:12, *Yes, woe to them when I depart from them!* The departure of the glory of God is clearly a fulfillment of God's promise.

APPLICATION

Chapter 10 clearly identifies God as a God of His word. 1 Kings 8:56 states: *There has not failed one word of all His good promise, which He promised through His servant Moses.* God desired a close, intimate relationship with the people He loved. He chose Israel not because they were more in number, nor because they were the greatest people, but because He loved them, Deuteronomy 7:7–8. God desires a close personal relationship with His children today, but He will not tolerate sin. 1 John 1 makes it abundantly clear that sin breaks our fellowship with God, and Romans 14:10 reminds us that we will be judged for our works after we are saved. Reading Ezekiel 10 should cause us to examine ourselves and confess sins and live for Christ.

Before leaving chapter 10, one more point needs to be made. Verse 4 states that He *paused over the threshold.* One gets a sense that as the glory is departing, the Lord stops before His exit, looks back at what He is leaving, and His heart is breaking for what has happened. To do so much and then to be thanked by having his people worship other gods, and even use his holy house to perform these detestable sins, must not only make our Lord angry, but must break His heart as well. We would do well before sinning, and when faced with the reality of our sin, not to linger and enjoy it for a season, but to repent immediately and restore the relationship that was fresh when you first trusted Christ. May God have mercy on us and may we never be guilty of breaking His heart.

Study Questions
1. How do you express your thankfulness to God?
2. Do you understand the effects sin has on our relationship with God?

EZEKIEL 11:1–25
SENTENCE UPON THE LEADERS

This chapter closes the section that began with chapter 8 and thus ends the vision and trip back to Jerusalem. This chapter also completes the departure of the Lord from His temple.

Verse 1
The glory of God pauses to look at the leaders. Ezekiel is brought to the *East Gate,* which *faces eastward.* The East Gate is significant in that this is where the elders of Jerusalem would sit in judgment over legal matters, like the courtroom of today.

Some believe this to be the porch of Solomon. Here we see twenty-five men, among them Jaazaniah and Pelatiah, called the *princes of the people*. They are described as *men who devise iniquity and give wicked counsel in this city*. (This is not the same Jaazaniah as found in 8:11, as they are said to have different fathers.)

Verses 2–3
These leaders are plotting their wickedness. This is made evident by what they say. This "slogan" would be a gross misuse of Jeremiah's words: *Build houses and dwell in them; plant gardens and eat their fruit* (Jeremiah 29:5). Jeremiah is writing out of his concern for the exiles and telling them to build and settle in the land of their exile. Here, these men are making a mockery of Jeremiah's counsel by having the people build in Jerusalem. According to Rooker, "The slogan represented a false sense of security among those who remained in Jerusalem and had not been exiled to Babylon. They believed they were the choice portions and were protected in the pot—Jerusalem. They thought things would soon return to normal and they would be able to build their houses again."[35]

Verses 4–13
The Lord commands Ezekiel to prophesy against these leaders. The accusation was harsh because these leaders were guilty of murder and had *filled the streets with the slain*. Using their own metaphor against them, the Lord states that it is the slain that are the *meat* and the city is the *caldron*, but it will not be long before all will be removed. The thing they feared the most will

---

[35] Rooker, 89.

be that which the Lord uses against them, the *sword.* In refuting their metaphor altogether, God states that the leaders will not be the meat, and the city will not be the caldron, because God will judge them *at the border of Israel.* He will deliver them into the *hands of strangers,* a reference to Nebuchadnezzar and Babylon, who will *execute judgment on them.* Again, the promise is that when this happens, *they will know the LORD is God.* They have behaved no better than the pagan nations that surrounded them. They were called to be different, but instead took on the same character as those around them.

As Ezekiel prophesied, Pelatiah, one of the leaders previously mentioned, died. The significance of this death is that it marks the beginning of the Lord's judgment. James 3:1 states: *My brethren, let not many of you become teachers, knowing that we shall receive a stricter judgment.* There is great responsibility in being a leader and it is the leader who will receive the greater condemnation. Ezekiel's response to the death of Pelatiah indicates his fear that even the remnant will be destroyed.

Verses 14–16
God reaffirms His promise and addresses Ezekiel's concern by reaffirming the preservation of the remnant. This is the first promise of restoration in Ezekiel. Feinberg notes that the "prophet's concern was to be not with those in Jerusalem but with those in exile with him."[36]

The promise given is that the Lord will be a *little sanctuary* for them while they are in exile. The term *little sanctuary* is sometimes translated as "holy place," but there has

---

[36] Feinberg, 65.

been some difficulty in finding its exact meaning. Block states: "Here Yahweh promises to be for the exiles what the temple has heretofore been for them in Jerusalem." [37] From the other perspective, Feinberg writes: "It is not a 'little sanctuary,' which could never be true of God, but 'for a little while.' No place would again be called God's sanctuary where He has set His name, but He would be accessible to any willing and obedient heart." [38] MacArthur likewise believes this to mean a "little while" and references the length of the captivity. [39] Because the Hebrew word can mean *asylum*, it might be best to understand this as meaning that while they are in exile, God will provide for and take care of them, and not to think of this as a temple *per se*.

Verses 17–18
The remaining verses of this section would have to have been an encouragement to those in exile. God had not departed the temple to go just anywhere; rather, He departed to the exiles to become their sanctuary. God has promised restoration and one day the land of Israel will be reoccupied by God's people. The captivity will not last forever. Not only will they reoccupy the land, but they will remove all those things that were an abomination to the Lord.

Verse 19
God makes four promises. It must be remembered that these promises are made to those already in exile and who remain faithful to the Lord. Promise #1: He will give them *one heart*. In other words, God will once again establish them as one nation.

---

[37] Block, 349.
[38] Feinberg, 65.
[39] MacArthur, 1165.

Promise #2: He will put a *new spirit* within them. Dyer writes: "Ezekiel's promise refers to the permanent indwelling of the Holy Spirit in Israel. Before the Church Age the Holy Spirit indwelt select individuals; this was generally a temporary enablement for a special task. However, in the Millennium, the Holy Spirit will indwell all believers in Israel."[40] This *new spirit* will result in a complete devotion of Israel to the Lord. Promise #3: He will remove the *stony heart.* Zechariah 7:12–13 states: *Yes, they made their hearts like flint, refusing to hear the law and the words which the LORD of hosts had sent by His Spirit through the former prophets. Thus, great wrath came from the LORD of hosts.* A stony heart is one that refuses to hear and obey the Word of God and God's promise is that when Israel returns to her land, that heart will be gone. They will long to hear the Word and want to please God. Remember the events of Nehemiah, when Ezra read the word and the people stood out of respect, and this went on from morning until midday (Nehemiah chapter 8).

Promise #4 is the reception of a *heart of flesh.* This is best understood in contrast to the *stony heart.* As one cannot live without a heart, so one cannot have a proper relationship with the Lord without a heart. "Heart" is, of course, a reference to the whole being, the inner man. When God removes the stony heart, He will replace it with a heart of flesh. It is the heart of flesh that can be responsive to God's voice and message if it seeks God without reserve.[41]

---

[40] Dyer, 1248.
[41] Feinberg, 66.

Verses 20–21

What follows are the results of a new spirit. First, they will walk in *God's statutes*, a reference to living a pure and holy life that is pleasing to the Lord. Second, they will keep *His judgments*. "Judgments" is another term for the Word of God. Psalm 119:30 states: *I have chosen the way of truth; Your judgments I have laid before me.* A new spirit results in being obedient to the Word. Paul said in Colossians 3:16 to *let the Word of Christ dwell in you richly,* and this is accomplished with a new spirit.

Third, they will *do God's judgments.* Knowledge without application does no good at all. This is the difference between knowledge and wisdom, as Solomon's understanding is set out in the book of Proverbs. It is one thing to know something; it is quite another to act upon what you know. Someone has said that knowledge without application is like a train off the tracks, which amounts to a whole lot of power that is unusable. Ezra understood this great truth. Ezra 7:10: *For Ezra had prepared his heart to seek the Law of the LORD, and to do it, and to teach statutes and ordinances in Israel.*

The ultimate result of a new spirit is found in the phrase *they shall be My people and I will be their God.* This is a reminder of God's promise in Exodus 6:7. Israel still awaits this promise and according to Jeremiah 31, this will happen when they recognize Jesus as their Messiah.

Israel is brought back to reality by the reminder that for any who are disobedient and follow detestable things, God will repay them their due. We would do well to remember the words of the author of Hebrews 10:31: *It is a fearful thing to fall into the hands of the living God.*

EZEKIEL 11:22–25
PASSING AWAY OF GOD'S GLORY

This is the end of the vision that began in chapter 8. We return to the Chariot Throne and the departure of the glory of God. God's presence stops upon the mountain east of the city, which would be the Mount of Olives. This is significant in that this is the place to which the Lord returns in Ezekiel 43:2. Rooker sums it up best: "Thus the glory takes the direction of David's flight from Absalom (2 Samuel 15:23–30) and comes to rest where Jesus ascended to heaven and promised to return (Acts 1:9–11; Zechariah 14:4). The vision ended as it began—with the Spirit transporting Ezekiel back to the exiles in Babylonia."[42]

APPLICATION

The application from this chapter is heart-wrenching. No one likes to be forgotten or, for that matter, left alone. It is hard to imagine what it would be like to have God depart, as He did with Israel, yet nowhere do we read that there was a great outcry from the people. In fact, it would be fair to assume that they might not even have been aware that God has departed. This only goes to show the depth of their sin. Three times in Romans 1, the phrase *God gave them up* or *God gave them over* is used. There are those who believe this is God's judgment of abandonment. In any case, it is true that God will and does depart from those He loves, if they are so entrapped by sin that they refuse to repent. For the Christian today, this does not amount to a loss of salvation (1 Peter 1:4, John 10, Ephesians

---

[42] Rooker, p. 92.

4:30), but can and does amount to a loss of fellowship (1 John 1) and a removal from the protection and power of God's grace. Let us claim 1 John 1:9 and daily confess our sins. Let us recall the words of Paul in Romans 6:12–14, *Therefore, do not let sin reign in your mortal body, that you should obey it in its lusts. And do not present your members as instruments of unrighteousness to sin but present yourselves to God as being alive from the dead, and your members as instruments of righteousness to God. For sin shall not have dominion over you, for you are not under law but under grace.*

Study Questions
1. Have you ever felt abandoned by God?
2. How do you explain the abandonment of God in Romans 1:24–32?
3. Define the phrase *"gave them up (over)"* in Romans 1:24, 26, and 28.

Ezekiel 12:1–28

Acting Out the Exile

Chapter 12 begins with an indictment against Israel. Israel is described as having *eyes to see but does not see* and *ears to hear but does not hear.* This condition is described by the Lord Himself as rebellious. This is very similar to what the Lord told Isaiah in chapter 6, verse 9: *And He said, Go, and tell this people: Keep on hearing, but do not understand; Keep on seeing, but do not perceive.* The second vision is now complete, Ezekiel is still in Babylon by the River Chebar, and again, he is being called upon to use drama to get the message of God to the people. The recipients are the exiles with Ezekiel in Babylon. Chapters 8 through 11 dealt with the sin of those in Jerusalem, whereas the focus starting with chapter 12 is now on the sins of those in exile.

EZEKIEL 12:1–11
THE PEOPLE OF THE EXILE

Verses 1–3
God commands Ezekiel to perform a visual sign of captivity. He is told to prepare his belongings for captivity. The King James Version translates the word "belongings" as *stuff* and the New American Standard Bible translates the word as *baggage.* This stuff, according to tradition, could have included no more than

water, a mat for sleeping, and a bowl for food. In other words, he was to take with him only the essentials and no more. Twice, the Lord tells him to do this in *their sight*, which emphasizes that this was to be a public display, in the sight of all. Feinberg writes: "In spite of their rebelliousness the people were to view the symbolical action, so that perchance some might yet heed; the possibility of repentance was still held out to them."[43]

Verse 4

By referencing both day and night, it is clear that Ezekiel was to make this an all-day affair. He was to make it obvious, by taking his belongings from one place to another, that he was acting out going into captivity.

Verses 5–6

With the exiles watching, he was to dig through the wall and carry his belongings through it. The walls of Jerusalem (or, for that matter, the houses of Jerusalem) were not all that easy to penetrate, so the digging through the wall is better understood as showing the desperation of the present situation. He was to have his face covered all the while he is carrying his belongings. So that there will be no guessing as to what is going on, Ezekiel is told plainly that he is being made a *sign to the house of Israel.*

Verse 7

Ezekiel's heart is on display as he performs as he was commanded. Again, at the risk of losing his dignity, he is completely obedient to the Lord. It was more important what

---

[43] Feinberg, 69.

God thinks about him than what the people thought. After all, it is the Lord that he answers to, not the people.

Verses 8–11
When Ezekiel is asked what he is doing, he is to explain that this is about the *prince in Jerusalem.* He is to explain, to those who are curious, that he is a sign to them and as he has done, so shall it happen to them. Without leaving anything to guesswork, Ezekiel is as plain as he can be: he tells them that they shall be carried away into captivity.

EZEKIEL 12:12–16
THE PRINCE OF THE EXILE

Here, Ezekiel is given more details about this drama. This is a reference to King Zedekiah, here referred to as the *prince.* Just as the Lord has instructed Ezekiel—to carry his belongings out in the sight of all, dig through the wall and exit through the hole, and then cover his face so he could not see the ground—so all of these things will happen to Zedekiah, the prince of Jerusalem.

2 Kings 25:1–7 gives us a good understanding of what is going here. In the ninth year of his reign, in the tenth month, on the tenth day of the month, Nebuchadnezzar, king of Babylon, and all his army came against Jerusalem and encamped against it; they built a siege wall all around it. The city was besieged until the eleventh year of King Zedekiah's reign. By the ninth day of the fourth month, the famine had become so severe in the city that there was no food for the people of the land. Then the city wall was broken through, and all the men of war fled at night by way of the gate between two walls, which was by the king's garden, even though the Chaldeans were still encamped

all around the city. The king went by way of the plain. But the army of the Chaldeans pursued the king, and they overtook him on the plains of Jericho. All his army was scattered from him. So, they took the king prisoner and brought him up to the king of Babylon at Riblah, and they pronounced judgment on him. Then they killed the sons of Zedekiah before his eyes, put out the eyes of Zedekiah, bound him with bronze fetters, and took him to Babylon.

Thus, all that Ezekiel had performed in his drama became a reality in the life of King Zedekiah. Ezekiel was to cover his face and not see the ground, thus representing the eyes of Zedekiah being gouged out. Zedekiah never saw the land of Babylon even though he was taken there as a captive. This whole account is repeated in Jeremiah 52:4–11. Make no mistake: this is an actual historical account of a true incident.

As for the prince's men, they were to be scattered to every wind and hunted down to be put to death. The promise of the Lord to Ezekiel is that He is going to spare a few, but only for the purpose of spreading the news. God wanted all to know what was happening so all would know that He is God.

EZEKIEL 12:17–20
THE PROPERTY OF THE EXILE

Ezekiel was to quake while eating his bread and tremble with anxiety while drinking his water. This is a vivid display. The word *tremble* is used to describe an earthquake and this sign was to represent the violent nature of the captivity, as devastating as an earthquake. The significance of eating bread and drinking water while quaking and trembling was not to show a famine, but to remind watchers that violence happens during the normal, routine parts of life. There will be an element of surprise: while they eat and drink, the captor will come. The result will be the devastation of the land. The cities will be laid waste and the land will be desolate. Not even the land will be spared in this judgment.

Again, we find the statement: *then they shall know that I am the Lord.* By now, one should get a sense of the heartbeat of God in all of this. We have seen this phrase some five times already and it will be mentioned again some twenty-one more times. God, being a jealous God (refer to chapter 8), wants the inhabitants of all the lands to know who He is. Because our God is the same yesterday, today, and forever (Hebrews 13:8), He to this day is consumed with people knowing that He is God. Those who know this truth need to be informing others.

EZEKIEL 12:21–28
THE PROVERBS OF THE EXILE

Two proverbs are mentioned, and, in both cases, God corrects or changes the proverb.

Verses 21–25
The first proverb—*the days are prolonged, and every vision fails*—speaks to the fact that those in exile believed that not all God has said through Ezekiel will come to pass. God rendered this proverb meaningless and replaced it with *The days are at hand, and the fulfillment of every vision.* God will put a stop to false vision and flattering, falsifying divination. Evidently there were other men proclaiming to be prophets and yet they were not proclaiming the accurate truth of God's word. We will find later that they were not proclaiming God's word at all; rather,

they were inventing these things to tickle the ears of the hearers. The time of judgment is at hand and there will be no delay.

Verses 26–28
The second proverb, similar to the first, was: *The vision that he sees is for many days from now, and he prophesies of times far off.* This speaks to a distant future and claims that God's judgments are way off in the future. This only addressed the timing of events yet to happen, whereas the first one addressed the doubt that this would happen at all. As in the first, God dismisses this proverb and changes it to say *None of My words will be postponed any more, but the word which I speak will be done.* Obviously, God is saying that delay is now over. The execution of all Ezekiel has prophesied concerning the coming judgment is a certainty. Remember that there were false prophets that were confusing these issues before the people.

APPLICATION

This is a confusion very similar to one that was addressed by the apostle Peter. It seems that false prophets also existed in Peter's day and they were teaching that because the Lord had not yet returned, He was never going to return.

2 Peter 3:3–7: *Knowing this first: that scoffers will come in the last days, walking according to their own lusts, and saying, "Where is the promise of His coming? For since the fathers fell asleep, all things continue as they were from the beginning of creation." For this they willfully forget that by the word of God the heavens were of old, and the earth standing out of water and in the water, by which the world that then existed perished, being flooded with water. But the heavens and the earth which*

are now preserved by the same word, are reserved for fire until the day of judgment and perdition of ungodly men. It is a dangerous thing to believe that God is not a God of His word. There is a saying, "God said it, I believe it, and that settles it." This should be good enough for anyone, especially for God's children, but because of sin and rebellion, we tend to forget what the Word of God says and start believing things that are easy and convenient to believe. As Paul told Timothy, there will be those who desire to have their ears tickled. We need to pray that we will have ears that hear and eyes that see.

Study Questions
1. Are you able to discern the false teachers from those who teach truth?
2. Do you ignore passages in the Bible that are hard to understand?

Ezekiel 13:1–23

Warning Against False Prophets

With the correction of false prophets closing chapter 12, Ezekiel now warns the exiles against these false prophets. False teaching has been a problem for God's people for centuries. We can trace this back to the Garden of Eden when Satan approached Eve (compare Genesis 3). He challenged the Word of God then and false teachers have been twisting and manipulating the Word of God in every generation since. God's Word is extremely blunt and plain to understand concerning false teaching. Galatians 1:9 states, *as we have said before, so now I say again, if anyone preaches any other gospel to you than what you have received, let him be accursed.* If God is this strong against those who would distort and malign His Word, then God's children ought to feel as strong against those false teachers as well. Our heart should be God's heart. As we approach chapter 13 of Ezekiel, we find a warning against the false prophets that were seeking to circumvent the teaching of the day. The message of this chapter is that a true prophet of God speaks God's heart and not his own.

Because Jeremiah was a contemporary of Ezekiel, he may have fought against some of these same false prophets. Some have compared Jeremiah chapter 23 to Ezekiel 13 and have noted several similarities. In any case, as we saw in Ezekiel 12:24, false teachers must be stopped—thus the warning of this chapter.

EZEKIEL 13:1–2
COMMAND TO WARN

This is one prophet against another prophet. The difference, of course, is that Ezekiel is the true prophet of God, and the others are false prophets. It is interesting to note that they are not called prophets of the Lord, but instead prophets of Israel. They prophesy from their own hearts instead of from God's heart. Peter, in describing the false teachers of his day, gives us a vivid picture in 2 Peter 2:1–3: *But there were also false prophets among the people, even as there will be false teachers among you, who will secretly bring in destructive heresies, even denying the Lord who bought them, and bring on themselves swift destruction. And many will follow their destructive ways, because of whom the way of truth will be blasphemed. By covetousness they will exploit you with deceptive words; for a long time, their judgment has not been idle, and their destruction does not slumber.*

EZEKIEL 13:3
CONTENT OF THE WARNING

Woe is an expression of pain or grief. The false prophet is one who dreams up his own message. They have received nothing from the Lord and they have seen nothing from the Lord, so they must invent a message from within themselves, from their own spirit and fantasies. Feinberg states: "They were misled by their own desires, which is the scriptural method of asserting they were not inspired of God. The wish was father to the thought, and they spoke accordingly."[44]

Here the Lord calls them *foolish*. The Hebrew (*nabal*) is defined by *Strong's Dictionary* as "stupid" or "wicked."[45] This is not a reference to mental stupidity, but to moral stupidity, in that they are breaking the law of God. There are several Hebrew words for "foolish," but according to *Vines Expository Dictionary*, *nabal* is most often used as a word for a serious sin.[46]

EZEKIEL 13:4
COMPARISON OF THE WARNING

The comparison is made between these false prophets and *foxes in the deserts*. Foxes in the desert make their home in desolate places and are mischievous and destructive. They break through barriers and destroy vineyards and gardens. As do these foxes, so do false prophets. They are destructive and reap havoc on God's truth as well as on God's people. Paul's warning to the elders of Ephesus was about these same kinds of men. Acts 20:29–30, *For I know this, that after my departure savage wolves will come in among you, not sparing the flock. Also, from among yourselves men will rise, speaking perverse things, to draw away the disciples after themselves.*

---

[44] Feinberg, 73.
[45] *Strong's*, #5036.
[46] *Vine's Expository Dictionary of Biblical Words* (Nashville, TN: Thomas Nelson, 1985).

EZEKIEL 13:5–23
CONDEMNATION OF THE WARNING

Verses 5–6

Israel is condemned for not filling in the *gaps* that were found in the wall. Using the wall as an illustration, Ezekiel is comparing the vulnerability of a city with a broken wall to that created by the spiritual condition of Israel. Israel was vulnerable, they were facing God's wrath for their idolatry and instead of preaching against idolatry, here referred to as gaps in the wall, they were responsible for making the gaps bigger. In fact, it was these very same false prophets who were responsible for making the gaps. The *battle* is the battle for truth. The *day of the Lord* is probably a reference to the Babylonian captivity and the attack on Jerusalem in 586 BC.

A false prophet is described as one whom the Lord has NOT sent. Thus, they were self-appointed, commissioning themselves to go forth and speak. They *envisioned futility and false divination* by declaring, *Thus, says the Lord* when indeed the Lord had not spoken at all. Their stating that they *hope that the word may be confirmed* simply underscores their own self-deception. While speaking lies, they in some perverse way were hoping upon hope that their words would come true. When one tells a lie often enough, one begins to believe one's own lie, and such is the case with the false prophets.

Verse 7

With two rhetorical questions, Ezekiel challenges their authenticity in verse 7. *Have you not seen a futile vision* and *have you not spoken false divination* can only be answered in the affirmative, and yet the false prophets attempt to attach God to their sayings as if He had spoken them when indeed He had not.

Verse 8
Then comes the scathing rebuke from the Lord: *I am indeed against you.* The Lord declares they have spoken *nonsense. Nonsense* is the same Hebrew word translated as "vain" in the third commandment in Exodus 20:7: *You shall not take the name of the LORD your God in vain, for the LORD will not hold him guiltless who takes His name in vain.* It means vain or empty and by declaring this against these false prophets, the Lord was condemning them for taking His name in vain, referring to their act of declaring "thus says the Lord" when the Lord has not spoken. The condemnation from the Ten Commandments could not be any clearer: the Lord will not hold him guiltless. Those who abuse and mishandle the Word of God will be held accountable because they are taking the name of the Lord in vain.

Verse 9
The Lord gives a three-fold condemnation. This, described as having the hand of God against them, involves not being included in the *assembly of the people.* This carries the idea of their losing the respect and authority of the people of Israel. Secondly, they *shall not be written in the record of the people.* The understanding of this is difficult to conclude with any certainty. Some believe this to mean they would be excluded from the coming kingdom. Others believe this to mean excommunication from the nation of Israel, and still others believe this could refer to Jeremiah 17:13, *O LORD, the hope of Israel, all who forsake You shall be ashamed. Those who depart*

from Me shall be written in the earth, because they have forsaken the LORD, the fountain of living waters. This would mean that their names would be erased from or not included in the registers of Israel.

The third part of this condemnation is that they shall not *enter in the land of Israel*. This is an obvious reference to the return to Israel after the captivity. Ezekiel is told that these false prophets will not return, either because they would have been put to death, or they simply will be left in Babylon. One thing is certain: the Lord desires all to know that He is the Lord God.

Verses 10–16
A wall is built with *untempered mortar*. Ezekiel is preaching destruction and these false prophets are declaring peace. Their ministry is as weak as this wall. The wall will fall. Destruction, described as *flooding rain, great hailstones, and a stormy wind*, will come and tear it down. These are all references to the anger and wrath of God. It is God Himself who will destroy the ministry of these false prophets, He will expose them for who they truly are and He will do this for one purpose and one purpose only: so they shall know that He is the LORD.

God will put an end to the false teachings and to those who are responsible for them. These are men who prophesy concerning Jerusalem and proclaim peace when there is not peace. This is what is called the "ostrich syndrome." The prophets were burying their heads in the sand and ignoring the reality going on around them. God was judging the nation for their sin of idolatry and instead of confirming this judgment; the false prophets were making the people feel secure and satisfied when they should have feared the wrath of God. It is the fear of God that will bring me to repentance.

Verses 17–23

It is not only men who are responsible for false teaching; there were female prophetesses as well. Women have been the object of God's rebuke in other places (compare Isaiah chapter 3 and Amos chapter 4), but this is the only place in Ezekiel where female prophetesses are mentioned. These women went further than just proclaiming "thus says the Lord"; they were involved in occult activities. *Magic charms* on their sleeves and *veils* on their heads were practices of sorcery. In fact, these women were more like witches than false prophetesses. They hunted for the souls of people. Their motivation was simply for *handfuls of barley* and *pieces of bread.* Some think that the barley was not used for compensation, but actual items used for their divinations.[47]

God announced that He was against them and He would cause their activity to cease. He declares, I will tear the souls you hunt from your arms; I will tear off your veils and I will deliver my people from your hands. God will hold them accountable for making the heart of the righteous sad and for strengthening the hands of the wicked, causing them to not turn from their wicked ways.

APPLICATION

Although we see God's condemnation of these wicked prophets and prophetesses, we have hope knowing that in destroying the

---

[47] Feinberg, 76.

works of the wicked, God delivers the righteous. The church today is in danger from similar false teachers. Paul warns us in his second letter to Timothy that perilous times are coming, and the evil men and imposters will grow worse and worse (2 Timothy 3:1). Jude tells us to contend earnestly for the faith (Jude 1:3). God desires all to know that He is God and the day will come when *at the name of Jesus every knee should bow, of those in heaven, and of those on earth, and of those under the earth, and that every tongue should confess that Jesus Christ is Lord, to the glory of God the Father* (Philippians 2:10–11).

Study Questions
1. Define false teaching.
2. Do you believe that it is unloving to identify false teachers by name?

Ezekiel 14:1–23

Warning Addressed to the Elders

Hypocrisy is a detestable sin in the eyes of God. Jesus had much to say about hypocrisy, as we read in the Gospels. In referring to the Pharisees, he called them hypocrites when they gave of their tithes and when they prayed (Matthew 6), in their dealings with others (Matthew 7), and in their keeping of their own traditions (Matthew 15). It is a hypocrite that destroys with his mouth (Proverbs 7), and he only deceives himself (Proverbs 26).

Chapter 14 is a sharp rebuke to the elders of Israel for their hypocrisy. The chapter opens with a visit to Ezekiel from the elders (verse 1). What they received was a lesson on hypocrisy and the need to repent. "Perhaps they were seeking a salvation oracle containing glowing promises for the future, like those the false prophets preached (13:16). If so, they are to be rudely disappointed. Perhaps they have not even expressed yet the object of their inquiry when they are accosted by Ezekiel for the divided loyalties of their hearts."[48]

The issue of chapter 14 is that of forgiveness. Proverbs 28:13 states, *He who covers his sins will not prosper, but whoever confesses and forsakes them will have mercy.* Also, in Psalm 66:18 we read, *If I regard iniquity in my heart, the Lord will not hear.*

---

[48] Brownlee, 200.

EZEKIEL 14:1
THE CONCERN OF THE ELDERS

We have seen these elders sitting with Ezekiel before, in chapter 8:1. The question one must ask is: why are these elders coming to a prophet of God if they have no desire to obey? This is reflective of their hypocrisy.

EZEKIEL 14:2–3
THE CONDITION OF THE ELDERS

In Israel, idolatry was on open display. In chapter 8, the leaders of Israel were portraying the idols on the walls of the temple and even had idols set up in their own homes. Now these men are in Babylon, under God's judgment. The idolatry was not as open and evident, but the Lord tells Ezekiel that they are still idolaters, in that they have *set up their idols in their hearts.* With man, it is the heart that is first corrupted, then the actions that follow. Proverbs 4:23 states: *keep your heart with all diligence, for out of it spring the issues of life.* These men's hearts were so corrupt with idolatry that it became a way of life. They worshipped their idols as easily as they breathed. It was a common way of life and they could not detach themselves from *stumbling into iniquity.*

God was not asking for Ezekiel's permission to answer these men. Rather, the statement is more, "Why should I allow Myself to be inquired of them?" This question of God to Ezekiel implies that these elders have come seeking a Word from God and wanting Ezekiel's counsel. Rooker observes: "The lack of spirituality exhibited by the leadership of the nation may help explain why the problem of false prophets in chapter thirteen was not corrected."[49]

EZEKIEL 14:4–6
THE CALL FOR REPENTANCE TO THE ELDERS

Verses 4–5

Repentance is ultimately God's desire. Peter states: *The Lord is not slack concerning His promise, as some count slackness, but is longsuffering toward us, not willing that any should perish but that all should come to repentance* (2 Peter 3:9).

God is calling for a change of heart which will result in a change of actions. He told Ezekiel *that I may seize the house of Israel by their heart, because they all are estranged from Me by their idols.* But make no mistake: God will punish sin and He makes it clear that the punishment will fit the crime. The more idolatry, the more severe the punishment. Hosea 4:17 states, *Ephraim is joined to idols, let him alone.*

Verse 6

The message to these elders is to *repent, turn away from your idols and turn your faces away from all your abominations.* Reading this, one gets a sense that God's heart is for a restored relationship with these men, but they are so engrossed in their sin that they do not hear what God is saying (compare Ezekiel 12:2). God did answer them, and would be satisfied with nothing less than thorough and complete repentance; anything else would be totally unacceptable.

---

[49] Rooker, 104.

EZEKIEL 14:7–11
THE CUTTING OFF OF THE ELDERS

Verses 7–8

The Lord makes his answer perfectly clear to these men: Either separate from idolatry or be separated from God. When anyone involved in the sin of idolatry comes to a prophet to inquire of God, God Himself will give the answer personally. The idolater, in direct opposition to God, will be made an example before all of Israel and God will *cut him off* from the nation.

Verses 9–10

God has already established his Word concerning the practice of idolatry. Deuteronomy 28:36–37 states, *The LORD will bring you and the king whom you set over you to a nation which neither you nor your fathers have known, and there you shall serve other gods—wood and stone. And you shall become an astonishment, a proverb, and a byword among all nations where the LORD will drive you.* Not only will God cut an idolater off from the nation, but if a prophet came to the Lord on behalf of the idolaters, God would destroy him from among the people of Israel. The message is that one who aids the idolater, even if not personally involved in idolatry himself, would be considered the same as an idolater. *The punishment of the prophet shall be the same as the punishment of the one who inquired.* Feinberg writes: "Just as God is impartial in His offers of grace, mercy and love, so is He no respecter of persons in judgment."[50]

---

[50] Feinberg, 80.

Verse 11
God gives clear purpose for being so stern. God desires for Israel to cease from their sin and return to be His people and He their God.

EZEKIEL 14:12–21
THE CERTAINTY OF JUDGMENT UPON THE LEADERS

Verses 12–14
Four specific judgments are mentioned in this section. God has been very direct in His dealing with sin in the past: Noah and the wicked generation, Sodom and Gomorrah and the perversity that existed, and the bondage of Israel by the nation of Egypt. Verse 13 is a direct statement that God will and does judge sin. Here the sin of Israel is referred to as *persistent unfaithfulness.* When this happens, God will stretch out His hand and unleash His wrath. The first judgment mentioned is **famine.**

God shows the certainty of His judgment by stating that even if three powerhouses of the faith, *Noah, Daniel,* and *Job* were present, it still would not prevent the coming judgment although they could *deliver only themselves by their righteousness.* This passage closely parallels Jeremiah 15:1–4. In Jeremiah, even Moses and Samuel could not prevent God's judgment.

Verses 15–16
The second judgment is **wild beast.** Again, the Lord mentions the three powerhouses of the faith and declares that they would not stop this judgment from coming to past: only *they would be delivered, and the land would be desolate.*

Verses 17–21

The third judgment is the **sword**, and the fourth judgment is **pestilence.** As with the first two, Noah, Daniel, and Job could not prevent this from taking place, and only they would be spared. Notice that they would be spared because of their righteousness.

According to Rooker, these judgments were well-known covenant curses: "famine is referred to in Leviticus 26:20, wild beast is found in Leviticus 26:22, the sword is found in Leviticus 26:25, 33 and pestilence is found in Deuteronomy 32:24."[51] With the mention of each judgment, Ezekiel emphasizes the utter despair and hopelessness of the condition of Israel. It will be worse for Israel because she does not in fact have these three giants of the faith to intercede on her behalf.

EZEKIEL 14:22–23
THE COMPASSION WITHIN THE JUDGMENT

The consolation comes when the captives in Babylon realize that some in Jerusalem have been spared and when they *see their ways and their doings.* These escapees will bring comfort to the captives because they will testify that God has *done nothing without cause* and is totally justified in all His doings. This will prove the righteous nature of God's judgment. It would be good at this point to remember Abraham's question to our Lord as he pled for Sodom and Gomorrah: *shall not the Judge of all the earth do right?* (Genesis 18:25). The answer is a resounding YES!

---

[51] Rooker, 106.

Study Questions

1. Do you believe that higher standards should be placed upon church leaders?

2. Is sin in the life of a believer viewed differently by God than sin in the life of an unbeliever?

Ezekiel 15:1–17:24

Parables Spoken Against Israel

In these next three chapters we find three parables: the parable of the useless vine, the parable of the unfaithful wife, and the parable of the two eagles. All three give one message: there is no hope of deliverance for Israel.

EZEKIEL 15:1–8
THE PARABLE OF THE USELESS VINE

Verses 1–2
This parable is about a vine, useless at first and even more useless after being burned. The people of Jerusalem were useless to God because of their idol worship, so they would be destroyed and their citied burned. Isaiah also likened the nation of Israel to a vineyard (compare Isaiah 5:1–8).

Verses 3–5
We find a series of five questions in verses 3 through 5. These are rhetorical questions to show the utter uselessness of a vine. The only purpose of a vine is *fuel for a fire,* and even for that it is no better than any other wood of the trees of the forest. No *object* can be made from it. No *vessel* can be hung on it. In fact, the vine is not useful for any *work.* Even after it is burned, it serves no purpose.

Verses 6–8

The application to Israel is that they are like the vine, useless to God. God has *set His face against them* and will make the *land desolate* because they have persisted in their unfaithfulness.

EZEKIEL 16:1–63
THE PARABLE OF THE UNFAITHFUL WIFE

Chapter 16 is one of the longest chapters in the book of Ezekiel. This chapter illustrates the unfaithfulness of Israel by using a prostitute as an example. Because of the graphic nature of this chapter, rabbis advise that it be read only by mature students. Unfaithfulness is often referred to in Scripture as "adultery." Hosea was told to take a harlot for a wife to demonstrate God's relationship with Israel.

EZEKIEL 16:1–7
ABANDONED BABY

Verses 1–5

Israel is pictured as an unwanted child of a mixed union. Ezekiel states that their father was an *Amorite* and their mother a *Hittite.* Feinberg observes: "The names Amorite and Hittite are to be understood as a taunt, as though they were not descended from Abraham, Isaac, and Jacob. It is a moral rather than a historical notation."[52] What Ezekiel is pointing out is that Israel was bent toward idolatry because of the inheritance they received from former generations.

---

[52] Feinberg, 86.

At her birth, she was rejected, thrown out into an *open field.* She was not cared for as a newborn babe but rejected and discarded. The language of verses 4 through 5 is graphic in illustrating this point.

Verses 6–7
God declares that when Israel was struggling in their own blood, trying to stay alive after being abandoned, He gave them life and made them grow into a beautiful and strong nation. Even then they were vulnerable and needed God's protection and provision.

EZEKIEL 16:8–14
ADORNED WIFE

Verse 8
In her abandonment, God saved her, nursed her to health, and made her grow. The language indicates that God made her ready to be His bride by entering into a covenant with her.

Verses 9–14
He adorned her and made her great among the nations. Most agree that the articles mentioned were gifts given in marriage and the *fine linen, silk,* and *embroidered cloth* took her to the status of a queen. Thus, she had gone from being an abandoned, illegitimate baby to being adorned as a young bride.

The language is full of symbolism that takes the reader through the history of Israel, from her birth (Genesis 13) to her finest hour of majesty under King Solomon. Israel should be thankful for all God has done for her, but instead, they repay His kindness with unfaithfulness and idolatry.

EZEKIEL 16:15–63
ADULTEROUS WIFE

Verses 15–22

Despite all God has done for the nation, they quickly turned to other lovers. Israel's beauty and fame—that which God gave her—evidently became her downfall. She turned to harlotry in the form of idolatry. It is not as if they were not warned, for we read in Deuteronomy 6:10–15, *so it shall be, when the LORD your God brings you into the land of which He swore to your fathers, to Abraham, Isaac, and Jacob, to give you large and beautiful cities which you did not build, houses full of all good things, which you did not fill, hewn-out wells which you did not dig, vineyards and olive trees which you did not plant—when you have eaten and are full—then beware, lest you forget the LORD who brought you out of the land of Egypt, from the house of bondage. You shall fear the LORD your God and serve Him and shall take oaths in His name. You shall not go after other gods, the gods of the peoples who are all around you (for the LORD your God is a jealous God among you), lest the anger of the LORD your God be aroused against you and destroy you from the face of the earth.*

Pride is an ugly thing and when it fills the person, things just get worse. They took the garments from God and made high places. They took the fine jewelry God gave them and made images of idols. They offered the food, oil, and incense that came from God to their idols. As if this were not evil enough, they sacrificed the children to the god Molech. They have forgotten all that God had done for them in their youth.

Verses 23–34
They offered themselves to their pagan neighbors and *multiplied their acts of harlotry.* All of this only served to provoke God to anger. God reviews His past judgments of giving them over to the Philistines and to the Assyrians. They erected shrines in the public squares. They engaged in prostitution with anyone who passed by. Their sin of harlotry was so wicked, they are compared to the exact opposite of what a harlot does. A harlot is enticed to become a harlot, but Israel entices others to come to her. A harlot is one who is paid for her services, but Israel was paying others to come to her.

Verses 35–36
The Lord now summarizes Israel's unfaithfulness. They were filthy, their nakedness was uncovered, and they gave up the blood of their children.

Verses 37–43
The court is convened, the verdict is given, and the sentence pronounced. God will gather all their neighbors and expose Israel for who she really is: a harlot. Israel will be *judged as women who break wedlock or shed blood are judged.* God will bring them down. They shall be *stoned and thrust through with their swords.* Their property will be destroyed, and they will stop playing the harlot. He will recompense their deeds on their own heads. Once this is accomplished, then God will cease judging and lay down His anger and His jealousy. All of this is to take place in the public arena and Israel will be made an example and warning to her neighbors.

Verses 44–50
Israel will be known by the proverb *"Like mother, like daughter!"* The Lord reminds them of their mixed heritage. The focus is on their bent toward evil. God compares them to Samaria in the north and to Sodom in the south and states that they have acted even more corruptly than those ill-fated peoples. God further clarifies the sins of Sodom and explains that He took them away as He saw fit.

Verses 51–58
The Lord gives yet another scathing rebuke. Israel's evil is so bad, they make the evil of the pagans look good. Therefore, they are to be disgraced and need to bear their own shame. Israel has followed in the pagan footsteps of her beginnings (compare Ezekiel 16:3).

Verse 59
The Lord makes it clear that they have broken the covenant by despising the oath. Israel could have been great, and the other nations would have answered to her, but because of her sin, she finds herself answering to the pagan nations.

Verses 60–63
This chapter ends with a message of hope and restoration. The final verses exhibit the heart and mercy of God. God will establish a new covenant with them because they broke the old one. God had made a promise to Abraham and the new covenant will be a reinstatement of the Abrahamic covenant. It is referred to in Jeremiah 31 as the New Covenant. Israel will be restored by grace and not by her own merit, because God will provide

atonement for all they have done. This, then, brings hope to an otherwise dark chapter.

EZEKIEL 17:1–24
THE PARABLE OF THE TWO EAGLES

Verses 1–6
The parable is stated, and we are told that this is both a riddle and a parable, in that there is symbolism which makes this more of an allegory than a parable. Here we see two eagles. The first eagle represents Nebuchadnezzar. He is referred to as the *great eagle with large wings and long pinions* which speak of his power and great dominion. The *feathers* represent the many nations that are subject to him. The *various colors* represent the many nationalities. *Lebanon* represents Jerusalem and the *highest branch* would be Jehoiachin, king at the time of captivity. Jehoiachin was replaced by Zedekiah who was set like a *willow tree* and became prosperous. Zedekiah was liked by Nebuchadnezzar and had he remained faithful, would have continued to enjoy his prosperity and would have been allowed to stay in Jerusalem.

Verses 7–8
Another eagle is introduced which represents Egypt. Egypt reached out to Zedekiah and Zedekiah looked to them for help to overthrow Nebuchadnezzar. There was no valid reason for this revolt: he was neither opposed nor treated unfairly. The desire for more and the lack of contentment led to his demise.

Verses 9–10
Zedekiah's survival depends on the strength of Egypt, but they will not endure. Nebuchadnezzar has pronounced judgment upon Zedekiah because of his rebellion. Zedekiah and his kingdom will *wither when the east wind* [Babylon] *touches it.*

Verses 11–21
The parable is now explained, and little is left to guesswork. A study of 2 Chronicles 36 will give complete understanding of this text.

Verses 21–24
The last section of this chapter begins a new movement of thought. This is obvious by the phrase, *Thus says the Lord God.* The last three verses represent a messianic prophecy and present a promise of future blessings for Israel. Referencing the royal line of David, the highest cedar, God states that He will *crop off from the topmost of its young twigs a tender one and will plant it on a high and prominent mountain.* This is a clear reference to a future event when Christ will establish His throne in Jerusalem on the seat of David. This event will fulfill the Davidic covenant in which God promises that his throne would be forever and ever (compare 2 Samuel 7:13).

Psalm 89:1–4, *I will sing of the mercies of the LORD forever; with my mouth will I make known Your faithfulness to all generations. For I have said, "Mercy shall be built up forever; Your faithfulness You shall establish in the very heavens." I have made a covenant with My chosen, I have sworn to My servant David: "Your seed I will establish forever and build up your throne to all generations."*

APPLICATION

To close this section, we turn to the words of Feinberg: "The Bible has one unified message whether before the cross, now after the cross, or in the future ages: there is blessing in the Lord Jesus Christ alone. His kingdom will fill all the earth with righteousness and equity for all the world. But personal participation in these assured glories comes only through personal faith in the Redeemer. How can men enter these joys if they believe not? We must face our responsibility to transmit the message to them."[53]

Study Questions
1. How is God ultimately pleased with us?
2. What is the basis for God's reward for your life? (Compare 1 Corinthians 4:1–2.)

---

[53] Feinberg, 98.

Ezekiel 18:1–32

Personal Responsibility

Concerning our sin, the Scriptures are very plain: each person is individually responsible for his or her own sin. The "blame game" will not work with our Lord. Romans 14:10–12 makes this point perfectly clear: *For we shall all stand before the judgment seat of Christ. For it is written: "As I live," says the LORD, "every knee shall bow to Me, and every tongue shall confess to God." So then each of us shall give account of himself to God.*

In chapter 18, the Lord reminds Ezekiel of the personal responsibility each of us has for our own actions.

EZEKIEL 18:1–4
RESPONSIBILITY DENIED

Here we find the denial of guilt: Israel was passing the buck or blaming others. We find Jeremiah stating the same thing in Jeremiah 31:29–30, *In those days they shall say no more: "The fathers have eaten sour grapes, and the children's teeth are set on edge." But everyone shall die for his own iniquity; every man who eats the sour grapes, his teeth shall be set on edge.*

The meaning of this proverb is that the children suffer because of the sins of the fathers. The father has sinned, *eaten our grapes*, but it is the children who suffer, *teeth set on edge*. The proverb was not accurate, but it was being used to ignore or evade personal responsibility. The idea is that they were suffering not because of what they had done, but because of what their ancestors had done (compare Lamentations 5:7).

God quickly corrects such attempts by stating that this proverb shall no longer be used in Israel. It is the *soul of the one who sins that shall die.*

EZEKIEL 18:5-20
RESPONSIBILITY DEFINED

Verses 5-9
It is the righteous man who lives. A righteous man, here referred as a man who is *just,* is defined as one who is not involved in idolatry, not involved in sexual immorality, and not involved in oppressing fellow Israelites. Cleary this is a man who does what is lawful and right.

Verses 10-13
The unrighteous man is described and faces the reality that *he shall not live.* This is the man involved in oppressing his fellow Israelite, practicing idolatry, and committing sexual immorality. God's word is plain to understand: *He shall surely die, and his blood shall be upon him.*

Verses 14-20
A righteous son is one who has an unrighteous father, and considers the sins his father has committed but does not do likewise. His father's sins are listed in some detail, but again God explains that the responsibility belongs to the father and says that the son shall not die for the iniquity of his father. Most children follow the example of the father, but there are times when this can be the wrong course. Verse 20 summarizes this

point: *The soul who sins shall die. The son shall not bear the guilt of the father, nor the father bear the guilt of the son. The righteousness of the righteous shall be upon himself, and the wickedness of the wicked shall be upon himself.*

EZEKIEL 18:21–31
REPENTANCE DEMANDED

The Hebrew word *shubh* is found some thirteen times in this chapter alone. It means "to turn" or "to return." "It is used extensively by the prophets and makes prominent the idea of a radical change in one's attitude toward sin and God. It implies a conscious, moral separation, and a personal decision to forsake sin and to enter into fellowship with God."[54] God reminds Ezekiel of four areas of God's character that are involved with repentance: God's mercy, verses 21–23; God's justice, verse 24; God's accusations, verse 25; and God's pleading, verses 26–32. God tells Ezekiel that He has no pleasure in the death of one who dies, therefore turn and live!

APPLICATION

Chapter 18 ends with great hope that there is forgiveness with the Lord. We would do well to remember verses like Psalm 103:12, *As far as the east is from the west, so far has He removed our transgressions from us.* Psalm 32:1–2 states, *blessed is he whose transgression is forgiven, whose sin is covered. Blessed is the man to whom the LORD does not impute iniquity, and in whose spirit, there is no deceit.* Solomon reminds us, in Proverbs

---

[54] International Standard Bible Encyclopedia Electronic Database (1996).

28:13, that *He who covers his sins will not prosper, but whoever confesses and forsakes them will have mercy.* There is forgiveness with our Lord! He desires that we cast away from us all the transgressions which we have committed and get ourselves a new heart and a new spirit.

Study Questions
1. Is there an unpardonable sin today (compare Matthew 12:31–32)?
2. Have you committed a sin that you believe God has not forgiven?

Ezekiel 19:1–14

Lamentation for Judah

This chapter has often been referred to as a lamentation. Ezekiel is told to take up a *lamentation for the princes of Israel.* A lamentation is a funeral song given in honor of the dead person. It is intended to express the good qualities of the deceased.

EZEKIEL 19:1–9
LAMENTATION FOR THE LEADERS

Verses 1–4
Ezekiel uses the term *princes* to refer to the kings of Israel. He uses the imagery of a lion cub and a vine to depict the failure of two of Judah's kings. The lioness in verse 2 represents the nation of Israel. The first cub mentioned in verse 3 was known for its fierceness and became strong and would tear apart its prey. He is captured in verse 4 and taken to Egypt. This is a reference to Jehoahaz, and 2 Kings 23:31–34 record the events. *Jehoahaz was twenty-three years old when he became king, and he reigned three months in Jerusalem. His mother's name was Hamutal the daughter of Jeremiah of Libnah. And he did evil in the sight of the LORD, according to all that his fathers had done. Now Pharaoh Necho put him in prison at Riblah in the land of Hamath, that he might not reign in Jerusalem; and he imposed on the land a tribute of one hundred talents of silver and a talent of gold. Then Pharaoh Necho made Eliakim the son of Josiah*

king in place of his father Josiah and changed his name to Jehoiakim. And Pharaoh took Jehoahaz and went to Egypt, and he died there.

Verses 5–9
This second lamentation is a reference to Jehoiachin. His account can be found in 2 Kings 25:27–30: *Now it came to pass in the thirty-seventh year of the captivity of Jehoiachin king of Judah, in the twelfth month, on the twenty-seventh day of the month, that Evil-Merodach king of Babylon, in the year that he began to reign, released Jehoiachin king of Judah from prison. He spoke kindly to him and gave him a more prominent seat than those of the kings who were with him in Babylon. So Jehoiachin changed from his prison garments, and he ate bread regularly before the king all the days of his life. And as for his provisions, there was a regular ration given him by the king, a portion for each day, all the days of his life.*

EZEKIEL 19:10–14
LAMENTATIONS FOR THE LAND

The symbolism changes, from the mother being represented as a lioness to her being represented as a vine. The vine represents Judah, and the branches thus represent the kings. This vine is *plucked up in fury, cast down to the ground* and the *east wind dried her fruit.* The result of this action is that her *branches were broken, withered,* and *consumed by fire.* This is a reference to the kings of Judea who were once powerful among all the nations. But they were overthrown and removed, and the vine was replanted in the *wilderness,* an obvious reference to Babylon. Feinberg suggests that the symbolism of this passage parallels that in 17:5–8. [55] The *rod* in verse 14 probably represents Zedekiah (see Ezekiel chapter 12). This marks the end of the Davidic kingship, and not until Christ returns will this throne be used again. Thus, a sad ending to a sad chapter: *this is a lamentation and has become a lamentation.*

---

[55] Feinberg, 106.

Ezekiel 20:1–24:27

History of Corruption

Chapter 20 is introduced with more dates. When compared with chapter 8:1, we see that eleven months have elapsed since the last dated prophecy. Once again, we see the elders coming to Ezekiel for information. They were seeking a word from God and by coming to Ezekiel, they at least recognized him as a man of God. Verses 1 through 17 deal with the sins of the first generation, while verses 17 through 32 deal with the sins of the second generation. Another division could be made: prewilderness wandering versus postwilderness wandering.

EZEKIEL 20:1–32
REVIEW OF PAST SINS

Verses 1–17
These verses deal with the sins of the first generation and rehearse the activities of Israel from the time of the Egyptian captivity, the exodus, and the wilderness wandering. It was in Egypt where the nation grew, multiplied in number, and became great. Seven times in chapter 20 the Lord refers to *raising His hand in an oath.* This gesture was used for making a solemn oath (compare Psalm 106:26) and was used of the Lord to confirm the oath of deliverance to bring them out of Egypt into a *land flowing with milk and honey.* The numerous repetitions of this phrase indicate that God is a God of His word and will keep His

promises. The content of this oath was the promise God made to Moses as found in Exodus chapter 3.

Verses 18–26
In return, Israel was to rid herself of her idols, keep God's judgments, walk in His statutes, and simply put, to do them. But they did not obey and instead rebelled against the Lord. Soon after leaving Egypt, when Moses was on the mountain receiving the Law from God, they returned to their idolatrous ways (Exodus chapter 32). God's response was to pour out His wrath against them, but for the sake of His name, that it should not be profaned among the Gentiles, he withdrew His hand. He did, however, pronounce them unclean because of their ritual gifts and *gave them up to statutes that were not good.*

This phrase, "gave them up," is like Paul's words in the book of Romans. In Romans chapter 1, three times we find *God gave them up* or *God gave them over*. "God's 'giving over' of the people to sin was His judicial act. Because they refused to follow His righteous ways, God would abandon them to the consequences of their actions."[56]

This section finishes by showing how Israel continued to rebel, even after they entered the promised land. Soon after entering, they forsook the Lord. God describes this to Ezekiel: *They saw all the high hills and all the thick trees, there they offered their sacrifices and provoked Me with their offerings. There they also sent up their sweet aroma and poured out their drink offerings* (verse 28).

God's answer to these elders is found in verse 31: *I will not be inquired of by you.* Their desire was to be like the Gentiles,

---

[56] Dyer, 1265.

to worship wood and stone. What a sad commentary when God's people are more satisfied by living with and like the world than by pleasing and honoring the Holy name of God! This is reminiscent of the time in Israel's history when they desired a king so as to be like the other nations (compare 1 Samuel 8:5).

EZEKIEL 20:33–21:32
REMOVAL OF FUTURE SINNERS

Verses 20:33–44
The people are assured that God will deal with them. God makes His position very clear: *surely with a mighty hand, with an outstretched arm, and with fury poured out, I will rule over you.* His purpose is for them to know that He has dealt with them for His name's sake.

Verses 20:45–49
God punishes the Southern Kingdom with fire. The fire will destroy everything from the *south to the north.* Once again, the fire is probably a reference to Nebuchadnezzar. The south is a reference to the land of Israel, specifically the kingdom of Judah. Three times the south is mentioned, and in each case, we find three different Hebrew words. The first, found in the phrase *set your face toward the south,* simply refers to the region on the left as one looks west. The second, *preach against the south,* is a poetic word and refers to the great land of God (compare Deuteronomy 33:23). In the last reference, *prophesy against the forest land, the South* is used as a proper noun and refers to the dry land known as the Negev (compare Joshua 15:21). The message is God's judgment on the land of Israel using the symbolism of fire, and it was during the third invasion of

Nebuchadnezzar where he destroyed the city in 586 BC: thus the three references to the south. This section closes with Ezekiel complaining that the people were not taking him seriously. They were saying, *does he not speak parables?*

Verses 21:1–7
Chapter 21 continues this same theme, but now we see that future sinners will be removed by the sword. The sword is drawn, and God gives a certainty of this judgment to come. It will be complete in that *all flesh from south to north* will be cut off, *both righteous and wicked.* The result will be that when they hear this prophecy, their *hearts will melt, their hands will be feeble, and their knees will be weak as water.*

Verses 21:8–17
The sword is now *sharpened* and *polished to make a dreadful slaughter.* The leadership will be affected by this sword. This is seen in the phrases *scepter of My son* and *princes of Israel.* The striking of the hands and the beating of God's fists together are best seen as an act of anger, God's anger. Again, we get a sense of the complete devastation to all of Israel from the statement *against all their gates.*

Verses 21:18–27
The message becomes more specific as we see that the sword is directed in two ways. It is first directed toward Judah and the sword is identified as the king of Babylon (verse 19). Again, Ezekiel is told to act out this judgment in the sense that he is to *make a sign and put it at the head of the road to the city.* It is interesting to note that Nebuchadnezzar thought he was getting his direction and guidance from divination and occultist

practices, when in fact it was the Lord God Who was directing his every step. This is not about what Nebuchadnezzar can do to Judah, but what God can and does do to Judah through Nebuchadnezzar. God makes it very clear that it is because of the sins of His people that Nebuchadnezzar is permitted to invade and destroy. This is all about God's judgment. This section finishes with a promise of the future return of the true King of Israel, the *One whose right it is*.

Verses 21:28–32
Chapter 21 closes with the sword directed toward Ammon. This is present-day Jordan. The Ammonites might have been thinking that since all of God's attention was focused on Judah, they would go unnoticed, but this is not the case. God has a plan for Ammon. Similar language is used against Ammon as was used against Judah, in that a sword is drawn for their slaughter. So complete and devastating will be their judgment that they will be remembered no more.

EZEKIEL 22:1–31
THE WHY, HOW AND WHO OF GOD'S JUDGMENT

Verses 1–16
The Lord explains the why of His judgment. This section reads like a litany of crimes against a criminal. Israel committed social injustice (verse 7), apostasy (verse 8), idolatry (verse 9), immorality (verses 10 and 11), and greed (verse 12). They abused family (verses 7–10), friends, and the feeble (verse 7).

The leaders were responsible for the moral climate of the nation because God chose them to lead. The same is true today. James 3:1 states: *My brethren, let not many of you become teachers, knowing that we shall receive a stricter judgment.* Unfortunately, many of the sins mentioned here have been committed by Christian leaders of today. If this text teaches us anything, it is that we must be faithful to pray for our pastors and leaders of our churches, that they be protected against the fiery darts of the wicked one (Ephesians 6:16).

Verses 17–22
The Lord explains the "how" of His judgment. The judgment of God was considered a refining process. As precious metals are refined with intense heat so that the impurities (referred to as *dross*) can be removed, so it is with the nation of Israel. Here God says that Israel has become *dross.* This image of a refiner's furnace is commonly used throughout the Scriptures; compare Isaiah 1:22–25, Jeremiah 6:27–30, Zechariah 13:9, and Malachi 3:2–4.

Verses 23–31
The Lord explains the "who" of His judgment. Reading through this text, we find several specific groups that were responsible for God's wrath being poured out. God describes the nation as a *land that is not cleansed or rained on in the day of indignation.* The groups responsible include the *prophets.* These were the men responsible for relaying a message from God to the people. They are guilty of *tearing the prey* like a lion, of *devouring the people,* of taking their *treasure and precious things* and making *widows* by killing the men. The next group mentioned are the *priests*, those responsible for communicating from the people to God, who *violated the law and profaned the holy things.* The *princes*, probably a reference to governmental leaders, are mentioned as being like *wolves,* shedding blood and destroying

people to get a *dishonest gain.* Finally, the *people* in general are mentioned. This would be a reference to all not previously mentioned. They are guilty of oppressing other people by robbing from them and mistreating the *poor and needy.*

The sin of these people was so widespread, so deep, that everyone was affected. The Lord *sought for a man,* anyone to *stand in the gap,* and found no one. Because He could find no one, He poured out His wrath upon the nation.

APPLICATION

What a sad commentary on the day, that among all the men of Israel not one could be found who would stop the downslide of moral decadence and uphold truth. One wonders what the result would be today. God is still looking for good men to stand in the gap!

Study Question
1. Are you willing to take a stand against moral decadence in our culture?

EZEKIEL 23:1–49
PARABLE OF THE TWO SISTERS

This is a rather long chapter that continues to detail the history of corruption of Judah. We see the promiscuousness of the nations (verses 1–21), the punishment of the sisters (verses 22–35), and the rehearsal of the sisters' sins (verses 36–49). God again gives a parable to Ezekiel (compare chapters 15–17). This parable is referred to as the Parable of the Two Sisters. Their names are *Oholah* and *Oholibah* and some rather graphic words are used to describe them and their deeds.

Verses 1–21

Ezekiel first recognizes the sisters in verses 1 through 4. They are referred to as *two women* who are the *daughters of one mother,* which makes them at least half sisters. They *committed harlotry in Egypt,* a reference to the Egyptian bondage. They *committed harlotry in their youth,* a reference to a time before the Egyptian bondage. Here we find some of the graphic language of the chapter. Rooker writes: "These two women became prostitutes while they lived in Egypt where their breasts were fondled, and their virgin bosoms caressed."[57]

Ezekiel also gives us their names which are based on the same Hebrew term for *tent. Oholah* means "her tent." *Oholibah* means "my tent is in her." Many recognize *Oholah* as referring to Samaria, the northern kingdom of Israel. They were drawn away from God by the Assyrians. The people coveted youth, strength, power, wealth, and pleasure, which are the same things people want today. But the Assyrians captured the heart of Israel and led them into captivity in 722 BC.

Oholibah is recognized by many as a reference to Judah, the Southern Kingdom, and she is shown to be worse because she did not learn from the judgment upon her sister but continued in her lust for the Assyrians and Babylonians. Therefore, her judgment was equally certain.

One is reminded of the admonition from Paul in 1 Corinthians 10:6, *Now these things became our examples, to the intent that we should not lust after evil things as they also*

---

[57] Rooker, 160.

lusted. We would do well to learn from the mistakes of the past. Just as Oholibah was privileged and should have known better, so we are privileged because we know about Christ. We need to be doubly sure that we follow Him.

The sisters' deeds are laid out for us in verses 5 through 21. The sin of Oholah is found in verses 5 through 10 and Oholibah's sins are found in verses 11 through 21.

Oholah is said to have lusted for her lovers, the neighboring Assyrians. She became enamored with their young men and committed harlotry with them by defiling herself with all their idols. God's pronouncement of judgment was clear: because of her harlotry and defilement with the idols, He delivered her into the hands of the Assyrians. They took away her innocence, took away her children, and killed many with the sword (compare 2 Kings 17).

Oholibah also lusted after the Assyrians. Much of what is said of Oholah is true of Oholibah as well. But she did not stop with the Assyrians: she *increased her harlotry* by observing the portrayals of images on the wall (compare Ezekiel 8:10) and lusting after the Chaldeans. The description of her lust for the Chaldeans is extremely graphic, as found in verse 20. Feinberg writes: "In Egyptian hieroglyphics the horse represents a lustful person. Asses and horses are proverbially lustful (Jeremiah 2:24; 5:8; 13:27). Thus was described the return to her first degradation."[58]

Verses 22–35

Next, we see the punishment of the sisters. This section predicts the last attack on Jerusalem that would destroy the city and

---

[58] Feinberg, 134.

bring to Babylon the third wave of captives in 586 BC (compare 2 Kings 25 and Jeremiah 52). Mentioned here are *Pekod, Shoa,* and *Koa. Pekod* means "inflictor of," *Shoa* is a reference to the rich, and *Koa* references the noble. These are possibly tribes of Babylon, but one would be hard-pressed to make this interpretation because we do not find these names in the geographical contents of Babylon. It is best to describe these names as allies of Babylon and leave it at that.

Much of the punishment mentioned was common punishments for prostitutes in those days. Oholibah is compared to her sister, but in a harsher way. The Lord holds Oholibah more accountable than Oholah because she followed the example of her sister and did not learn from her sister's mistakes; therefore, she will drink from her sister's cup. The verdict is in and the pronouncement of her judgment is final. The Lord said, *Because you have forgotten Me and cast Me behind your back, therefore you shall bear the penalty of your lewdness and your harlotry* (verse 35).

Verses 36–49
Chapter 23 ends with a rehearsal of the sisters' sins. They had gone so far as to sacrifice their own children to idols, and then to sacrifice to the Lord on the very same day (verse 39). This made a mockery of worship. The chapter continues by rehearsing all the sins that had been committed. Ezekiel thus details in summary the entire case against God's people. What a sad commentary! This nation, whom God has chosen to be special and a people for His own, are now worshipping other gods and putting these gods on the same level as Jehovah God.

What a fitting end to an otherwise sad chapter when the Lord states, *They shall repay you for your lewdness, and you shall pay for your idolatrous sins. Then you shall know that I am the LORD GOD* (verse 49).

APPLICATION

The lesson to learn is that we cannot praise God and willfully sin at the same time. That would be like celebrating one's wedding anniversary and then going to bed with the neighbor.

Study Question
1. Do you believe your sin affects your worship (compare Matthew 5:21–26)?

EZEKIEL 24:1–27
THE POT AND THE PROPHET

Chapter 24 not only finishes the discussion of the history of Israel's corruption, but also finishes the first major division of Ezekiel. This chapter has two main themes: the seething pot (verses 1–14) and the stoic prophet (verses 15–27). Chapters 20 through 23 are prophecies given during the seventh year of King Jehoiachin's captivity (compare Ezekiel 20:1), whereas now we are in the *ninth year, in the tenth month on the tenth day of the month,* which is some two years later. Many agree that this is equivalent to January 15, 588 BC. Ezekiel makes it clear that this is the day the king of Babylon started his siege against Jerusalem (compare 2 Kings 25:1).

Verses 1–14
To understand the parable of the seething pot, it is important to identify the different elements used therein. The pot represents

Jerusalem. The *choice cuts* represent the leadership of Judah and the *bones under it* represent the people of the nation. Two times the Lord pronounces woes upon the city. The people in Judah thought they were the choice meat because they had not been taken into captivity when the Babylonians last invaded the land. Ezekiel has used this picture before, in chapter 11, to show that though the people thought they were safe and secure, the *pot* would in fact be their place of destruction. The pot was to be set empty upon the fire, where its bronze would burn, its filthiness would melt, and its scum would be consumed. This represents a thorough cleansing of Jerusalem, the city that had to be destroyed to remove all its impurities. Israel, so deep in rebellion, would not be cleansed anymore, therefore God caused His anger to come upon them. God had been patient, but His patience has been exhausted. He has spoken, it will come to pass, He will do it and will not hold back His anger. *They* [the Babylonians] *will judge you, says the Lord God.*

Verses 15–27
An interesting ending comes with the death of Ezekiel's wife. Here we see God's instruction to Ezekiel to become stoic. God told Ezekiel that his wife would die and that he should not grieve for her. Even more interesting is the fact that Ezekiel obeyed God fully. This is reminiscent of God telling Hosea to marry an unfaithful woman (compare Hosea 1:2–3). Both illustrate God's relationship with His people. Obeying God will sometimes incur a high cost. Ezekiel is told to *sigh in silence, make no mourning, bind his turban on his head, put his sandals on his feet, not to cover his lips and eat no bread of sorrow.* Everything culturally done in a time of mourning and grief, Ezekiel was to avoid. The

reason for this is found in verse 24: these were to be a *sign* to the people of Israel.

When all of this is accomplished, one will escape to run and tell Ezekiel. It is at this point that Ezekiel will no longer be mute (compare Ezekiel 3:25–27). He himself will become a sign and by all of this it will be known that the God of Israel is the Sovereign Lord of the universe.

This section of Ezekiel is best summarized by Feinberg:

> No human heart could fathom what this act meant to the heart of God. God had condescended to make Himself known in His temple, accepting godly worship here, ordering the ritual, and protecting the sacred place from foreign intruders. But when sin mars the spiritual value of temporal ordinances, God casts them off, for at greatest sacrifice God always maintains the righteous requirements of His law. That is why Christ died even though it broke the heart of God and Christ. How much does it mean to you and me? Does it command our conformity to His will in every aspect of life?[59]

"Surely there is a message in all this for us today. We who call ourselves Christians have drifted far from the truth as set forth in the Word of God. How can we hope to escape when He arises to deal in judgment with those who have turned after the things of the world, thus dishonoring His name? Oh, that there might yet be a great returning to God and His Word, that there might

---

[59] Feinberg, 141.

come revival and blessing ere the close of this dispensation of grace!"[60]

APPLICATION

The message for us is that when we face tough times, we need to allow sin to be burned from our lives. When these times come, unnecessary priorities and diversions are purged away. We can and should re-examine and reorder our lives so that everything we do really matters for the glory of our Lord.

---

[60] Ironside, 165.

Ezekiel 25:1–7

Ammon

Verses 1–2
The Ammonites were mentioned before by Ezekiel in chapter 21. As noted earlier, Ammon is present-day Jordan. Genesis 19 reveals that the Ammonites were descendants of Lot, brought about by an incestuous relationship with his two daughters. They have been in conflict with Israel since Jephthah during the period of Judges (compare Judges 10:6—11:33). They were finally conquered by King David (see 1 Chronicles), only to regain strength and join with the Moabites and the Edomites in attacking Judah (unsuccessfully).

They do appear again in Jeremiah 25:1–7, where they join forces with Judah to fight against Babylon. This only proves that anyone will fight together when they have a common enemy.

Verses 3–7
The charge against Ammon is that they delighted in the demise of Israel. Instead of compassion and grief, they rejoiced over the desolation of the land. "They clapped and cheered at the desecration of the Temple, the desolation of the land of Judah and the deportation of the Judeans to Babylon."[61] God had made it very clear in His Word that anyone who curses Israel will be

---

[61] Derek Thomas, *God Strengthens* (Darlington, England: Evangelical Press, 1993), 186.

cursed. Genesis 27:29: *Let peoples serve you, and nations bow down to you. Be master over your brethren and let your mother's sons bow down to you. Cursed be everyone who curses you and blessed be those who bless you!*

God seems ready to deal with this kind of behavior, not only because of who these people represent, but also because He will not tolerate ridicule on the part of Israel's enemies.[62] As their judgment, God states that He will deliver the Ammonites into the hands of the men of the East. He would turn their land into a pasture for the Easterners' flocks and their capital city, Rabbah, into a stable for their camels. The destruction would be so complete that they would be given as plunder or spoils to their enemies. They would also cease to be counted among the peoples of the earth, evidently by being totally and utterly destroyed. Verses 5 and 7 make very clear the objective the Lord has in mind: then *you shall know that I am the Lord.*

APPLICATION

Israel has always been God's chosen nation and people. We would do well to remember that this has not changed. Romans 11:1: *"I say then, has God cast away His people? Certainly not!"* The context of this verse defines "His people" as Israel. We need to have the same attitude toward Israel that God demanded of the nation in the Old Testament and remember that *"I will bless those who bless you, and I will curse him who curses you; and in you all the families of the earth shall be blessed"* (Genesis 12:3).

---

[62] Ironside, 170.

Study Questions

1. Do you believe that the Old Testament promise to Israel still applies today?

2. Do you believe that God continues to hold accountable those who have disdain for Israel?

Ezekiel 25:8–11

Moab

Verse 8a
The beginning of the Moabites is found in Genesis 19:37–38. As was the case with the Ammonites, the Moabites were also products of an incestuous relationship between Lot and his daughter. The main location of the Moabites was an area along the lower region of the Dead Sea.

Isaiah expresses his thoughts concerning Moab in Isaiah 16:6: *We have heard of the pride of Moab—He is very proud—Of his haughtiness and his pride and his wrath; But his lies shall not be so.* They were an arrogant people who gloried in their strength and thought they were impregnable, but God would soon show them that they were powerless against His wrath.

One of the better-known Moabites is Balak, referred to as the King of Moab in Numbers 22:4. It was Balak, king of the Moabites, who contracted with Balaam to bring a curse upon Israel as Moses was leading them through the wilderness. The full account of this story can be found in Numbers 22–24. In the book of Judges, God uses the Moabites to judge Israel. Ruth was a Moabitess and part of the royal line of Christ. 2 Samuel 8:2 describes King David's conquering of Moab.

Verses 8b–11

The sin of Moab was to treat Israel like all the other nations. God considered this disrespectful of His people and a direct assault against His very character. Roy Gingrich writes: "They (Moabites) believed that Judah had no special relationship to God or else God would have protected her from the calamities inflicted [on] her by Nebuchadnezzar."[63]

Their punishment was to be the same as the Ammonites. They would be absorbed by the men of the East and cease to exist as a nation.

Study Questions
1. Is there such a thing as righteous pride?
2. Explain the difference between righteous pride and unrighteous pride.

---

[63] Roy Gingrich, *The Book of Ezekiel* (Memphis, TN: Riverside Printing, 2005), 38.

Ezekiel 25:12–14

Edom

Verse 12a
In giving the genealogy of Esau, Genesis 36:1 states that Esau is Edom, and for this reason many believe that Edom is more closely related to Israel than either Ammon or Moab (compare Deuteronomy 23:7). The Edomites were longtime enemies of Israel. It was Edom that refused to allow Israel to cross their territory while traveling to the land of promise (compare Numbers 20:14–21). The entire book of Obadiah is devoted to the coming judgment of Edom because of her despicable actions against Judah.

Verses 12b–14
The reason for Edom's judgment is because they took vengeance on Israel. According to Obadiah 1:14, *they* [the Edomites] *stood at the crossroads to cut off those among them who escaped and delivered up those who remained in the day of distress.* The phrase *taking vengeance* literally means "taking vengeance with a vengeance" and is to be understood as the worse kind of vengeance. It is for this reason that the Lord judges them.

When God finishes with them, they will be desolate of man and beast. The text clarifies that they will become *desolate from Teman; Dedan shall fall by the sword.* There is no doubt that these are Edomite cities, although their exact location is unknown. According to Dr. John MacArthur, *Teman* was possibly 200 miles east of the Dead Sea in the Arabian Desert and *Dedan* was possibly located 100 miles south of *Teman*, yet far east of the Red Sea.[64] "The Bible does not promise to them an eventual restoration as a people (as it does the Ammonites and the Moabites) but the desolated land of the Edomites will be possessed by the Israelites at the time of Israel's restoration to her land, Isaiah 11:14."[65]

Because of their savage vengeance, God will pour out His own vengeance by the hand of the Israelites. Notice that in verse 14 God refers to Israel as His people, which personalizes the attack previously mentioned in Obadiah. Deuteronomy 32:41 states: *I* [God] *will render vengeance to My enemies, and repay those who hate Me.* Jeremiah 46:10 states: *For this is the day of the Lord GOD of hosts, a day of vengeance, that He may avenge Himself on His adversaries. The sword shall devour.* Romans 12:19 states: *Beloved, do not avenge yourselves, but rather give place to wrath; for it is written, 'Vengeance is Mine, I will repay,' says the Lord.* We will see judgment upon the Edomites mentioned later in chapters 35 and 36 of Ezekiel.

---

[64] MacArthur, 1187.
[65] Gingrich, 38.

Ezekiel 25:15–17

Philistia

Verse 15a
The Philistines are the longest known enemy of Israel. They are mentioned many times throughout the Old Testament. One of the more infamous Philistines is Goliath, the giant whom King David slew. The Philistines were an uncircumcised people inhabiting the shore plain between Gezer and Gaza in southwestern Palestine.[66] This is the first group of people mentioned in this chapter who are not directly descended from Israel.

Verses 15b–17
The Philistines, like the Edomites, were accused of taking vengeance on God's people. Here, though, the wording is more severe. They *took vengeance with a spiteful heart.* This means they had malice in their hearts toward Israel, which amounted to nothing less than spite. As noted earlier, vengeance is prohibited for man in Romans 12:19.

They also sought to destroy because of the *old hatred.* This word is the same word translated as *enmity* in Genesis 3:15 to describe Satan's continual opposition to God. The Philistines were a proven enemy of Israel throughout all of the Old Testament, being a constant thorn in their flesh. Therefore,

---

[66] International Standard Bible Encyclopedia Electronic Database.

because of their constant attack on God's people, God would cut off the Cherethites and all those living along the coast.

The Cherethites originated in Crete but became a part of the Philistines. At one time, they were a part of King David's bodyguard (compare 2 Samuel 8:18). Their name is a play on words, having the literal meaning that God will "cut off the cutters-off." The Lord makes it perfectly clear that He will pour out His vengeance with *furious rebukes*. Speaking of the unrighteous, Psalm 50:21 states: *I will rebuke you and set them in order before your eyes.* Negative judgments may lead to rebuke, especially by God. Such divine rebuke may be physical, as indicated in Job 5:17, *Behold, happy is the man whom God corrects; therefore, do not despise the chastening of the Almighty.* However, those who understand Scripture know that the Lord rebukes him whom He loves. Compare Proverbs 3:12 and Hebrews 12:5–6. It should be noted that again the Lord gives His reason for His discipline: *they shall know that I am the LORD.* He will not tolerate anyone taking vengeance upon His people.

Ezekiel 26:1–28:19

Tyre

Verses 26:1–2
This section begins with a specific time in view. Ezekiel refers to the *eleventh year on the first day of the month* but does not specify the month. The *eleventh year* of Jehoiachin's captivity was the year 587–586 BC. 2 Kings 25 describes the fall of Jerusalem which took place on the seventh day of the fifth month. It is probably these events that prompted the prophecy of Ezekiel (compare Jeremiah 25).

Tyre was the commercial center of the ancient Middle East, and the next three and a half chapters are devoted to it. In fact, Ezekiel gives more attention to the city of Tyre than does any other prophet, which indicates its importance during his day. Tyre, the wealthy capital of Phoenicia, was an industrious, resourceful city, with many inhabitants skilled in arts and crafts. The Old Testament refers to it as a fortified city as well as a stronghold (compare Joshua 19:29 and 2 Samuel 24:7). It is interesting to note that the last phrase of each section dealing with Tyre states that it will become a terror and will be no more forever. Each section is clearly marked by the phrase *The Word of the Lord came to me again.* Whereas the previous chapter had dealt largely with the violence of the nations to the east of Judah, chapters 26 through 28 focus on corruption in the commercial life of the nations to the northwest.[67]

Tyre had not always been an enemy of Israel. During the reigns of David and Solomon, it enjoyed a good relationship with God's people, or at least it seemed to. There is no record of war between these two nations. In fact, it is worth noting that Tyre provided wood and manpower for Solomon to build the Temple and, according to 1 Kings 9:27, Hiram, king of Tyre, *sent his servants with the fleet, seamen who knew the sea, to work with the servants of Solomon.*

Tyre's sin, like that of Ammon (compare Ezekiel 25:3) was that it expressed joyfulness at the destruction of Jerusalem. Note verse 2:, *Aha! She is broken who was the gateway of the peoples; now she is turned over to me; I shall be filled; she is laid waste.* With Jerusalem in ruins, the Tyrians anticipated that businessmen would take new interest in Tyre. Wherever money is involved, it seems greed follows, and when Tyre saw an opportunity to take advantage of Israel's misfortune, it wasted no time in doing so. Without Jerusalem, the reality was that more products would be shipped by sea, so Tyre saw the fall of Jerusalem as an opportunity to corner the market on trade.[68] God's disdain for those who mock the misfortunes of others is clearly seen in Scripture. Proverbs 17:5 states, *He who mocks the poor reproaches his Maker; He who is glad at calamity will not go unpunished.* Because of Tyre's disdain for Jerusalem, it will face the judgment of God and will be forever destroyed.

---

[67] Thomas, 189.
[68] Dyer, 1278.

Verses 26:3–6

Even though Tyre is not accused of taking part in the destruction of Jerusalem, its joy would be punished by the Sovereign Lord of the universe. God would raise many nations to come against Tyre; in fact, we are told in verse 3 that the punishers would flow over Tyre *as the sea causes its waves to come up*. This is a fitting description: for as the sea was Tyre's means of income; its destruction would come as the waves of the sea. Verse 4a says that these nations will *destroy the walls of Tyre and break down her towers*. Her destruction will be so complete that she will be made *like the top of a rock* (verse 4b). This again is an interesting analogy, as the name "Tyre" means "rock" and her destruction will leave her as a rock. The location of the city will become a place for fishermen to spread their nets. Fishermen usually spread their nets on rocks or barren land to allow them to dry. This prevents them from becoming entangled in brushes or trees. The judgment here is that the once vibrant, commercial city of Tyre would be reduced to a barren, dry piece of real estate that will be worthless except for the spreading of nets by the local fishermen. According to Feinberg, "Mainland Tyre has been so thoroughly devastated that the ancient site cannot longer be identified with exactness."[69]

We should also be reminded of God's faithfulness to His people. What we are seeing is a fulfillment of the promise that God made to Abraham. In Genesis 12:3, God states, *I will bless those who bless you, and I will curse him who curses you.* Clearly, Tyre, in mocking the demise of Israel, is considered as cursing them, so the promise of God applies as much to them as to

---

[69] Feinberg, 148.

anyone else. They cursed Israel and God cursed them: it is just that simple.

The daughters of Tyre, mentioned in verse 6 as well as verse 8, should be considered to be her surrounding communities. As is common today, major metropolitan cities had many suburbs which were considered a part of that city. In fact, to live in one of these suburbs would be considered the same as living in the city. The same would apply to the daughters of Tyre. One could substitute the name *daughter* for the word *suburb* and not lose anything in meaning. So complete was the destruction of Tyre that even her surrounding communities were *slain by the sword.*

God's purpose in all of this is not just to keep His promise to Israel; in addition, by keeping this promise, all would know that He is Lord, Jehovah, or the Great I am.

Verses 26:7–14

We are now told how God intends to accomplish the destruction of Tyre. Nebuchadnezzar will be used by God to accomplish His purpose. This should clearly answer any question as to whether God uses the unrighteous to fulfill His desires. It is obvious from this text that He does. But let us not make a mistake here: even though Nebuchadnezzar is the one who invades Tyre, it is the Lord who is doing the work and the destruction of Tyre clearly is the work of God. In these verses, we are provided with a vivid description of the events that take place. We have references to *horses, chariots, wagons, horsemen, the sword, a siege mound, battering rams*, and *axes.* Tyre was no match for the mighty Babylon. The king who destroyed Jerusalem would now destroy Tyre.

After destroying Jerusalem, Nebuchadnezzar moved his army north in 585 BC and kept the city of Tyre under attack for some thirteen years. The strength of Tyre was in her navy, so supplies continued to come in from the coast to keep Tyre strong for the fight. Nebuchadnezzar, however, played havoc with the mainland according to the text of Ezekiel. We are told that he slayed the *villages of the fields*. He built a *siege mound*, which would have been used both as a defense wall and as an approach to the city for attack. *Battering rams* were used to break through the wall of Tyre and once in, the towers which were considered their strength would be torn down. Once the city was breached, the enormous army would invade and trample the streets and kill the people. Some have considered verse 10 an exaggeration, but it is not too difficult to understand as a literal fulfillment. The walls would literally shake at the number of horsemen that would invade the city. Tyre would be destroyed even to its *pillars,* which would fall to the ground. These pillars were probably like those mentioned in 1 Kings 7:15–21, which were built by Huram of Tyre for Solomon's Temple.

There is a distinct difference in pronouns from verses 7 through 11 and verse 12 and following. Ezekiel moves from *he* to *they*. Some see this as looking beyond the invasion by Nebuchadnezzar to the others who would come along later to finish the destruction begun by Nebuchadnezzar. More specifically, this is probably a reference to Alexander the Great, who later conquered Babylon. *For Tyre built herself a tower, heaped up silver like the dust, and gold like the mire of the streets. Behold, the LORD will cast her out; He will destroy her power in the sea, and she will be devoured by fire* (Zechariah 9:3–4). "In 332 BC, when Alexander the Great besieged the island city of Tyre for seven months, he finally captured it when he built a causeway from the mainland to the island. Hauling cedars from the mountains of Lebanon, he drove them as piles into the floor of the sea between the mainland and the island. Then he used the debris and timber of the ruined mainland city as solid material for the causeway. Hence, the remarkable prophecy of Ezekiel was completely fulfilled." [70] Feinberg comments: "The American archaeologist Edward Robinson saw forty or fifty marble columns beneath the water along the shores of Tyre. With the destruction of the city there would be no occasion for mirth."[71]

Tyre, which was once filled with *songs and the sounds of harps*, would be silenced, and the day would come when they were never heard from again. Songs and harps were evidently an important part of life at Tyre, for Isaiah describes that at the end of seventy years, she will be remembered with melody and songs. *Now it shall come to pass in that day that Tyre will be forgotten seventy years, according to the days of one king. At the end of seventy years it will happen to Tyre as in the song of the harlot: 'Take a harp, go about the city, you forgotten harlot; make sweet melody, sing many songs, that you may be remembered.' And it shall be, at the end of seventy years that the LORD will deal with Tyre* (Isaiah 23:15–17).

Verses 26:15–21

This section shows the commercial importance of Tyre. The response of her coastland neighbors reflects their total dependence on this great city. Tyre cannot be destroyed without

---

[70] *Nelson's Illustrated Bible Dictionary* (Nashville, TN: Thomas Nelson, 1986).
[71] Feinberg, 149–150.

causing utter chaos in the commercial world. These neighbors would see her fall as a world calamity.

The reference to the princes of the sea can be best understood by looking at Jonah 3:6–9, *Then word came to the king of Nineveh; and he arose from his throne and laid aside his robe, covered himself with sackcloth and sat in ashes. And he caused it to be proclaimed and published throughout Nineveh by the decree of the king and his nobles, saying, 'Let neither man nor beast, herd nor flock, taste anything; do not let them eat, or drink water. But let man and beast be covered with sackcloth, and cry mightily to God; yes, let everyone turn from his evil way and from the violence that is in his hands. Who can tell if God will turn and relent, and turn away from His fierce anger, so that we may not perish?'* This reference describes the response of the king of Nineveh at their predicted destruction; his arising from his throne is an indication of the seriousness of the event. Sitting in mourning was a common way to express one's grief and the princes of the sea were no exception. It should be noted, though, that this is a selfish grieving: they are not as concerned for the city itself as they are for their own welfare.

Tyre's fall is now complete. She will be covered with great waters and her end will come when she is brought down into *the Pit,* a reference to the place of the departed dead in their total separation from Jehovah God. "Tyre was to join the dead in Sheol, becoming a nonentity as they were, and to exchange the land of the living for the land of the nether places. The once virile city would leave behind an uninhabited ruin."[72] This is in full agreement with the Psalmist who wrote: *The wicked shall be turned into hell, and all the nations that forget God* (Psalm 9:17).

---

[72] Allen, "Ezekiel 20–48," in *Word Biblical Commentary* vol. 29 (Waco, TX: Word Books 1990), 76.

This prophecy has proven to be true as Tyre fell and never rose again. Her destruction was complete and thorough.

APPLICATION

This should also serve as a reminder to any who would turn their back on a Holy God. He will not be mocked; any who would curse Him or His people shall themselves be cursed. Thus Tyre, in her greed and selfishness, found herself at the mercy of a just God who is also a God of His promises. We are reminded that *God has chosen the weak things of the world to put to shame the things which are mighty* (1 Corinthians 1:27). Thomas reminds us that behind all this is a general warning to the wicked of what lies in store for them. "There is life after death, no matter what, but the quality of that life depends upon what we have done with God's offer of forgiveness in this life. Those who die in their sins will be sent, as Jesus warned, 'into the darkness, where there will be weeping and gnashing of teeth' (Matthew 8:12)."[73]

Study Question
1. Is it possible to discuss the mercy of God apart from the justice of God?

Verses 27:1–7
This chapter is a funeral dirge over the loss of Tyre. Although it had not yet come to completion, Ezekiel lays out a complete description of the city and its demise and by doing so reminds us that pride cometh before the fall. The apostle Paul told the church of Corinth in 1 Corinthians 10:12, *Therefore let him who*

---

[73] Thomas, 193.

thinks he stands take heed lest he fall. Tyre was a prideful city and full of greed. She thought of herself as indestructible and was certain of her lasting existence.

We will see several movements of thought in chapter 27, from a detailed description of Tyre's beauty to her final demise. It is clear from the text that these are not Ezekiel's words, but God's words given to Ezekiel to speak. The Lord reminds them of their pride in verse 3. Scriptures are clear concerning God's attitude toward pride. *Pride goes before destruction and a haughty spirit before a fall. Better to be of a humble spirit with the lowly, than to divide the spoil with the proud* (Proverbs 16:18–19). *A man's pride will bring him low, but the humble in spirit will retain honor* (Proverbs 29:23).

Because Tyre was a seaport city, it makes sense to use descriptions associated with the sea. In these verses she is described a beautiful ship. The best of wood was used to build her, her planks being furnished from the *fir trees of Senir.* According to Deuteronomy 3:9, the Amorites referred to Mt. Hermon as Senir, and it lay north of the Sea of Chinnereth which was later named the Sea of Galilee.[74]

Her *mast* was made of *cedar from Lebanon.* The cedar trees from Lebanon were commonly used for construction because of their height and strength. 1 Kings 5 describes the request from King Solomon to King Hiram of Tyre for cedar trees in order to build the Lord a house. *The cedars are tall—whose height was like the height of the cedars* (Amos 2:9; 2 Kings 19:23); majestic (2 Kings 14:9), and excellent (Song of Solomon 5:15). The Assyrian power is compared to *a cedar in Lebanon with fair branches and with a forest-like shade, a high stature;*

---

[74] Dyer, 1280.

and its top was among the thick boughs ... its stature was exalted above all the trees of the field; and its boughs were multiplied, and its branches became long (Ezekiel 31:3–5). They are God's trees: *The trees of Yahweh are filled with moisture, the cedars of Lebanon, which he hath planted* (Psalm 104:16).[75]

Her oars were made from the oaks of Bashan. Bashan was an area east of the Sea of Chinnereth and was famous for its oak forests. Isaiah 2:13 notes *all the cedars of Lebanon that are high and lifted up, and upon all the oaks of Bashan.* Zechariah 11:2 states, *wail, O oaks of Bashan, for the thick forest has come down.*

Her planks have been inlaid with ivory from the coasts of Cyprus. This is a reference to the deck of the ship. The use of ivory for ships and home was developed to a high degree in Tyre as we see with King Ahab. He built an ivory palace after his marriage to a Sidonian queen, according to 1 Kings 22:39. Some scholars describe this ivory as boxwood. "According to the historian Pliny the best boxwood came from Cyprus. Kittum (or Chittim, verse 6) in this instance may have included not only Cyprus but other areas as well (Daniel 11:30)."[76]

The catalogue of Tyre's splendor continues with a description of her sails and coverings. The linen was a fine embroidered cloth from Egypt as well as from Elishah. Egypt was known for its fine linen, as seen in the royal garment of Joseph (compare Genesis 41:42) and Proverbs 7:16 mentions the colored coverings of Egypt. The coverings, a reference to the awnings of the ship, were tent-like canopies that protected the crew during rainstorms. These were supplied from the *coasts of Elishah*, a location that is relatively unknown. Because the dye

---

[75] International Standard Bible Encyclopedia Electronic Database.
[76] Feinberg, 153.

industry was common in the Mediterranean area, some have suggested that *Elishah* is a reference to Greece, Italy, or Syria, but the exact location cannot be known for certain.

Verses 27:8–11
The first group of support personnel mentioned is the *oarsmen*. These were men from Sidon and Arvad and are described as *wise men* who became her *pilots*. Many agree that these men would have been the "cream of the crop." Sidon was another seaport city located twenty miles from Tyre and is considered by most to be Tyre's twin city. They are often mentioned together in the New Testament as Tyre and Sidon (compare Matthew 11:21, Luke 6:17, and Acts 12:20).

Arvad, however, was an island off the coast of Syria. It was known for its powerful navy and its ships are mentioned in the monuments of Egypt and Assyria. Arvad would have produced some of the finest sailors and ship captains in that time and it is no wonder that Ezekiel refers to them as *wise men.*

The second group of support personnel is the *elders of Gebal*, the builders and/or repairmen of the ships. Gebal was an ancient Phoenician city, situated at the foothills of Lebanon, overlooking the Mediterranean. It was a principal seaport of Phoenicia and had a small but good harbor for smaller ships. These men are said to have *caulked the seams* of the ship. This refers to repairing the weak spots in the vessel. Solomon used men of Gebal to help build the Temple of God (compare 1 Kings 5:18).

The third group of support personnel is the *army*. From *Persia, Lydia,* and *Libya,* men were obtained to serve for the defense of the great city. According to Jeremiah 46:8–9, these same cities also supplied soldiers for the Egyptian army. Persia, along with the Medes, ultimately became a world empire by defeating Babylon in 539 BC. *Lydia* is often translated as Lud and is often associated with Punt or Somalia in East Africa. Joining these men were the men of Arvad (see earlier description), who were posted on the walls surrounding the city along with the men of *Gammad* (unknown) who were posted in the towers to serve as watchmen. In the Revised Standard Version of the Bible, *Gammad* is translated as "valorous men," which led some to believe that this is not a proper name but a reference to men previous mentioned. This cannot be known for certain, so it is best not to press the meaning of *Gammad*.

What is known is that they decorated the wall with their shields. "Hanging the shields and helmets in the city, to ornament its walls, appears to have been a Phoenician custom, which Solomon also introduced into Judah (*1 Kings 10:16–17, Song of Solomon 4:4)*, and which is mentioned again in the times of the Maccabees (*1 Maccabees. 4:57)*."[77]

Verses 27:12–24

In these verses we have a list of some twenty-three different locations that traded/bartered with Tyre. It is an impressive list and provides a commercial catalog of all the products that were bought and sold there.[78] (Refer to Table 1.)

Table 1. Tyre's Trading Partners

Name	Location	Merchandise
1. Tarshish	Spain (?)	Silver, iron, tin, lead

---

[77] *Keil and Delitzsch Commentary on the Old Testament*. [electronic database], 1996.
[78] Dyer, 1281.

2. Greece	Modern Greece	Slaves, bronze implements
3. Tubal	Eastern Turkey	Slaves, bronze implements
4. Meshech	Central Turkey	Slaves, bronze implements
5. Beth Togarmah	Eastern Turkey	Work horses, war horses, mules
6. Rhodes*	Modern Rhodes	Ivory tusks, ebony
7. Aram (or Edom)**	Syria (or Jordan)	Turquoise, purple fabric, embroidered work, fine linen, coral, rubies
8. Judah	Palestine	Wheat, olive oil, balm, confections, honey
9. Israel	Palestine	Wheat, olive oil, balm, confections, honey
10. Damascus	Syria	Wine, wool
11. Danites~	Aden (?)	Wrought iron, cassia (a bark for perfume), calamus (an herb)
12. Greeks^ from Uzal	Yemen (or southeastern Turkey)	Wrought iron, cassia, calamus
13. Dedan	Arabia	Saddle blankets
14. Arabia	Arabia	Lambs, rams, goats

15. Kedar	Arabia	Lambs, rams, goats
16. Sheba	Southern Arabia	Spices, precious stones, gold
17. Raamah	Southern Arabia	Spices, precious stones, gold
18.–23. Haran, Cannen, Eden, Sheba, Asshur, Kilmud	Mesopotamia	Blue fabric, embroidered work, multicolored rugs

* The Hebrew has *Dedan* (dᵉdan) while the Septuagint has *Rhodes* (rodan). The difference in the Hebrew consonants is between a "d" and an "r". Because "Dedan" occurs again in verse 20, it is better to see "Rhodes" here.

** Most Hebrew manuscripts have "Aram" (`aram) but some Hebrew manuscripts and the Syriac read "Edom" (`edom), and the Septuagint reads "men" (adam). The difference in the Hebrew consonants is between "r" and a "d".

~ The "Danites" are not the tribe of Dan, which had already been taken into captivity. The NASB translates the word as "Vedan." The best conjecture is that it should be associated with the city of Aden on the Persian Gulf.

^ "Greeks" is the translation of "Javan" (*cf.* v. 13), but the Javan in verse 19 must be different from that of verse 13. "Javan" could be referring to a tribe by that name in Yemen, or "Uzal" could refer to the city of Izalla in the Anatolian foothills of Asia Minor.

Verses 27:25–33

The picture here, of Tyre's downfall and destruction, is as a shipwreck on the sea. The sea is her glory, her place of wealth, and it is ironic that the sea becomes her ultimate doom. She will be broken by the *east wind*, which usually causes great damage to ships because of the strength and violence of its gust. Compare Psalm 48:7: *As when You break the ships of Tarshish, with an east wind.*

Her destruction will be so complete so that all her support personnel will be cast into the sea and drowned. There will be a great mourning from all who witness this great destruction, from the surrounding land (verse 28) and from the men of the sea of whatever rank or station (verse 29). They will cry out bitterly, cast dust on their heads, roll in ashes, and shave the hair from their head to become completely bald, wear sackcloth and wail bitterly, all which was the culture of the day. The (Mosaic) Law specifically dealt with unlawful mourning, and shaving the head to become bald for the purpose of mourning was prohibited by the Lord. *You are the children of the LORD your God; you shall not cut yourselves nor shave the front of your head for the dead. For you are a holy people to the LORD your God, and the LORD has chosen you to be a people for Himself, a special treasure above all the peoples who are on the face of the earth* (Deuteronomy 14:1–2).

When Tyre was a wealthy prosperous city, all the merchants loved her. She satisfied the people and enriched the kings. But in her destruction, many will be troubled and astonished at seeing her destruction. However, her rival merchants will *hiss* (whistle through the teeth) at her; that is, they will celebrate with a malicious joy and celebration. In the end, Tyre will become a terror to the people and they will be frightened at seeing her demise.

APPLICATION

There is much to learn in the destruction of Tyre. Her economic strength allowed her to control other kings and lands. But she was a pagan city and her pride would not allow her to recognize the power and strength of the Lord. Riches and prosperity without the recognition of God are unable to satisfy the heart of man, and it is these very riches that keep the heart from serving God. The sins of any nation are great and unless a nation repents and falls on its face before a holy God, it will ultimately meet God's wrath and He will bring them to their end.

Tyre was full of conceit and pride and boasted that they were *perfect in their beauty* (verse 27:3). The Word of God teaches us that it was pride that brought the downfall of Uzziah and Hezekiah (compare 2 Chronicles 26:16; 32:25). It is pride that prevents a person from trusting Christ as Savior (Psalm 10:4) and God says He hates pride (Proverbs 8:13). When we look around us today, we see that our world is full of conceit and pride, but soon God will arise and destroy the proud and the arrogant, and those whose hope and security are found in "things" rather than in a living holy God will ultimately meet the wrath of God and be cast into a place called the "Lake of Fire," completely separated from God for all eternity. This will surely be the day when wailing and weeping will be common among the people.

The Lord told the church of Laodicea in Revelation 3:15–17, *I know your works, that you are neither cold nor hot. I could wish you were cold or hot. So then, because you are lukewarm, and neither cold nor hot, I will vomit you out of My mouth. Because you say, "I am rich, have become wealthy, and have need of nothing"—and do not know that you are wretched, miserable, poor, blind, and naked.*[79]

Study Questions
1. Do you recognize that God has provided everything you have?
2. Do you allow your possessions to interfere with your relationship with God?

Verses 28:1–3
This section has been the subject of much discussion. To understand this passage, it is best to understand the meaning of "dual fulfillment." Most understand the first ten verses as a reference to the actual king of Tyre at the time of his destruction, but verses 11 through 19 show a dramatic change in description that is difficult to accredit to any human. This is where the principle of dual fulfillment is important. While Ezekiel continues to have the king of Tyre in mind, he reverts to a discussion of the power or authority behind the man. Most scholars have no difficulty attributing the description found in the latter part of this section as referring to Satan, his initial creation, and his ultimate fall from glory. "The Tyrian king seems to symbolize Satan in Ezekiel 28:11–19, and he is said to have fallen because of these things (great prosperity and beauty); compare 1 Timothy 3:6."[80]

---

[79] It should be noted that God's wrath will ultimately be poured out on the earth during the seven-year period called the Tribulation. The church will be raptured (1 Thessalonians 4:15–17), and those who remain, the unrighteous, will be ushered into what Daniel calls the "seventieth week" (Daniel 9:24-27) at which time there will be great distress and tribulation upon the earth for seven years.

[80] Henry Clarence Thiessen, *Lectures in Systematic Theology* (Grand Rapids, MI: Eerdmans, 1979), 137.

We see something very similar in Isaiah 14:12–15. Although many describe this passage as the "Five 'I Wills' of Satan"—and correctly so—there is dual fulfillment, in that Isaiah has the king of Babylon in view. In this case, the king of Babylon is symbolic of Satan.

"The real-world rulers of the great earthly powers are not the men who seem to hold the reins of government and dominate the nations. These men are often but puppets under the control of Satan's minions, angelic personalities and powers who are doing all that they can to thwart the carrying out of God's counsels."[81] Thus, as we study this section, it is best to understand it as a two-fold discussion. The main character is the present king of Tyre, Ithobal II, and includes the entity behind the man, Satan. This is not a new interpretation; it was common among leading Christian scholars of the fourth century, among them Jerome. The date of the prophecy is shortly before the siege of Tyre by Nebuchadnezzar (585–573 BC). There is plenty of symbolism and, according to Feinberg, the chapter is also permeated with much irony.[82]

In verses 1 through 10, we find a direct message to the king of Tyre from God through the prophet Ezekiel. The message is a rebuke and judgment of his pride. The king refers to himself as a *god,* who sits in the *seat of gods*, but the Lord reminds him that he is just a man and not a god. He also considers himself the wisest of the land, *wiser than Daniel!* The phrase shows how far Daniel's fame has spread, even beyond the bounds of his own people. The irony was that Ithobal II felt his wisdom exceeded even that of Daniel, who served the country that would ultimately defeat Tyre. Daniel, who attributed all his wisdom to

---

[81] Ironside, 187.
[82] Feinberg, 158.

God (compare Daniel 2:27–28), was much wiser than Ithobal II, who claimed to be a god.[83] We see this same spirit in Satan, even with the first man and woman upon the earth. In the conversation between the serpent and Eve in Genesis 3:5 we read, *For God knows that in the day you eat of it your eyes will be opened, and you will be like God, knowing good and evil.* Both aspects are seen here. Satan, in the form of a serpent (compare Revelation 12:9), tempted Eve by telling her that she could become like God and have the wisdom of knowing good and evil.

This tactic of Satan is alive and well today. In fact, he has continued to convince people of all generations that they have no need for a deity in their lives, as they are or can become their own god. Self-deification is nothing new, but it is the one sin that keeps individuals from turning to the one and only true God of the Bible. Through the ages, humankind has become more and more independent, and as technology continues to advance, humankind is going to continue to become even more independent and think that we have less and less need for God. If Satan can accomplish his goal of making man more self-dependent and less dependent upon God, he can fulfill his goal (1 Peter 5:8) of leading mankind into destruction and devouring us all.

Verses 28:4–5
The Lord continues with the condemnation of Ithobal II. Through his fleshly effort, Ithobal has become rich and powerful, and his pride and self-righteousness because of this great wealth will become his downfall. We see a very similar problem in the life of King Nebuchadnezzar some years later. Nebuchadnezzar

---

[83] Dyer, 1282.

was the king of Babylon who invaded and captured Tyre. After his capture of Israel in 586 BC, when things appeared to be going "well," he looked around at his empire and stated: *Is not this great Babylon, that **I** have built for a royal dwelling by **my** mighty power and for the honor of **my** majesty?* (Daniel 4:30, emphasis mine). It was while he was still speaking these words that the Lord spoke and removed his kingdom from him and he was stricken with a condition called "insania zooanthropy," in which a man becomes a beast.

Proverbs 16:5 states: *Everyone proud in heart is an abomination to the LORD. Though they join forces, none will go unpunished.* It is the pride of the king of Tyre that becomes his downfall, and the following verses describe in detail the judgment of God upon Ithobal II.

Verses 28:6–10

These verses present a prophecy of invading armies who come and overthrow Tyre. Interestingly, the attack is *against the beauty of their wisdom* and against their *splendor*. The very things that made the king of Tyre prideful are the very things that cause his downfall. The king will be humbled and his pride stripped, as it will be revealed that he is not a god as he thought but a mere man who shall *die the death of the uncircumcised, by the hands of the aliens.* Although these aliens are not mentioned by name, Biblical record teaches us that it is Babylon under King Nebuchadnezzar who defeated Tyre (compare Jeremiah 27:6). Thus the Tyrians died a death of shame and scorn.

The phrase *die the death of the uncircumcised* is an expression that the Jews would understand as an insult. It was King Saul who would rather die than fall into the hands of the uncircumcised (compare 1 Samuel 31:4). Circumcision was a sign of identity and of belonging to the God of Israel as well as a seal of the covenant God made with Abraham and his descendants. It not only carried national significance, but held spiritual meaning as well. To die an uncircumcised death was to die the death of an unbeliever. The finality of this judgment is found in the words, *For I have spoken, says the Lord God.*

APPLICATION

There is tremendous peace and comfort in these words, as we can be confident of God's final victory over sin and evil. Even the wicked will meet their judgment. We are reminded in Scripture that Jesus Christ came to destroy the works of the devil. 1 John 3:8 states: *For this purpose, the Son of God was manifested, that He might destroy the works of the devil.* For the Christian, victory is not an event that might happen but is a certainty. Victory is assured. Everyone who has trusted Christ should live their lives as if they have already won, because they have. 1 Corinthians 15:57 states: *But thanks be to God, who gives us the victory through our Lord Jesus Christ.*

Study Question
1. Does your walk with Christ reflect victory or defeat?

Verses 28:11–19
Ezekiel now shifts from the man of Tyre, Ithobal II, to the power behind the man, namely Satan. As stated earlier, this should be understood as the principle of dual fulfillment or meaning. The *King of Tyre* mentioned in verse 12 is therefore the true king, the man behind the man, the source of all evil and the driving force. Rooker, in his commentary, suggests that these verses

depict the king of Tyre as compared to Adam, the first man and along with Eve, the only human resident of the Garden of Eden. He states: "Echoes of the original Adam are evident in the characterization of the prince of Tyre in the first panel (28:1–10) and the description of the cherub in the second (28:11–19)."[84] He continues: "One issue in favor of this view is that the king is described as one involved in a thriving trade practice, which would be questionable for Adam and well as Satan, but certainly characteristic of the King of Tyre."[85] Thomas sees the transition in descriptions as somewhat similar. He states: "In order to establish the relevance of the story to his readers, Ezekiel compares the King of Tyre to a primeval man in the Garden of Eden … What Ezekiel is portraying in these poetic and difficult lines is the idea of a great fall from a 'perfect' existence. The king seemed to have everything: he is bedecked with the finest jewelry—and falls. Adam had everything—and fell."[86] Some relate this view to a mythical tale of Phoenician origin which states that this primal being was driven out of garden through pride.

      Both of these views seem confusing at best; this author feels it is better to interpret this as a switch from a literal reference to the actual king of Tyre to a symbolic reference to the king (namely, Satan) who actually represents the true power behind this evil human king. Gingrich was right when he said, "Many of the statements made in these verses cannot be applied to the king of Tyre but have reference to Lucifer who through his fall became Satan."[87]

---

[84] Rooker, 199.
[85] Rooker, 199.
[86] Thomas, 197.
[87] Gingrich, 40.

Though it is true to the text to maintain an understanding of this as the Garden of Eden, and the wording of these verses in Ezekiel certainly would allow for this, the place is not so much in question as is the person who occupies this place. While the human king of Tyre is clearly on Ezekiel's mind, it is the driving force behind this king that attracts his attention and gives us an understanding of complete opposition to God. Certainly, the king of Tyre becomes a symbol for Lucifer and the similarity between the two is unquestionable. But if, as suggested, Lucifer (Satan) is the driving force behind this evil king, then there would naturally follow the similarity we see. In fact, Ezekiel saw the work and activity of Satan emulated by the king of Tyre in many ways. Feinberg correctly maintains that there is little difference between this text and that of Matthew 16:21–23 where Peter was rebuked by our Lord Jesus.[88] In the Matthew passage, Christ was not saying that Peter *was* Satan, but that the driving force behind Peter's so-called good intentions was Satan himself, to thwart God's plans at Calvary.

As we begin to unpack these verses, we see a description of the finest of God's creation, Lucifer, and his ultimate fall from heaven. Of interest here is that the Lord is not calling for his condemnation, but instead for a lamentation to be taken up. Isaiah 28:21 describes God's judgment work as unusual and implies that God does not delight in punishing the wicked. According to Micah 7:18, *He* [God] *does not retain His anger forever, because He delights in mercy.* The description that follows is very telling.

In verse 12 Lucifer is described as *the seal of perfection, full of beauty and perfect in beauty.* This is quite the opposite of

---

[88] Feinberg, 161.

a description of man (compare Romans 3:10–18, 23). This, of course, is a description of this being before he became full of pride and was cast out of heaven. God did not create some sinister being full of evil. Lucifer was created as a wonderful and beautiful being that later became full of pride and sinned against a holy God.

Verse 13 tells us that this being was in the Garden of Eden. This is not difficult to ascertain by anyone's definition. We read in Genesis 3 that the serpent came and tempted Eve; when correlated with Revelation 12:9, we can connect the identity of the serpent with that of the fallen Lucifer, Satan. It is at this point that one must begin to see the symbolism, as the literal king of Tyre, Ithobal II, never resided in the Garden of Eden. We know from Genesis that the only two humans ever to occupy this garden were Adam and Eve. Ironside interjects the suggestion that perhaps Lucifer might have been the one appointed from the beginning to take charge of this world, but he is equally careful to point out the danger of being too dogmatic in this approach.[89]

We also see a description of this man in relationship to precious stones. Again, this cannot refer to Adam, as there is no account anywhere in Scripture of Adam's clothing being covered by every precious stone. Here, though, we have a description of the beauty of this king. Ezekiel lists nine precious stones, all of which, along with three that are not mentioned here, were worn on the breastplate of Israel's high priest. Exodus 28:15–21, *You shall make the breastplate of judgment. Artistically woven according to the workmanship of the ephod you shall make it: of gold, blue, purple, and scarlet thread, and fine woven linen, you*

---

[89] Ironside, 192.

shall make it. It shall be doubled into a square: a span shall be its length, and a span shall be its width. And you shall put settings of stones in it, four rows of stones: The first row shall be a sardius, a topaz, and an emerald; this shall be the first row; the second row shall be a turquoise, a sapphire, and a diamond; the third row, a jacinth, an agate, and an amethyst; and the fourth row, a beryl, an onyx, and a jasper. They shall be set in gold settings. And the stones shall have the names of the sons of Israel, twelve according to their names, like the engravings of a signet, each one with its own name; they shall be according to the twelve tribes.

The precious stones enhanced the beauty and symbolized the high position that Lucifer enjoyed before his fall. It is interesting to note that these same stones were used in the description of the wall of Jerusalem in Revelation 21. This is yet future and speaks of a New Jerusalem that will be built for all eternity, after the great Millennial Kingdom. It is not surprising, then, to suggest that these stones reveal the glory of God. "Fire is a well-known symbol of God Himself (Hebrews 12:29), and the manifestation of His glory is represented under the figure of beautiful stones (Exodus 24:10, 17)."[90]

Many today think of Lucifer (Satan) as a cartoon character with a red suit, a long-pointed tail, horns, mustache, and a three-pronged pitchfork, this description could not be further from the truth. In many ways, this is the world's attempt to minimize the importance as well as the danger of this creature and the destruction he can cause when given a chance. Satan was originally created as a consummately beautiful creature and, as we will see, given a high position with much authority.

---

[90] Feinberg, 163.

Verse 13 ends with a reference to *timbrels and pipes*. Some suggest that a reference to musical instruments indicates that Lucifer oversaw the music and praise among the other angelic beings. Some even suggest that these are references to females, indicating that he was surrounded by women. This seems improbable unless you continue to accept the text as referring to Ithobal II, which we have already established as highly unlikely. It is best to understand these as a continuation of the description of Lucifer's beauty and majesty, especially given how the verse ends: *on the day you were created.*

Verse 14 informs us of the position that Lucifer enjoyed before his fall. Here we have a reference to Lucifer being responsible for guarding the throne of God. We know from Genesis 3:24 that cherubim were posted at the gate of the Garden of Eden to guard against anyone entering. It seems that the ministry of the cherubs was to guard, and in this instance the superior cherub, Lucifer, was responsible for guarding the throne. It is God who created, established, anointed, and chose him for this position. That he was allowed direct access to the throne of God is suggested by the phrase *you walked back and forth in the midst of fiery stones.* This is not the first reference to cherubs. In chapters 1 and 10 of Ezekiel we saw four living creatures who are called cherubs. They too were responsible for guarding the throne, but also, more particularly, for its transportation.

Verses 15 through 18 complete this description by referring to Lucifer as being perfect until iniquity was found in him. It is obvious that Satan was created with a free will to choose and he chose to sin. The sin that corrupted him was his pride (compare 1 Timothy 3:6). His position became his downfall and his splendor became his spoil. A study of Isaiah 14:12–15, a parallel passage, indicates that Satan had visions of grandeur. *I will ascend into heaven; I will exalt my throne above the stars of God; I will also sit on the mount of the congregation; I will ascend above the heights of the clouds,* and finally, *I will be like the Most High.* He sought equality with God and his judgment was expulsion from the mountain of God. In Luke 10:18, Christ says, *I saw Satan fall like lightning from heaven.*

    A clarification is in order at this point, for many believe that Satan was expelled from heaven once and for all when he sinned against the holiness of God. A quick study of Job chapters 1 and 2 will dispel this notion, as Satan, even after his expulsion, had access to God. He was under God's control and still had to report to God and give an account of all his actions. It is not until the seven-year tribulation period, specifically described in Revelation 12, that Satan is thrown out of heaven never to return. In fact, his ultimate fate is to be cast into the lake of fire for all eternity, but not until he makes one last-ditch effort to rebel against God. Christ will return after the seven years of tribulation to establish His Kingdom on the throne of David in Jerusalem (Revelation 19:11). At this time, Satan will be cast into a bottomless pit where he will remain until after the thousand-year reign of Christ (Revelation 20:1–3). When the thousand years are over, Satan will be released. He will at this time gather an army from among the people of the earth to stage one final battle against Christ. He will be sorely defeated, and it is at this time that he will be cast into the lake of fire (compare Revelation 20:10). All this because of pride. Is it any wonder that of the things that are an abomination to the Lord, the first listed is a proud look (Proverbs 6:16–19)?

    There seems to be a transition back to the literal king of Tyre beginning in verse 18, or at least the case can be made that both Lucifer and Ithobal II are referred to here. Tyre boasted numerous *sanctuaries* and temples and according to Feinberg, this is the reason the city was called the Holy Island by the ancients.[91] She ultimately was destroyed by fire and became a pile of ashes and a public spectacle of shame. Ezekiel begins this section by dealing with the ultimate ruler of Tyre, who is Lucifer (Satan), and he finishes by describing the utter destruction of the city itself. Those who knew her would be astonished, as many had profited from her great wealth, and yet they became full of horror and fear knowing they could face the same fate. So complete was her destruction that *she shall be no more forever.*

This finishes the long discussion of the destruction of Tyre. However, it should be noted that Tyre was an active, vibrant city at the time of the New Testament. Matthew 15:21 states that *Jesus went out from there and departed to the region of Tyre and Sidon,* and in Acts 12:20, we are told that Herod became angry with the people of Tyre and Sidon. Feinberg notes: "The geographer Strabo said it had two harbors. The town was in Saracen hands from A.D. 636–1125. Saladin could not capture it in A.D. 1189, but in A.D. 1291 it fell into Egyptian hands. Gradually its strongholds were reduced, and it became an obscure site. Present (location of) Sur has no ethnic connection with the prosperous Phoenician city of antiquity."[92]

Study Questions
1. Do you believe that Satan is a real person?
2. If you answered "yes" to question 1, then do you believe that Satan is alive and active today?
3. Explain the implications of 1 Peter 5:8.

---

[91] Feinberg, 164.
[92] Feinberg, 164.

Ezekiel 28:20–24

Sidon

Verses 20–21
Sidon is a sister city to Tyre, located some twenty miles north of Tyre, and may have been the lead city. She was founded by Canaan's firstborn (Genesis 10:15). Sidon is closely related to Tyre in her actions. Although her sins are not mentioned here, it is obvious that she shared some of the same sins and therefore similarly faced the wrath of God. Judges 10:6 refers to the gods of Sidon and 1 Kings 11:33 refers to Ashtoreth, the goddess of the Sidonians, which would indicate (among other things) that idolatry was prevalent among the people of Sidon; it is even possible that Sidon was the headquarters of idolatry connected to Baal, Ashtoreth, and Tammuz.

Verses 22–24
Here we see the purpose of God's judgments. God will be *glorified*, and the surrounding nations will know that He is God. God's judgments upon this city as well as all the others will bring God the consecration and purity that is so deserving of His name. God does not execute judgment because it brings Him pleasure to inflict pain, but because His great love and His great holiness must be satisfied. We are told by the author of Hebrews that God loves those whom He chastens (Hebrews 12:5; compare Proverbs 3:12). This judgment would come by way of *pestilence* and the

sword. The result of this judgment was to remove the *pricking brier* and *painful thorn* from among Israel. These two terms are used by the Lord to describe those who despise Israel. Again, we see the fulfillment of the Abrahamic Covenant from Genesis 12:3 where the Lord states: *I will bless those who bless you, and I will curse him who curses you.*

A quick look at the world's current situation makes it obvious that all of Israel's enemies have yet to be destroyed. At the time of the writing of this commentary, the Middle East is much turmoil, with war in Iraq, war in Afghanistan, and threats from Iran to attack Israel. This author clearly remembers Iraq invading Kuwait in 1990, and when the coalition forces responded, Iraq retaliated by bombing Israel. Israel has long been the object of hatred among most countries in the Middle East, and several countries would be elated if Israel were completely annihilated. That Israel's enemies will be completely removed is a fact, but this will not become a reality until after the Tribulation Period as defined in the book of Revelation. Then and only then will the whole word know that God is Lord of all (compare Philippians 2:10–11).

Verses 25–26
This chapter ends with a pronouncement of future blessings for Israel. God will scatter Israel's enemies, and will restore Israel to her rightful place of prominence. This, in its historical fulfillment, was realized upon the return from captivity in Babylon, but even then not all Israel returned. Some became so attached to the world in Babylon that they refused to return to the land the Lord had given them. The full realization will come when God regathers all of Israel into His kingdom when Christ returns after the Tribulation. They will *dwell safely*, *build*

houses, and *plant vineyards*. Israel is not dwelling securely at present, but when God's ultimate judgment upon this earth comes, this prophecy will be fulfilled. Then it will come to pass that *they shall know that I am the Lord their God.* Thus says the Lord! Amen!

Ezekiel 29:1–32:32

Egypt

Verses 29:1–2

Again, we are faced with a rather long section dealing with one nation. This is the longest of the prophecies in Ezekiel against any nation and is made up of seven separate and distinct shorter prophecies. Verse 1 gives us a good record of the time frame involved with the prophecy. Many would agree that for the most part these prophecies occurred between 587–585 BC, during the time Jerusalem began to fall and taken captive by Nebuchadnezzar, which was ultimately completed in 586 BC. Before Babylon, the Persians were in power and Egypt was somewhat a servant to the Persian Empire.

Israel's history with Egypt dates to the days of Abraham. It was not until the time of Joseph, however, that Egypt became a constant thorn in the side of Israel. Egypt was a place of refuge for many of the patriarchs, but it was God's intervention that had Israel living in Egypt, to preserve the nation against the famine (Genesis 46–47). God miraculously delivered the Jews from Egypt by means of the exodus, but the Egyptians were always lurking to inflict pain upon Israel. At the time of Ezekiel's writings, there was conflict for power over the land. First Assyria invaded Judah and became a force to be reckoned with; then Babylon grew in strength and power and invaded not only Assyria, but all that Assyria had controlled, and seized its power and authority. Judah became immersed in the conflict and was taken captive by Nebuchadnezzar, with Judah's final destruction coming in 586 BC. Throughout these times, Egypt had sought to be allied with Israel's enemies, or at least to make Israel subservient to them.

The Pharaoh King of Egypt referred to in verse 2 is a reference to Pharaoh Hophra. Feinberg gives us a good understanding of the persons involved:

> Pharaoh Necho had been defeated by Nebuchadnezzar at Carchemish (605 B.C.). He was succeeded in 594 B.C. by his son Psammetik II who died in 588 B.C. His son Pharaoh Hophra (Jeremiah 44:30; the Apries of Herodotus) followed him. He besieged Tyre and Sidon, was unsuccessful against Cyrene and was deposed by Amasis in 569 B.C. Zedekiah, as his predecessors Hezekiah (Isaiah 30) and Jehoiakim (Jeremiah 46), sought Egyptian help against the Babylonians. Ezekiel predicted Egypt would be a poor support in time of need. Isaiah (31:1) and Jeremiah (2:36) before him had condemned Egypt.[93]

In the end, Pharaoh Hophra withdrew his army, leaving Judah to the mercy of the Babylonians (Jeremiah 37:5–7, 44:30).

Verses 29:3–16

The first prophecy is directed against Pharaoh Hophra. He is referred to as the *great monster who lies in the midst of the rivers*. *Monster* is a reference to dragon and possibly means

---

[93] Feinberg, 167.

crocodile of the Nile. This same word is used to describe Aaron's rod when the Lord transformed it into a reptile in Exodus 7:9–10. The crocodile was symbolic of power and strength and the Egyptians believed that their pharaoh could conquer this great sea monster. Ironically, the Lord calls the pharaoh the monster, thus implying that the conqueror becomes the conquered. Isaiah made the same prophecy in Isaiah 27:1.

We have already seen how pride contributes to the downfall of great leaders, and this pharaoh is no exception. Pharaoh believes he created the great river (compare verse 9). Herodotus stated that Pharaoh Hophra considered himself so strongly entrenched in his realm that no god could displace him, but it is the Lord who will bring him down by putting hooks in his jaws. This is how you capture a crocodile, and the terminology would have had much significance to those who heard.

The *fish* mentioned in verse 4 would be the people or followers of the pharaoh. They were loyal: so much so that they become recipients of God's judgment as well. The monster, along with the fish that stick to his scales, will be cast up out of the river and thrown into the desert and there shall they die. They will become food for beasts of the field and birds of prey.

In verse 6, as we have seen in past judgments, in this judgment the purpose is to put God's glory on display so the recipients will know that God is Lord indeed. Here they are called a *staff of reed* which is an expression referring to a supporting stick, like a cane or walking stick. Israel had used Egypt for support at a time when they needed it the most, but Egypt removed the support (verse 7). Egypt was notorious for breaking treaties with other nations (compare 2 Kings 18:21 and Isaiah 36:6). She broke her promise to Judah in her hour of need and as a result, Babylon came and broke Judah and made all their backs quiver. Isaiah 30:7 states: *For the Egyptians shall help in vain and to no purpose. Therefore, I have called her Rahab-Hem-Shebeth.* This is to be translated as "Rahab the Do-Nothing."[94]

Because of Egypt's lack of support, God will bring her down with the sword (verse 8) and make her *desolate and a waste, from Migdol to Syene, as far as the border of Ethiopia* (verses 9–10). The *forty years* mentioned in verse 11 are not to be confused with the forty-year captivity of the Jews in Babylon; that said, however, it would be appropriate to understand this as the forty years during which Babylon enjoyed world dominance, which would have had ill effects on Egypt as well. Verse 12 was easily fulfilled during the reign of Babylon. As with Israel, Egypt was scattered throughout the land and much of her country was laid desolate and barren. Feinberg notes that "Berosus, the historian of Babylon, states that Nebuchadnezzar, after he had conquered Egypt, took great numbers of the captives to Babylon. Others, undoubtedly, fled to neighboring areas as in similar case."[95]

After the forty-year period, God promises to restore Egypt: not to what she had been, but to a much weaker nation, one that will be the *lowliest of the kingdoms.* She shall never be as great as she once was. Israel, then, will no longer be dependent upon Egypt and use her as a support. Egypt is never to rule over any nations again. Egypt will exist to be a continual reminder to God's people of their sin when they return to follow them. Their sin was putting their trust in man and not in God. God desires and demands His people to look to no one and nothing other than

---

[94] Thomas, 202.
[95] Feinberg, 169.

Him. He declared to Israel, back at Mount Sinai in the giving of the law, that He was a jealous God and would not share with anyone (Exodus 20:5). Deuteronomy 4:24: *For the LORD your God is a consuming fire, a jealous God.* Nahum 1:2a: *God is jealous.*

Verses 29:17–21
The second prophecy begins with yet another date, almost seventeen years after the first prophecy. This is the latest recorded prophecy of Ezekiel and some scholars agree that the date places the timeline around the twenty-sixth year of Ezekiel's exile. It is noteworthy that Ezekiel is still serving the Lord faithfully over these many years, which stand as a testimony to his longevity of service.

Here we have the "who" of the judgment of verses 1–16. It is Nebuchadnezzar himself who would attack Egypt. Verse 18 refers to the long, drawn-out battle that Nebuchadnezzar had with Tyre. *Bald* heads are a reference to the results of the helmets of war being worn for such long periods and *shoulder rubbed raw* refers to chafing caused by carrying armor, weapons, and supplies. The results were not good. Tyre had sent most of its wealth to Egypt, so Nebuchadnezzar was not able to acquire any booty and therefore could not pay his men. There simply was no reward for their strenuous and prolonged labor of war. In response, Nebuchadnezzar attacked Egypt to take its wealth. Verse 19 clearly shows the irony of all this. It was the Lord who was using Nebuchadnezzar as an instrument to judge Egypt and therefore, unknowingly, he was doing the work of the Lord. It was the Lord's plan for Nebuchadnezzar to take the wealth of Egypt to be used for wages for his army. The wealth and the land were rewards to Nebuchadnezzar from the Lord (verse 20).

Many have questioned whether God uses the unrighteous to complete His plans and accomplish His goals. This text should serve as proof to all who have any doubt about this, as the Lord clearly states: *They* [the Babylonians] *worked for Me.*

Verse 21 has given readers some difficulty over the years as to what exactly the Lord is saying. To keep it in context, *that day* should be taken as referring to the downfall of Egypt. The *horn* has been used throughout Scriptures to refer to power or strength. It is best to understand this as a sort of revival among Israel, in that they will give more heed to Ezekiel and his prophecies, especially when some of what he has said comes to pass. This will to give him more credence among his people and they will listen even more. He may have felt constrained before because of the people's unbelief and their initial response to his messages, but now he could command a certain confidence and boldness in speaking for the Lord to the people. Prophecy was meant to glorify God, to warn and comfort the people, and to minister to the servant of God at the same time.[96]

Verses 30:1–19

Unlike the other six prophecies, the prophecy in these verses is the only one not dated. Although we have no timeline, this prophecy divides nicely into four sections, each starting with the phrase *thus says the Lord God.* What is obvious from this prophecy is that Egypt's influence was keenly felt in the world around her and many would suffer judgment from the hand of the Lord for allowing themselves to be so closely connected.

Verses 2 and 3 refer to *the day* and are a reference to the time that Babylon will invade and destroy Egypt. The warning

---

[96] Feinberg, 171.

is that this time is very near and preparations need to be made. They should wail and mourn the day as it approaches. It is referred to as *a day of clouds.* Clouds often picture doom and gloom. Joel 2:2 states: *A day of darkness and gloominess, a day of clouds and thick darkness, like the morning clouds spread over the mountains. A people come, great and strong, the like of whom has never been nor will there ever be any such after them, even for many successive generations.*

Zephaniah 1:15 states: *That day is a day of wrath, a day of trouble and distress, a day of devastation and desolation, a day of darkness and gloominess, a day of clouds and thick darkness.* The "day of the Lord" is an expression that often refers to God's judgment. Many have confused the phrase as found here with the time of the Great Tribulation, when God brings all nations under His hand of judgment (compare Daniel 11:42–43). However, as we have seen before, we must remain true the context of this prophecy; which indicates that the "day of the Lord" refers to the judgment and ultimate desolation of Egypt. It is now time for Egypt to face the fierce hand of the Lord's judgment.

Time of the Gentiles should not be taken out of context either. While it is true that the Lord used this same phrase in Luke 21:24, He was referring to the entire period during which Palestine, the city of Jerusalem, and the people of the Jews are under Gentile domination. This began with the rise of Nebuchadnezzar, and is still in progress, and will continue until the day when the Lord Himself appears from heaven in His glorious second advent to execute judgment upon the nations and to set up His own heavenly kingdom over all this lower universe.[97]

The *sword* in verse 4 is a reference to the invading armies of Babylon—but it is not only Egypt that will suffer, as there shall be great anguish in all of Ethiopia (verse 5). Men will be slain, the city will be plundered and ransacked, and her very foundations will be destroyed. The area lands include *Ethiopia*, *Libya* (Put), *Lydia* (Lud), and *Chub*. Also mentioned are all the *mingled people*, which leaves out no one in the surrounding lands contiguous to Egypt, including all those who allied themselves with Egypt. This is truly guilt by association.

The identifications of Ethiopia, Libya, and Lydia are all easy to ascertain because we see them in other prophecies. Jeremiah 46:9 states: *Come up, O horses, and rage, O chariots! And let the mighty men come forth: The Ethiopians and the Libyans who handle the shield, and the Lydians who handle and bend the bow.* These would be a band of soldiers, or a private army fighting alongside the Egyptian forces. The difficulty comes in identifying Chub and the mingled people. In fact, it is basically impossible to come to a definitive conclusion as to their identity. They should, however, be included in this private army with the others. Secular sources have confirmed that Egypt used hired soldiers from different backgrounds; this is probably the case here and would serve to give us a clearer understanding as to who these men are. But no amount of help will protect Egypt from the hand of God: as with the Egyptians, they shall fall by the sword.

Before leaving these verses, it should be noted that the Revised Standard Version translates *the men of the land who*

---

[97] Ironside, 203.

are allied as *the people of the land that is in league,* which in the original text would allow the reading to be "children of the land of the covenant." This could thus be a reference to Jews who fled Jerusalem and settled in Egypt. Jerome and others have accepted and taught this view. Jeremiah 42–44 could be used to support such a position. Jeremiah 42:15–17: *Then hear now the word of the LORD, O remnant of Judah! Thus says the LORD of hosts, the God of Israel: 'If you wholly set your faces to enter Egypt, and go to dwell there, then it shall be that the sword which you feared shall overtake you there in the land of Egypt; the famine of which you were afraid shall follow close after you there in Egypt; and there you shall die. So, shall it be with all the men who set their faces to go to Egypt to dwell there. They shall die by the sword, by famine, and by pestilence. And none of them shall remain or escape from the disaster that I will bring upon them.'*

As this prophecy continues, verse 6 reminds us that there is no power greater than the hand of God. All who come to the aid of Egypt will themselves be destroyed. From *Migdol* [the tower] *to Syene* indicates that from the north to the south—the extreme outer limits of the Egyptian power—no country will be left untouched.

Verses 7 and 8 use language as we have seen before (compare Ezekiel 28:18). Fire is an all-consuming enemy that leaves nothing untouched, and as with fire, so it will be with God's judgment. Again, these verses remind us that Egypt's allies would be of no help. The strong arm of the Lord is undefeatable and regardless of the size of the army, and how many years a nation spends building up its defenses, nothing will protect it against God's judgment.

Verse 9 speaks of messengers going from Egypt to the Ethiopians. The indication is they will be heralding the news of Egypt's destruction, but they only manage to bring further fear and anguish to the Ethiopians. Previously, the Ethiopians felt secure because they had Egypt to protect them and to function as a "big brother." Now that Egypt has been destroyed and its men have fled to Ethiopia, their security is gone, and they must fear for their own lives. As a fire spreads quickly from location to location, God's judgment is meted out, and there is no escaping. *The day of Egypt* could serve as a reminder of what Jehovah accomplished when freeing the Jews during the Exodus and the great power and miracles He exhibited to accomplish His will. As it was then, so shall it be now!

Verses 10 through 12 continue to describe the complete and utter destruction of Egypt but give more detail as to whom it is the Lord uses to destroy them. Multitudes will cease to exist, and Nebuchadnezzar will be used of God to execute God's wrath. Three times in these verses alone we see the phrase *I will*. The irony is sweet, in that a pagan king who will not acknowledge the creator God is being used by this great God to accomplish His will and plan. One might wonder whether, if Nebuchadnezzar had had some inkling as to what was really happening, he would have resisted his destiny and refused to attack Egypt. We will never know!

Babylon was a ruthless nation that treated captives cruelly, and thus is described as *most terrible of the nations*. We read in 2 Kings 25 that when Nebuchadnezzar invaded Judah, he forced King Zedekiah to witness the slaying of his two sons, and then immediately gouged out his eyes so that the last thing he saw was the death of his sons.

The description of the rivers drying is a reference to the many branches of the Nile River. This river was the life source for Egypt; without it; they were no more than a barren, dry land. Take away the Nile and Egypt quickly ceases to exist; they would have to sell the land to accumulate any wealth, so the land would be occupied by aliens and foreigners. All this will come to pass, because *I, the LORD have spoken.*

In the final verses of this third prophecy, Ezekiel mentions the principal cities that are to be destroyed—in fact, they are to be annihilated. They range in geographic location from Upper Egypt to Lower Egypt. The focus on these cities is their involvement in idolatry. Feinberg informs us that the "Greek historian Herodotus related how Cambyses of Persian, son of Cyrus the Great, took Pelusium by setting before his army cats and dogs, sacred to Egypt, which the Egyptians would not attack."[98]

Noph is a reference to Memphis, which was the first capital of Egypt as well as serving as its religious center, the focus of idolatrous worship. God will cause her images to cease. *Pathros,* located midway between Cario/Aswar in Upper Egypt, would become desolate and *Zoan,* located in the Delta region and serving as the residence for all royalty, was to be destroyed by fire. *No*, also known as Thebes, was in Lower Egypt, some 400 miles south of Cairo, and was where God would execute His judgment and cut off the multitude from her.

God will also pour out His fury on *Sin,* referred to here as the *strength of Egypt. Sin*, also known as Pelusium, was located one mile from the Mediterranean Sea; it was a major military center and served as a guard post for the north entrance into

---

[98] Feinberg, 175.

Egypt. *Sin* will experience great pain, *No* will be split apart, and *Noph* will be in constant distress.

Aven, or Heliopolis, in Upper Egypt, was a religious center where sun worship flourished. *Pi Beseth,* another religious center and a place where cats were mummified, was located northeast of Cairo. It was in *Pi Beseth* where festivals were held annually, with gatherings of around 700,000 people to worship and honor the cat-headed goddess Ubastet. The Lord states that these two cities were to fall by the sword and be taken into captivity.

Tehaphnehes was located near what we now know as the Suez Canal. This city was named after the Egyptian queen Tahpanhes, and is the city where the pharaohs resided. Jeremiah 43:8–9 states: *Then the word of the LORD came to Jeremiah in Tahpanhes, saying, 'Take large stones in your hand, and hide them in the sight of the men of Judah, in the clay in the brick courtyard which is at the entrance to Pharaoh's house in Tahpanhes.'* The city's day was to be darkened, which was to serve as a sign of the judgment to come.

Finally, the stronghold of Egypt will be broken, and her strength will be ripped away. Again, we see the analogy of cloud covering representing a dark day approaching for Egypt. The assurance that these events will come to pass can be found in the words of the Lord: *Thus, I will execute judgments on Egypt, then they shall know that I am the Lord.*

APPLICATION

The major thrust of this third prophecy centers upon idolatry. We have noted earlier that our God is a jealous God and will share His due with no one or nothing. How senseless are humans in their perversion to worship that which is created rather than the Creator? The apostle Paul refers to them as fools who were not thankful but are futile in their thoughts and have foolish hearts being darkened. They choose to worship and serve the creature rather than the Creator because of their great sin of idolatry, and God will judge them severely (Romans 1). Egypt now understands this very well, as they became the recipients of God's wrath.

Study Questions
1. Explain the jealousy of God.
2. Can you name idols that people worship today?

Verses 30:20–26
The fourth prophecy is dated the eleventh year of the captivity, which would be 587 BC. This is around the same time that Jerusalem fell into the hands of the Babylonians. Some in Judah may have felt that Egypt would be their knight in shining armor and come to their rescue. According to Jeremiah 37:5, when the Chaldeans were besieging Jerusalem, Pharaoh's army came up from Egypt and the Chaldeans departed Jerusalem. However, had they continued to study the prophecy of Jeremiah, they would have learned that the Lord also said that the Egyptians would return to their land and the Babylonians would return (Jeremiah 37:6–8).

Pharaoh's army was not strong enough to hold back the forces of Nebuchadnezzar. In fact, the text in Ezekiel tells us that the Lord would render Egypt powerless against her enemies. Pharaoh's arm has been broken and it would not be attended to: *it has not been bandaged for healing, nor a splint* (bandage) *put on to bind it, to make it strong enough to hold a sword.* The Lord has spoken and there is no way to reverse the outcome.

Verse 22 refers to the breaking of the arms of Egypt; *both the strong one and the one that was broken.* The former arm is a reference to Pharaoh Hophra as seen in Jeremiah 37 (discussed earlier), and the latter may be a reference to Pharaoh Necho at Carchemish (2 Kings 24:7 and Jeremiah 46:2). As part of Egypt's judgment, the Lord promises to *scatter the Egyptians among the nations and disperse them throughout the countries,* and He will use the Babylonians to accomplish His plan and purpose. The Lord will put His sword into their hands and in so doing; He will break Pharaoh's armies. Egypt will groan but to no avail.

APPLICATION

It is amazing that men who have no desire for a relationship with a sovereign God are controlled and used by this very God to accomplish a greater purpose. When will we learn that God is sovereign, and we are powerless to accomplish anything outside of His divine plan and purpose? When God arises to judge, neither the forces of heaven, earth, or hell can stay His hand. At whatever cost, men must learn that God is Lord and in absolute control.

Another application to recognize at this point speaks to all those who would conclude that God is not interested in and does not concern Himself with the affairs of nations. We have seen time and time again, throughout the written pages of Scripture, that God is sovereign not only over the affairs of men but also over those of governments and nations. Thomas explains: "In a day when Christians are apt to confine God to purely personal issues, we need to regain the cosmic perspective of the prophets as they speak of the Lord of the universe intimately involved in the international issues of the day. There is not an item of news that the Lord is not involved in."[99]

Study Questions
1. Is there any event in your life that God does not control?
2. Explain Colossians 1:15–18 in relationship to the sovereignty of God.

Verses 31:1–18
When we look at the timing stated in these prophecies, it becomes obvious that they are not in chronological order. The fifth prophecy is given in the *eleventh year, the third month,* which would be about two months before Jerusalem fell to the Babylonians. This prophecy is a parable or analogy that compares the nation of Egypt to the great trees of the forest.

The Lord begins this prophecy by reminding Egypt of the greatness of the Assyrians and the fact that she was still broken and defeated by the Chaldeans. He refers to Assyria as a *cedar in Lebanon* and is comparing Egypt to Assyria. The cedar surpassed all other trees in greatness, both in height and beauty, with some growing to as much as eighty feet tall. The cedar was known for its interwoven branches which provided much-needed shade (verse 3). The reason for its tremendous height and majesty was the water that supplied its nourishment. The *rivers* (verse 4) are a reference to the Tigris River with its many branches.

---

[99] Thomas, 206.

Some scholars understand the waters to be a reference to people: more specifically, to the surrounding nations who contributed to the greatness of Assyria so that she became *exalted above all the trees of the field* (verse 5). The birds of heaven in verse 6, who made their *nests in its boughs* and the *beasts of the field*, who *brought forth their young* under the cedar are references to all the nations that looked to Assyria for protection and support.

This tree (a reference to Assyria) is described as the most beautiful tree in God's entire creation (verse 8). The others in the surrounding area could not hide her. No tree even in the garden of Eden could compare to it; in fact, all the other trees envied her (verse 9). The analogy could not be any clearer. Assyria stood as the greatest nation of her time. She was the envy of all those around her. Yet in all her pride, she fell and was judged by the Lord.

Ezekiel, having opened his prophecy with the question of whom Pharaoh with his might resembles (verse 2), moves on to depict Assyria as a mighty towering cedar (verses 3–9) which has fallen and been cast down by a *mighty one of the nations* on account of its height and pride (verses 10–14). Everything mourned over its fall, because many nations went down with it to hell (verses 15–17). The question is then repeated in verse 18, and from the preceding comparison the conclusion can be drawn that Egypt will perish like that lofty cedar (Assyria). The fall of that great empire was still so fresh in people's minds at the time that the memories could not fail to make a deep impression upon the prophet's hearers.

That a nation should be compared to a great tree is not that unusual. In Daniel 4, King Nebuchadnezzar had a dream that troubled him, and he went to Daniel to find an interpretation. This is what Daniel told him:

> *The tree that you saw, which grew and became strong, whose height reached to the heavens and which could be seen by all the earth, whose leaves were lovely and its fruit abundant, in which was food for all, under which the beasts of the field dwelt, and in whose branches the birds of the heaven had their home—it is you, O king, who have grown and become strong; for your greatness has grown and reaches to the heavens, and your dominion to the end of the earth.* (Daniel 4:20–22)

We find similar wording in the text of Ezekiel as the Lord compares Assyria to the great cedar tree. What is being addressed here is the pride and arrogance of Egypt, as she is asked to consider with whom she compares. God was in effect saying to Pharaoh and his people, "If you are inclined to pride yourself on your glory as a mighty empire, just consider what happened to Assyria, described under the figure of a cedar."[100]

Some conclude that Assyria is not mentioned here but rather that Assyria is the name of the tree. However, if this is so, the question in verse 2 would be rather pointless. At the time of this prophecy, Assyria was, for all intents and purposes, totally destroyed and the comparison should not be missed. Egypt is clearly being warned to look to Assyria as an example. Assyria was a great nation, but because of its pride it fell—and

---

[100] Feinberg, 177.

the same fate will come upon Egypt for the same reasons. As Assyria went, so goes Egypt, as the Lord says in verse 18.

"Let Pharaoh learn from what had taken place in Asia and understand that however he might seek to guard against destruction, so long as he lifted himself up against the God of Israel he but exposed himself to the same doom as that which had overtaken Assyria. This says the prophet, is Pharaoh and all his multitude, for they, too, must suffer in the same way as their great sister kingdom."[101]

APPLICATION

To leave this passage without the solemn awareness that God hates pride is to miss entirely what the Spirit teaches us. God hates pride but loves humility. James 4:10 states: *Humble yourselves in the sight of the Lord, and He will lift you up.* It can be correctly concluded that he who refuses to humble himself will not be lifted up. In fact, James and Peter quote Proverbs 3:34, *God resists the proud, but gives grace to the humble* (James 4:6 and 1 Peter 5:5). We should daily ask God for the humility needed to serve Him and glorify His name so that in due time, we may be exalted (1 Peter 5:6).

Study Questions
1. Do you pray daily for humility to please man or to glorify God?
2. Name the dangers of pride.
Verses 32:1–16
The date of this sixth prophecy is 585 BC, approximately eight months after the fall of Jerusalem. According to Ezekiel 33:11,

---

[101] Ironside, 213.

it took some two months after the fall of Jerusalem for word thereof to arrive among the exiles in Babylon. This prophecy gives a thorough and complete picture of the destruction of Egypt in graphic terms and, as with the seventh prophecy, comes in the form of a lament.[102]

In the sixth prophecy, a lament is called for the Pharaoh King of Egypt, who is compared to a *young lion among the nations* and a *monster in the seas* (probably the crocodile; compare Ezekiel 29:3–5). A lion is well known for its ferocity and power and the crocodile for its quickness, power, and strength. The analogy points out that on land, Pharaoh is ferocious and powerful, and on the water he is quick and powerful. He is feared both on land and on sea. He causes turmoil and chaos among his neighbors. The term *bursting forth* gives us a picture of the quickness of the crocodile as well as the lion. Both, when stalking their prey, can remain silent and extremely still until the moment comes to attack. At that point, the predator is very quick and precise, pouncing on its prey with such speed and precision that the prey is unable to defend itself.

God refers to His *net* as a *company of many people* (verse 3). By using the possessive pronoun, the Lord intends to make it clear that this is His operation. He is in charge and controls the thoughts and movements of nations. The *many people* is a reference to Babylon as led by King Nebuchadnezzar. Pharaoh's army was disturbing the international scene as he tried to defend himself against an invading Babylonian army.

Verses 4–6 supply us with some graphic details of the extent of the destruction. As this lion or sea monster is captured

---

[102] Some suggest, as does Feinberg, that the sixth is the final prophecy and contains two lamentations, but this author prefers to view these as two separate prophecies.

and destroyed, she will be laid in an *open field* for the vultures to feast on. Her corpse will supply food enough to *fill the beasts of the whole earth.* Her destruction will be so complete that the valleys will be filled her carcass. The land will be watered with her blood, which will flow even to the mountains and the riverbeds will be full. To some, these words seem a bit much, and a question arises as to how exaggerated this text is or has become. All one must do is compare this to Revelation 14:20 to see blood as deep as the *horses' bridles, for one thousand six hundred furlongs.* God's judgment is exact and complete and there can be no exaggeration as to the extent of the devastation.

The analogy now changes to that of luminaries. Darkness will prevail and cover the land as God *covers the heavens and makes its stars dark* (verses 7–8). The sun is to be covered by clouds and the moon will not give off her light. Darkness will be the order of the day as even the bright lights of the heavens are made dark. Some suggest, as does Ironside, that this section is not to be taken literally; they think it indicates the "destruction of delegated authority and the gloom that would settle down upon the hearts of men because of the ruin that was to fall upon the land."[103] However, referring to Revelation, we see similar wording in the sixth-seal judgment of the tribulation period in Revelation 6, the fourth-trumpet judgment in Revelation 8:12, and the fifth-bowl judgment of Revelation 16:10. It is not too difficult to take this passage literally, as our God, who is the God of all creation, can and does use His creation to accomplish His judgment upon the earth. It should be noted that this figure is also used in connection with the day of the Lord in Joel 2:10.

---

[103] Ironside, 216.

Verses 9–10 display for us the emotions involved during that time. *Astonished, horribly afraid*, and *trembling* are among the responses from the surrounding nations. This further emphasizes the complete and utter destruction that will come upon Egypt and the effect it will have on her neighbors and even countries that are not known by Egypt. They will tremble every moment for their own lives.

Verses 11–14 reveal to us the complete and utter destruction the Lord will bring upon Egypt. He will use Babylon to complete His judgment upon them and it will be swift and thorough. According to *Strong's* dictionary, the Hebrew word used for *multitude* in verse 12 is "hamown," which can be used to describe not only a crowd of people but also an abundance of riches.[104] In other words, not only will throngs of people be destroyed, but the economy of the nation will also fall. This is further evidence of the complete annihilation of Egypt.

Babylon will be ravaged so completely that the waters of the Nile will become completely clear. This is made possible by the absence of both men and animals. In other words, the waters will settle when the waters are no longer trampled and the mud is no longer stirred; they will settle into clear water that will *run like oil*. In verse 2, Egypt is described as a sea monster that troubles the waters with her feet and causes the waters to be foul, but according to the text here, the Lord will put an end to this and the waters will run free and smooth.

Verses 15–16 are clear: it is the Lord who is doing the destroying. In fact, in this sixth prophecy alone, the word *I* appears some twenty times, each referring to the Lord and making perfectly clear His intent to destroy Egypt. He will

---

[104] *Biblesoft's New Exhaustive Strong's Numbers and Concordance* (1994/2003).

completely devastate the land and Egypt will become a land of waste. All of Egypt, as well as the surrounding nations, will mourn for her loss. After all, they have a stake in this as well, as their livelihoods and economic prosperity come from Egypt; with her gone, they are in danger of annihilation as well. Therefore, there will be great weeping and wailing heard throughout the land.

Verses 32:17–32
This seventh prophecy came in the *twelfth year, on the fifteenth day of the month*. Even though the month is not named, many agree that the author is referring to the same month as had been mentioned in previous prophecies. If this is true, then the date of this prophecy would be around March 17, 585 BC, approximately two weeks after the preceding message.

When reading this seventh and last prophecy of chapter 32, one cannot help but be struck by the number of references to *pit* and *hell*—references to the place of the dead—in contrast to references to *land of the living*. Some six times we find a reference to the *land of the living* and some nine times we find a reference to *depths, pit,* or *hell*. In fact, according to Feinberg, this seventh prophecy has been characterized as "the most solemn elegy over a heathen people ever composed."[105]

Verses 17–21 are a reference to Egypt being cast down into the depths of the earth. She is to be placed among the uncircumcised. She is to be among all those nations who assisted and partnered with her and the power and strength of Egypt will become equal to those of the others. Pharaoh's pride will be destroyed, and he will be brought to his knees in humility.

---

[105] Feinberg, 184.

We are told that these nations will speak to the King of Egypt out of the midst of hell. Sheol or Hell in the Old Testament is the place where the unrighteous go at the time of their death. Clearly, there is consciousness in hell or the pit; there is existence beyond the grave. Derek Thomas states:

> What is depicted in these chapters in Ezekiel is the condition of certain individuals and groups of people after death. Though much of the language is poetic, it is reasonable to conclude even from these verses that existence in which men are conscious of their shame (32:24) is in view. This is not annihilation! Jonathan Edwards once wrote that "God hath had it on His heart to show to angels and men, both how excellent His love is, and how terrible His wrath is." Here we are meant to be horrified at the end of the wicked and weep for them.[106]

Ezekiel may have had Isaiah 14:15–20 in mind here as well. In fact, some believe that Ezekiel may have been developing this text further and depending on the words of Isaiah to help him describe Egypt's final plight. Isaiah states:

> *Yet you shall be brought down to Sheol, to the lowest depths of the Pit. Those who see you will gaze at you, and consider you, saying: "Is this the man who made the earth tremble, who shook kingdoms, who made the world as a wilderness*

---

[106] Thomas, 208.

and destroyed its cities, who did not open the house of his prisoners?" All the kings of the nations, all of them, sleep in glory, everyone in his own house; but you are cast out of your grave like an abominable branch, like the garment of those who are slain, thrust through with a sword, who go down to the stones of the pit, like a corpse trodden underfoot. You will not be joined with them in burial, because you have destroyed your land and slain your people. The brood of evildoers shall never be named.

Because Egypt and her king did not learn from history and realize or acknowledge the power of the mighty and sovereign God, the nation would be destroyed, along with its king. Thus God would make His message plain: do not trust in one's own power or strength, because He hates pride and arrogance.

This message should resonate with us today as we read in 1 Corinthians 1:26–29: *For you see your calling, brethren, that not many wise according to the flesh, not many mighty, not many noble, are called. But God has chosen the foolish things of the world to put to shame the wise, and God has chosen the weak things of the world to put to shame the things which are mighty; and the base things of the world and the things which are despised God has chosen, and the things which are not, to bring to nothing the things that are, that no flesh should glory in His presence.*

In Ezekiel, what follows is a list of those nations that are designated as helpers and who are already occupants of the pit.

The descriptions are similar, as each is said to be surrounded by their own graves. Egypt will simply join them.

Assyria is first mentioned in verses 22–23. Her fall has already taken place and she is mentioned first because she is fresh in the mind of Ezekiel. Assyria is mentioned in chapter 31. They are said to have caused terror to the living, and now her previous powerful armies are lying in their graves surrounding their once powerful leader and are set in the recesses of the pit. She now is but a dim memory.

Verses 24–25 are a reference to Elam, a recognized nation at the time of Abraham. We read in Genesis 14 of wars between nations, one of which included Elam. This would have been the time when Lot was taken captive and Abraham rescued him from the hands of the enemies. Jeremiah prophesied the defeat and destruction of Elam in Jeremiah 49:34–39. Elam was known for her expertise in archery and Jeremiah states that her bow would be broken.

As with Assyria, Elam will be surrounded by the graves of her armies and will be cast down into the pit. Similar language is used with each of these helping nations and Elam is no exception. She will bear her shame and be held accountable for her actions. Twice Ezekiel states that she caused terror among the land of the living, twice he refers to them bearing their shame, and twice he states that they will go down into the pit. The purpose of these repeated statements is to emphasize God's destruction upon those uncircumcised nations who warred against Israel and joined forces with Egypt.

Verses 26–27 are a reference to two nations by the names of Meshech and Tubal. These two nations were mentioned earlier (Ezekiel 27:13) as those who traded with Tyre and thus were included in the iniquity of Tyre. There is some disagreement as to the exact identity of these two nations, but most scholars conclude that the intended reference is the northern nations that lay between the Black and Caspian Seas. Again, their graves will surround their land, as they will be slain by the sword because they caused terror in the land of the living.

What distinguishes Meshech and Tubal from the rest is that we are told they would *not* lie with the mighty. They would *not* lie among the uncircumcised who have gone down to hell nor with those who have *laid their swords under their head.* This means that they would not have separate tombs, but were instead to be buried in a common and promiscuous manner.[107] We are told that *their iniquities will be on their bones:* a statement expressing their complete accountability for the destruction and terror they caused. Their once great and powerful rule has come to an end and they are met with the wrath and fury of God's judgment. More will be said of Meshech and Tubal when we examine chapters 38 and 39.

Many understand verse 28 as a direct statement to Pharaoh. He is being reminded of the fate of the other nations and that he will meet the same doom.

Verse 29 is a reference to Edom. Edom was referred in chapter 25. She, like the other nations, will also meet the same fate. No amount of power will rescue her from her impending doom. Her kings and princes will go down to the pit, and there await the arrival of Egypt.

Verse 30 includes the *princes of the north* along with the *Sidonians.* These would include the Phoenician cities. They too meet a similar fate because of the terror they caused by abusing

---

[107] Feinberg, 186.

their mighty power: they will be cast into the pit to await the arrival of Egypt.

This seventh and final prophecy ends with the author's attention drawn back to Egypt, more specifically to Pharaoh himself. The text here may seem a little confusing, in that we are told that Pharaoh would be comforted when he sees them. But in a strange and bizarre way, when he sees all his allies and soldiers there in *the pit,* he will be comforted in knowing that he is not alone and that he will have companions in hell. He will not be alone in his humiliation.

APPLICATION

This section of Ezekiel now ends. We began in chapter 25 with a parade of nations and the pronouncement of doom upon each of them. During this time, Ezekiel has been relatively silent regarding Israel, but as we arrive at chapter 33, his full attention will once again be directed to Israel and her future blessings. If we have learned anything from these past few chapters, it is that God's wrath is swift and sure and none will escape. God will punish sin, make no mistake about it, and in so doing, He will be glorified, and all will know that He is God!

Study Questions
1. Define God's wrath.
2. Will believers ever have to face the wrath of God?

Ezekiel 33:1–34:31

Blessings On Israel

RECOMMISSIONING OF THE WATCHMAN

We have seen that Ezekiel was appointed a watchman over Israel (Ezekiel 3:17). We noted earlier in this commentary that in the days of Ezekiel, the cities were protected by great walls. The watchmen who were posted on these walls were to watch for approaching danger and to warn both those who were outside the protection of the walls as well as those who were on the inside. According to Isaiah 56:10–11, a watchman was a leader or shepherd. Jeremiah 6:17 tells us their purpose was to warn. Psalm 127:1 states: *Unless the LORD builds the house, they labor in vain who build it; unless the LORD guards the city, the watchman stays awake in vain.* To get a clear illustration of the work of a watchman, read 2 Samuel 18:24.

EZEKIEL 33:1–9
AUTHORITY OF THE WATCHMAN

This section begins a new direction in Ezekiel's prophecies. Ezekiel is reminded that he is the nations' watchman. Before Jerusalem's fall, he told the people of their punishment and dispersion. Now he is to proclaim the hope of restoration, but even this message does not improve the people's response. They listen to him with curiosity and then live as they please. We see similar responses today, in that as the message of God's forgiveness is proclaimed throughout the earth, people listen, some seem interested, and yet most ignore it and live their own lives.

As mentioned earlier, this chapter marks a new direction in Ezekiel's message. Up to this point, he has been preaching doom and gloom as he described the coming judgment upon Judah (Ezekiel 1–24) and then on the surrounding nations (Ezekiel 25–32) because of their sins. After Jerusalem fell, Ezekiel turns from his doom and gloom to comfort, hope, and future restoration for the people of God (Ezekiel 33–48). God had previously appointed Ezekiel as watchman over Israel (Ezekiel 3); now He is recommissioning him to the same task, but this time his message was to be one of hope. God will and does remember those who are faithful to Him. We must pay attention to both aspects of Ezekiel's message: warning and promise. Those who persist in rebelling against God should take warning. Those who remain faithful to God should find encouragement and hope.

The message of this section is like the message in Ezekiel chapter 3. The watchman in chapter 3 was to warn against sin. The watchman in chapter 33 is to warn of approaching attacks of the enemy. The protection of those living within the city walls is the responsibility of the watchman and he has been given authority over them. The instructions are clear. When the watchman sees the enemy approaching with swords drawn, he is to blow the trumpet and warn the people of the impending attack. When one hears the trumpet but chooses to ignore the warning, then if he is killed, his blood shall be on his own head. If he hears the trumpet and heeds the warning, then he shall save his own life.

What about the alternative: if the watchman sees the enemy approaching with swords drawn and does not sound the trumpet warning and the people are not properly warned of the impending danger? In that case those who are killed in the attack will become the responsibility of the watchman and the Lord will require their blood at the watchman's hand; he is responsible for those deaths.

The Lord then applies the authority of the city watchman to that of the spiritual watchman. When the Lord speaks to Ezekiel and gives him a warning about the sin of the people, it then becomes Ezekiel's responsibility to warn the people. If he does not warn them and they die in their sin, their blood will be required at the hand of Ezekiel. Nevertheless, if upon hearing the warning they refuse to heed that warning, then they will die in their sins, but Ezekiel will not be held responsible. The responsibility clearly rests with those who were warned.

APPLICATION

The apostle Paul used similar words in Acts 20:26. In an emotional speech to the elders of Ephesus, he declared to them, *Therefore I testify to you this day that I am innocent of the blood of all men.* Paul had warned the people of their sin, he preached the good news of the gospel message; therefore, it became the responsibility of the listeners to heed the warning or die in their sins. As Paul told the church of Corinth, one plants, another waters but it is God who gives the increase (1 Corinthians 3:6). We must always remember that God has called us to proclaim the good news, but the people's response is not the heralder's responsibility: that belongs solely to the listeners. Pastors and teachers today would save themselves a lot of grief if they would just understand and grasp this main point.

Study Questions
1. Why do you find it difficult to warn people of their sin?
2. When sharing the good news of the gospel, are you willing to share the bad news as well as the good news?

EZEKIEL 33:10–20
THE ACCOUNTABILITY OF THE WATCHMAN

Verses 10–11
In these verses we see a key turning point in the attitude of Israel. Before, we have witnessed a people that had refused to face their sin and repent. They would not accept the responsibility. Now, the exiles seem to be discouraged by their sins and seemingly want to correct the problem by coming to the Lord in repentance. They ask the question, *If our transgressions and our sins lie upon us, and we pine away* (vanish) *in them, how can we then live?* They apparently felt heavy guilt for rebelling against God for so many years. Therefore, God assures them of forgiveness if they repent. God desires for everyone to turn to Him (2 Peter 3:9).

God reminds them that He takes no pleasure in the death of the wicked, a truth He has spoken to them before (Ezekiel 18:32). It is God's desire that they turn from their wickedness and, as a result, live.

APPLICATION

One gets the sense of God's compassion and tenderness. God is pleading with them to repent because after all, He is ready to forgive! It makes no sense at all that any should die in their sins when all they have to do is repent: God will forgive and then, as a result, they live! This is such a simple truth, yet so hard for the sinner to grasp. This truly displays the absolute depravity of man (Romans 3:10–18). Forgiveness is available to all who simply ask. A sporadic, inconsistent life is not pleasing to our Lord, as God has expressed here in verse 11: *Turn, turn from your evil ways.*

Study Questions
1. What would you say is the main reason people find it hard to repent of their sins?
2. Should there be a noticeable change in a person's life after salvation?

Verse 12
It should be noted at this point that the eternal destiny of the soul is not in question. Notice that those mentioned here are called *righteous*. A man's eternal destiny is determined by his faith. At the time of Ezekiel, they were under the Mosaic Law, the sacrificial system, and their faith was to be directed toward God through this system. The judgment of death is speaking of this life only, so when our Lord pleads with them to live, He is pleading with them to enjoy the blessings and benefits that He offers them while on this earth.

Clearly, past righteousness will not deliver a man presently in sin any more than a man's past wickedness will condemn him in the day he repents. Some may think they have done enough good deeds to overshadow the sins they do not desire to give up. This is like storing up several good deeds with the intent to be evil later, and then call upon those earlier good deeds to save you from God's judgment. There is no "get out of jail free" card or "collect two hundred dollars when you pass go" award; it simply does not work that way with our Lord. We are held accountable for our present actions and cannot call upon past righteousness to deliver us.

Verse 13
The Lord is very emphatic. He states that when a person attempts to call upon past righteousness to deliver him, none of his past righteousness will be remembered. God desires a wholehearted love and obedience.

Verses 14–16
So, what is required of the wicked? Five things are mentioned here in our text. First, he must turn from his sin. This is full repentance. The Hebrew word used here for *if he turns* is *shuwb*. According to Strong's dictionary, "shuwb is a primitive root which means to turn back, hence, away literally or figuratively and not necessarily with the idea of returning to the starting point. The word generally means to retreat."[108] Thus, the first requirement of the wicked is to retreat from their sin and desist from their wicked activity.

The second thing is he must do what is right—not only turn from his wicked way, but start doing what is *lawful and right*. It is worth noting that the Bible seldom tells one to turn

---

[108] *Biblesoft's New Exhaustive Strong's Numbers and Concordance.*

from something without showing what to turn to. Here, the wicked man is told to turn from the sin but start doing the right things.

The third thing required of the wicked is that he must *restore the pledge*. This refers to the pledge originally made to the Lord to walk in His ways, to live a righteous life and please God in all he does. By turning from righteousness to wickedness, he has reneged on this pledge, so the sinner must turn to righteousness to restore that pledge.

Fourthly, he must *give back what he has stolen.* This is a matter of making past offenses right. True repentance will drive a person to make up for past mistakes, either by asking for forgiveness from offended parties, or as the text suggests, making reparations for taking what was originally not ours. This is nothing new. It was already required in the law (Exodus 22:1–2 and Numbers 5:6–7), and we see in the Gospel of Luke that when Zacchaeus came to faith, his immediate response was to make reparations (Luke 19:8).

Finally, not only should the wicked turn from his sin, do what is right, restore the pledge, and make reparations, but he should also *walk in the statutes of life without committing iniquity.* This is not to say he would never sin again, but that the desire of his heart should be to walk uprightly before the Lord and purpose in his heart not to allow sin to have dominion over him (compare Romans 6:12–14). The promise to the person who accomplishes this is that his past sins will not be held against him and he shall live.

Verses 17–19

The people of Israel thought God to be unfair. They either did not understand what the Lord was telling them, or they just plain did not like it. They thought God to be inequitable, a contention to which God was quick to point out that it is their way that is unfair. God's way was simple and straightforward. When the righteous turns to wickedness, he shall die, or when the wicked turns to righteousness, he shall live.

APPLICATION

There is nothing unfair about the way God treats us. In fact, what is unfair is the way we treat God. He will deal with us each according to our own ways. 2 Corinthians 5:10 states, *For we must all appear before the judgment seat of Christ, that each one may receive the things done in the body, according to what he has done, whether good or bad.* Romans 14:10b states, *For we shall all stand before the judgment seat of Christ* and a little later, in verse 12, we read, *so then each of us shall give account of himself to God.* These verses are a reference to the Bema where God's children will be judged for the works they do after they are declared righteous, when they put their faith and trust in the blood shed by Jesus Christ.

It is important to take the time here to clarify that a person is not saved by good works. Ephesians 2:8–9: *For by grace you have been saved through faith, and that not of yourselves; it is the gift of God, not of works, lest anyone should boast.* Again, in Romans 3:20 we read, *Therefore, by the deeds of the law no flesh will be justified in His sight, for by the law is the knowledge of sin.* Even the Old Testament saints were counted righteous because of their faith, as Genesis 15:6, speaking of Abraham, clearly states: *and he believed in the Lord, and He accounted it to him for righteousness.*

However, good works are clearly to be a part of the life of all believers. Ephesians 2:10 states, *For we are His workmanship, created in Christ Jesus for good works, which God prepared beforehand that we should walk in them.* Titus 2:14 states that Jesus Christ *gave Himself for us, that He might redeem us from every lawless deed and purify for Himself His own special people, zealous for good works.* In our caution to make sure works are not a part of salvation (and they are not), we have gone to the opposite side of the spectrum and almost entirely downplayed good works. Israel is reminded that God will judge each one according to his ways, and we must remember that this still holds true today. Good works are to be a part of every believer's life. We are not saved "by" works, but we are saved "to" work.

Study Questions
1. Have you ever thought that God was unfair?
2. Name some works that some believe might save them.

EZEKIEL 33:21–33
THE AUDIENCE OF THE WATCHMAN

Verses 21–22
Near the beginning of his ministry, Ezekiel was stricken dumb by the Lord and was unable to speak to Israel (Ezekiel 3:25–27). After some seven years, and in fulfillment of Ezekiel 24:26–27, there were some who escaped the destruction of Jerusalem for the purpose of reporting to Ezekiel that the city had been taken captive. In these verses we are told it was the twelfth year of captivity, in the tenth month, that Jerusalem fell. This would put the date at 586 BC. Feinberg explains: "The Syriac version

and some Hebrew manuscripts read eleventh instead of twelfth year, which would allow six months rather than a year and a half for the news of Jerusalem's fall to reach the exiles, and many accept this date. The captivity referred to was that of Jehoiachin (see 1:2)."[109] No longer needing to prove himself, Ezekiel was free to offer God's message of restoration and hope to the people of God.

Verses 23–29

Here the Lord describes the causes for the fall of Judah. Israel shows her arrogance by stating she is stronger than Abraham. He was one, we are many, was their cry; therefore, they concluded they would possess the land. What pride they exhibited to think they could have something that God said He would take away! They were unworthy to have the land. They abhorred God's law by eating meat with blood (compare Leviticus 3:17), and they worshipped false gods and shed blood (compare 2 Chronicles 28:1–4). They were prideful in that they relied upon their own strength and committed abominations and adulteries. They did not deserve the land and yet they were too arrogant to understand this. They had learned nothing.

God promised to make the land desolate, to make the people weak, to cause the beasts of the fields to devour them; those who thought they could hide in the caves would be destroyed by disease. No one who chooses to stay in Judah and defy the living God would escape. Clearly, God defeated them because of their sin and when it is all said and done, they will know who the Lord of Lords truly is.

---

[109] Feinberg, 191.

Verses 30–33

The people refuse to act upon Ezekiel's message. They apparently flocked to hear his message and showed much interest, maybe even realizing that they were listening to a message from God, but when it came time to act upon that message, they refused. They had very little interest in obeying God. They were much like those to whom James referred, *hearers but not doers* (James 1:22).

I remembers a time in my teenage years (still unregenerate), when I would listen to the rock music of my day. The music was sweet, the melody was great, but I had no idea what the words were. Thus it was with Israel. The music of the message was sweet, they enjoyed the melody and the rhythm of the voice, but in the end, they had no clue what the words were nor did they care to find out. Their hearts professed something that was nonexistent, and it is the heart that truly matters to our Lord. Solomon said, *for as a man thinks in his heart, so is he* (Proverbs 23:7).

Through Ezekiel, God promises that His Word would come to pass, and the sad reality is that when it does, they will then know for certain that a true prophet of God has been among them. Some suggest he was referring to his prophecy against the remnant in Judah, but it is doubtful that a message of judgment on that remnant would have had any greater impact on those in captivity than the fall of the city. Therefore, Ezekiel was probably referring to the fact of individual responsibility and judgment that God imposes on all people.[110] This would make more sense given the preceding context.

---

[110] Dyer, 1294.

APPLICATION

In sad reality, we are seeing much of the same today. With the introduction of the "seeker friendly" churches came contemporary music; a relaxed, informal worship environment; and a flippant attitude toward how we approach our God. Many today attend church to be entertained. Good, solid fundamental Bible-preaching churches are losing people to music and the desire to be self-fulfilled, and the truth does not seem to be a part of the church message. Pragmatism is the order of the day and worshipping in spirit and truth does not seem important (compare John 4:24).

Today, many are not interested in hearing the Word of God and putting it into practice. They enjoy the music, the people, and the activities, but they do not take the basic message to heart. They do not seek to be challenged or to serve. Woe to us if we reduce the worship of the Lord to self-fulfilling activities and refuse to hear what God has to say!

Study Questions
1. What does it mean to worship in spirit and truth?
2. What should be the main component of any worship service?

EZEKIEL 34:1–31
CONTRAST OF THE SHEPHERDS

In chapter 34, we find a contrast between the shepherds of Israel and the True Shepherd of Israel. A shepherd is to tend to his flock, to feed it, to protect it and see that it is well cared for. A shepherd even risks his own life to protect his sheep from the predators that would come and destroy the flock. For a shepherd, his one and only concern is for his sheep.

The rulers of Israel are called shepherds. In referring to King David, the psalmist writes, *He also chose David His servant and took him from the sheepfolds; from following the ewes that had young He brought him, to shepherd Jacob His people, and Israel His inheritance. So, he shepherded them according to the integrity of his heart and guided them by the skillfulness of his hands* (Psalm 78:70–72). Feinberg notes that as Christ chose fishermen to become fishers of men, he chose a shepherd to shepherd his people.[111] Speaking of Moses, Isaiah states, *Then he remembered the days of old, Moses and his people, saying: "Where is He who brought them up out of the sea with the shepherd of His flock? Where is He who put His Holy Spirit within them?"* (Isaiah 63:11). In Jeremiah chapter 23 and then again in chapter 25, the rulers of Israel are referred to as shepherds.

These shepherds were to be strong, caring, compassionate leaders whose first interest was to serve their sheep by guarding and protecting them. Ezekiel begins chapter 34 by looking at the false shepherds whom God would later judge.

EZEKIEL 34:1–10
FALSE SHEPHERDS

Verses 1–6
In condemning these false shepherds, the Lord identifies their sin. Ezekiel is told to prophesy against the shepherds of Israel and to speak boldly to them. It is interesting to note that when

---

[111] Feinberg, 195.

confronting sin, he does not make a general statement such as, "Oh, by the way, you have sinned," but rather a direct statement identifying the specific sins that had been and were being committed.

The sins committed include the fact that instead of feeding the sheep, they *feed themselves*. A good shepherd will not put his own interest above that of his sheep. These shepherds were guilty of self-interest, putting their own desires above those of the people, which included making sure they were well fed and well clothed.

Secondly, they were heartless, not caring for the sheep or tending to their needs. We find four specific groups that were neglected by these shepherds: *the weak* were not strengthened and nurtured to learn to survive, *the sick* were not healed, *the wounded* were not restored, and *the lost* were not sought after and brought back. Instead, these shepherds were ruthless, ruling by force and with cruelty. The result was that the sheep were scattered, left defenseless, and became food for the beasts of the field as they wandered about the countryside. The indictment against the shepherds points out that no one sought the sheep, no one went after them, no one cared enough to come out of their own comfort zone and tend to the sheep.

The implication is clear. These "shepherds" represent the rulers of Israel, so these rulers are to be held accountable for Israel being taken captive, not only by the Assyrians, but ultimately by the Babylonians. In these captivities, Israel was scattered. It was the shepherds' responsibility to prevent such a catastrophe and thus they will be judged by the one and only true Shepherd. The Great Shepherd will pour His wrath upon these false shepherds.

Verses 7–10
God pronounces judgment upon the shepherds. Those shepherds who failed their flock would be removed from office and held responsible for what had happened to the people they were responsible for leading. As the Lord pronounces His judgment, He reiterates their sins. What sobering words to hear: *Behold, I am against the shepherds and I will require My flock at their hand.*

APPLICATION

Woe to us if the Lord should ever say the same regarding our ministry. Christian workers must heed this warning. This was one of the apostle Paul's main concerns as he reflected upon his own ministry. 1 Corinthians 9:24–27: *Do you not know that those who run in a race all run, but one receives the prize? Run in such a way that you may obtain it. And everyone who competes for the prize is temperate in all things. Now they do it to obtain a perishable crown, but we for an imperishable crown. Therefore, I run thus: not with uncertainty. Thus, I fight not as one who beats the air. But I discipline my body and bring it into subjection, lest, when I have preached to others, I myself should become disqualified.*

Study Questions
1. Who among the church should be responsible for "checking" the pastor?
2. What course of action should you take if your pastor is unfaithful to the truth?

EZEKIEL 34:11–24
FAITHFUL SHEPHERD

Verses 11–16

Contrasting the True Shepherd to the false shepherds, the Lord promises to intervene and to bring an end to their captivity Himself. He promises to search for His sheep and return them to the flock. The Babylonian captivity is described in verse 12 as a *cloudy and dark day*. He promises to feed them in their own land, in the valleys and throughout all the inhabited lands. They will be nurtured well because it is the Lord Who will accomplish this. Israel will return to the land God promises to give them and they will once again find themselves in the security of the Lord's protection.

Israel's shepherd promises to be their nurse. He will *bind up* their wounds (34:16). He will be their rescuer (34:11, 12), protector (they will *lie down* in safety, 34:15), provider (34:13, 14), and guide (their exile had been because of their desire to stray from God's path, 34:11, 16).[112] These words were not ultimately fulfilled when Israel returned to her land and will not be fulfilled until Israel's future is totally completed when the Lord regathers her in the Millennium Kingdom (compare Ezekiel 37 and Revelation 20).

These should have been encouraging words for Israel to hear. They were not being cared for, the enemy was surrounding them, and they were living in extremely dark days. To have the Lord state that He Himself (note that *I* is used some twenty-four times in the last half of chapter 34) is coming to rescue them and return them for a dark and cloudy day should have lifted their

---

[112] Thomas, 221–222.

spirits and encouraged them to remain faithful even in the darkest of days. He would be a shepherd to the shepherdless.

APPLICATION

One cannot help but think of Psalm 23 in which David refers to the Lord as his shepherd and upon realizing this great truth states: *and I shall not want.* Under the loving care of our Great Shepherd, we should have no wants. All our desires and needs have been fulfilled through our shepherd. In the Gospel of John, chapter 10, Jesus refers to Himself as the good shepherd (John 10:11), and it is the good shepherd who gives his life for his sheep. What comfort this should bring! What peace we should have! Understanding that we are under the care of our shepherd, Jesus Christ, we should then *Be anxious for nothing, but in everything by prayer and supplication, with thanksgiving, let our requests be made known to God and the peace of God which surpasses all understanding, will guard your hearts and minds through Christ Jesus* (Philippians 4:6–7).

Study Questions
1. Define the difference between a good shepherd and a hired shepherd (John 10:11).
2. Study and explain John 10:11–16.

Verses 17–23
God assures them even further by promising to judge the false shepherds. He will judge them because they have trampled down the pasture and made it difficult to find food and have fouled the clear water, making it unpleasant to drink. He further explains that He will judge between the sheep, between the rams

and the sheep and between the fat and lean sheep. Some understand this to be a reference to lesser officials who had mistreated their fellow countrymen. The basic message is that God will judge between one class (the weak and the helpless) and another (the strong and the oppressive).

APPLICATION

Today, we see bad shepherds who are not only selfish but destructive as well. The pastor who muddies the waters for others by raising unnecessary doubts, teaching false ideas, and acting sinfully and selfishly is destroying his flock's spiritual nourishment. He too will be judged by the Lord.

It would be correct to apply these words of Ezekiel to the pastor/teacher, elders, or any Christian worker of the New Testament church. In all ages it has pleased God to place upon certain men the responsibility of ministering to and caring for the temporal and spiritual needs of their fellows. God holds these men to a high standard, and their accountability to their sheep is just as important. Clearly 1 Peter 5:2 commands these men to shepherd the flock of God because God has made them overseers. 1 Timothy 3 and Titus chapter 1, in referring to these as overseers, bishops, and elders, delineate the distinction of these men.

Jesus refers to a shepherd who is not a shepherd as one who does not own his sheep and has no care for them. In fact, at the first sign of danger, this shepherd, whom the Lord calls a hireling, flees and protects his own life. A true shepherd will own his sheep and risk his life to protect them.

Too many today are calling themselves pastors when there is no call in their life, and they serve with a self-righteous and self-serving attitude. The focus is not upon the sheep God has called them to protect, but on themselves: how much money they can accumulate or how many accolades they can collect. They presently have their reward: the reward of men. A true shepherd will seek to please God rather than man. The alternative is a sad one: *they have no reward from heaven (Matthew 6:1)*. See Table 2 for a comparison.

Table 2

Bad Shepherds	*Good Shepherds*
Take care of themselves	Take care of their flock
Worry about their own health	Strengthen the weak and the sick and search for the lost
Rule harshly and brutally	Rule lovingly and gently
Abandon and scatter the sheep	Gather and protect the sheep
Keep the best for themselves	Give their best to the sheep

Rich rewards belong to those who serve in the fear of God and out of love for the people of the flock, as we see in 1 Peter 5:1–4, where the faithful elder is promised a crown of glory at the appearing of Jesus Christ.[113]

Study Questions

1. Why do you believe that God sets such high standards for pastors and elders?
2. Does your church use these standards when selecting spiritual leaders?

---

[113] Ironside, 234.

Verse 24
For Israel to hear that the Lord would bring them back to their own land had to be gratifying; then to hear God's promise to establish David as His one and true shepherd should have been exhilarating. Dr. John MacArthur suggests that this refers to the greater One in David's dynasty (compare 2 Samuel 7:12–16), the Messiah who will be Israel's ultimate king over the millennial kingdom (31:24–26; Jeremiah 30:9; Hosea 3:5; Zechariah 14:9).[114] Feinberg is quick to point out that the usage of the verb *"set up"* (King James Version) in verse 23 does not imply the resurrection of David himself, but instead the appointment of another similar person. He further states that if this does in fact refer to David himself, it is very strange that there is nothing at all concerning this resurrection.[115] The name "David" has been used in Scripture to refer to the coming Messiah (Isaiah 55:3–4), and is also used to refer to his dynasty (2 Samuel 20:1). Israel during the time of the reign of David, has been referred to by many as the Davidic Kingdom. Amos 9:11, *On that day I will raise up the tabernacle of David, which has fallen down, and repair its damages; I will raise up its ruins and rebuild it as in the days of old.* Zechariah 12:8, *In that day the LORD will defend the inhabitants of Jerusalem; the one who is feeble among them in that day shall be like David, and the house of David shall be like God, like the Angel of the LORD before them.* By referring to *one shepherd*, there should be no doubt that the Lord means one nation instead of a divided nation.[116]

---

[114] MacArthur, 1201.
[115] Feinberg, 198.
[116] Refer to this commentary's segment on Ezekiel 37:15-28 for a "literal David" view.

EZEKIEL 34:25–31
GOD'S COVENANT

Verses 25–29
After bringing the nation under one shepherd, He will then establish a *covenant of peace* with them. The words of verse 25 and following appear to be Millennium Kingdom descriptions. All that Israel had feared in the past will no longer be a problem. No more wild beasts (a reference to invading nations), the ability to roam the countryside in peace, the cleansing showers (called *showers of blessings*), trees yielding their fruit, the earth increasing its yield, no more slavery, freedom from oppression, and no more need to be afraid. Hunger and shame will not be arise in these days, as the Lord will provide for their needs in both sustenance and protection.

These words are like Isaiah's words in Isaiah 11:3–10: *His delight is in the fear of the LORD, and He shall not judge by the sight of His eyes, nor decide by the hearing of His ears; but with righteousness He shall judge the poor, and decide with equity for the meek of the earth; He shall strike the earth with the rod of His mouth, and with the breath of His lips He shall slay the wicked. Righteousness shall be the belt of His loins, and faithfulness the belt of His waist. The wolf also shall dwell with the lamb, the leopard shall lie down with the young goat, the calf and the young lion and the fatling together; and a little child shall lead them. The cow and the bear shall graze; their young ones shall lie down together; and the lion shall eat straw like the ox. The nursing child shall play by the cobra's hole, and the weaned child shall put his hand in the viper's den. They shall not hurt nor destroy in all My holy mountain, for the earth shall be full of the knowledge of the Lord as the waters cover the sea.*

And in that day, there shall be a Root of Jesse, Who shall stand as a banner to the people; for the Gentiles shall seek Him, and His resting place shall be glorious.

It is obvious from a study of history that when Israel returned from Babylonian captivity, only a few of Isaiah's prophecies came true, thus indicating that his words refer to conditions yet to come in the future, to be fulfilled in the Millennium Kingdom where Christ will sit upon the throne of David and reign with a rod of iron (Psalm 2:7–9).

Verses 30–31
Undoubtedly, this refers to the great day when Israel realizes once and for all that the Lord is their God and acknowledges this together as a nation. Israel will finally be established as a nation once again and will realize that they are God's flock and He is their God—thus says the Lord (compare Jeremiah 31:31–34).

APPLICATION

There are those today who would not call themselves dispensationalist and would hold to a symbolic view of this passage. I argue that if the literal sense makes sense, then seek no other sense. Clearly, the events of Ezekiel 34 have not taken place in totality; because the Word of God is without error and God cannot lie (compare Titus 1:2), we must understand that the promise of the covenant of peace refers to the future.

Jeremiah 33:1–26 promises the permanence of this covenant. In fact, part of that promise is that *David shall never lack a man to sit on the throne of the house of Israel; nor shall the priests, the Levites, lack a man to offer burnt offerings before Me, to kindle grain offerings, and to sacrifice continually*

(Jeremiah 33:17–18). Jesus Christ will fulfill this prophecy as King and High Priest forever. *I have made a covenant with My chosen, I have sworn to My servant David: 'Your seed I will establish forever and build up your throne to all generations.'* (Psalm 89:3–4).

In his commentary, "God Strengthens," Derek Thomas discusses the fallacy of believing in a future literal Millennium Kingdom as described in Isaiah 11. He equates the promise that God gave to Abraham in Genesis 12 with a picture of the paradise God originally gave to Adam and Eve; thus, the promise of Palestine was in effect a promise of paradise![117] He further states that the dimension given of Jerusalem in Revelation 21:16 is a problem for a literal Palestine. (See my comments of this subject in the chapters concerning Ezekiel 40–45.)

He concludes his discussion by stating it is a mistake to believe that God has a different purpose for Israel from the one He has for the church. He also states it is a mistake to think that the Old Testament expects a future earthly millennial kingdom, or to believe that these passages in Ezekiel go beyond what happened during the days of Ezra and Nehemiah, because this would mean little to Ezekiel's immediate listeners.[118]

Again, I counsel that if the literal sense makes sense, then seek no other sense. The promises to Israel in Ezekiel 34 were not fulfilled then and have not been fulfilled yet, which should clearly indicate that they are promises concerning what

---

[117] Thomas, 228–230.
[118] Having met Derek Thomas and heard him preach, I have much respect for him. I would not want my disagreement with him to be understood as arrogance on my part or as a lack of appreciation for his ministry. I just happen to disagree with his eschatology.

is still to come in the future. The dimension of Jerusalem in Revelation 21:16 should not cause a problem, as God can do whatever God desires to do. The seemingly difficult correlation between having a Millennial Temple and animal sacrifices can be easily rectified when one understands that Jesus Christ has provided that perfect sacrifice and has perfected forever those who are being sanctified (Hebrews 10:14). Because of what Christ has done, He will be that perfect sacrifice and there will be no need to offer animal sacrifices in the Millennium Kingdom for the atoning of sin; this would only disgrace the sacrifice provided by Christ (Hebrews 10:29). Why are we so set on thinking that if we have a Millennium Temple, animal sacrifices should serve the same purpose as the Old Testament sacrifices? Pre-Calvary, yes, but post-Calvary, they will not be necessary to cover sins.

Study Questions
1. Why are there sacrifices in the Millennium Kingdom (compare Ezekiel 43).
2. Read Isaiah 11. Describe the conditions of the Millennium Kingdom.

Ezekiel 35:1–15

The Destruction Of Edom

Verses 1–2
Mount Seir is to be understood as referring to the mountain range where the Edomites lived, south of the Dead Sea. Thus, a reference to Mount Seir is a reference to Edom. The Edomites were descendants of Esau, Jacob's brother.

The Lord now pronounces a second prophecy against Edom. Not only did Ezekiel prophesy against Edom, but so did Isaiah, Jeremiah, and Obadiah. Why? Edom becomes an example to all of Israel's enemies as a fulfillment of Genesis 12:3, *I will bless those who bless you, and I will curse him who curses you; and in you all the families of the earth shall be blessed.* Ezekiel is told to set his face against them and to prophesy against them. Each prophecy is divided into three parts, each marked by *they shall know that I am the Lord.*

EZEKIEL 35:1–4
DESOLATION OF THE LAND

Verses 3–4
In the first part of this prophecy, God says, *Behold, O Mount Seir, I am against you.* He promises to make their land desolate, meaning that when God is done with them, their land would be a desert, it would bleak and uninhabited. Edom was to be isolated from its neighbors.

This prophecy has been fulfilled literally. Edom was first conquered by Babylon, then the Medo-Persians, and then in 126 BC by John Hyrcanus the Hasmonean, who compelled them to become Jews.[119] There is no trace of the Edomites today. By His doing as He promised, they learned that God is the Lord.

EZEKIEL 35:5–9
DESTRUCTION OF THE PEOPLE

Verse 5
God explains the why of the destruction of Edom. They had an everlasting history of hating God's people and killed many Hebrews while they tried to escape the Babylonians. Because they slaughtered God's people, God promises to slaughter them.

Verses 6–9
It is interesting to note that four times in verse 6 alone, the word *blood* or *bloodshed* is found. Some suggest that this might be a play on words, as the name Edom means "red."[120] Edom, with its red mountains, is red with blood. She will suffer the same fate as she inflicted upon Israel. Ezekiel prophesied not only against the people of Edom, but also against their mountains and land. Their home territory was Mount Seir.

Mountains, symbols of strength and power, represented the pride of these people who thought they could get away with evil. Edom's desire for revenge turned against them. They received the punishment they were so hasty to mete out to others. As a result, Edom would become isolated, cut off from those who

---

[119] Feinberg, 202.
[120] Dyer, 1296.

leave and from those who return. The Lord promises to make it an everlasting desolation.

A similar warning, but in more detail, is given to the Edomites in Obadiah 1:10–16: *For violence against your brother Jacob, shame shall cover you, and you shall be cut off forever. In the day that you stood on the other side—In the day that strangers carried captive his forces, when foreigners entered his gates and cast lots for Jerusalem—Even you were as one of them. But you should not have gazed on the day of your brother in the day of his captivity; nor should you have rejoiced over the children of Judah in the day of their destruction; nor should you have spoken proudly in the day of distress. You should not have entered the gate of My people in the day of their calamity. Indeed, you should not have gazed on their affliction in the day of their calamity, nor laid hands on their substance in the day of their calamity. You should not have stood at the crossroads to cut off those among them who escaped; nor should you have delivered up those among them who remained in the day of distress. For the day of the LORD upon all the nations is near; as you have done, it shall be done to you; your reprisal shall return upon your own head. For as you drank on My holy mountain, so shall all the nations drink continually; yes, they shall drink, and swallow, and they shall be as though they had never been.*

APPLICATION

One can't help but remember the words of the author of Hebrews, who states, *It is a fearful thing to fall into the hands of the living God* (Hebrews 10:31) and later, *For our God is a consuming fire* (Hebrews 12:29). God has a way of turning our treatment of others into a boomerang, so we must be careful how we deal with others (compare Matthew 7:1–5).

Study Question
1. Read Romans 12:9–21 and explain it in your own words.

EZEKIEL 35:10–15
DESIRE TO INHERIT THE LAND

Verse 10
Clearly Edom was wrong in desiring to possess the land of Canaan. This belonged to Israel and God desired her to share it with no one. The *two nations* and the *two countries* referred to the divided kingdom, Judah, the southern nation; and Israel, the northern nation. The arrogance of Edom was evident as they desired to possess these lands even though the Lord was there. They had no regard for the God of Israel. This land belonged to Israel, and even though Israel sinned, and God judged them by allowing them to be taken from their land, He never reneged on his promises to once and for all give them that land. Certainly, God did not intend for anyone or any nation to possess this land other than His chosen people.

Verses 11–13
The measure of punishment doled out to Edom was to be proportionate to their anger, envy, and hatred expressed toward Israel. Edom sought to take advantage of Israel's weakness at the time of their Babylonian captivity, but the Lord knew the intention of their heart. He heard all the blasphemies of Edom against Israel. In making themselves great, they made their judgment/punishment even greater.

Verses 14–15
God promises to make Edom an example to all those around her. As she desired to make Israel desolate, God would return the favor and make her desolate. Edom then becomes a literal object lesson for all to see and witness. Thus, we see a fulfillment of Matthew 25:31–46, where Christ speaks of His second coming at which time He would establish His Kingdom.

Other nations would do well to heed the warning of Ezekiel. As stated earlier, the Lord is a God of promise and One who does not and cannot lie. He told Abraham in Genesis 12:3 that *I will bless those who bless you, and I will curse him who curses you; and in you all the families of the earth shall be blessed*, and this is exactly what the Lord meant; we see that fulfillment in the words of our Lord to Edom. God's judgment will be measured out according to their actions and it is irrevocable. Nation after nation has experienced this judgment in the past and nations today should take notice, or they will experience the same from our Lord.

For the third time in this chapter, the Lord states, *"Then they shall know that I am the Lord."* It is God's desire to be glorified. It is also His desire to be shared with no one. He is a jealous God and when a nation—or any individual, for that matter—defames His glory, they become subject to His wrath (compare Ezekiel 36:5). Exodus 34:14 states, *for you shall worship no other god, for the LORD, whose name is Jealous, is a jealous God.* Again, in Nahum 1:2–3a, the Lord says, *God is jealous, and the LORD avenges; the LORD avenges and is furious. The LORD will take vengeance on His adversaries, and He reserves wrath for His enemies. The LORD is slow to anger and great in power and will not at all acquit the wicked.*

Ezekiel 36:1–38

The Restoration of Israel

This chapter is a detailed layout of the plan of redemption, both for Israel and, by way of application, for all who desire to be saved. This is such an organized treatise that many have referred to Ezekiel as "the first dogmatic theologian." In fact, according to Feinberg, no prophet before Ezekiel assigns the ministry of the Holy Spirit in regeneration such a precise place as does Ezekiel.[121]

This chapter also adds validity to a dispensational position that a literal Israel is in view. Those who teach otherwise are hard-pressed to make a sound argument.

As this chapter unfolds, there is a stark contrast between the mountains of Edom and the mountains of Israel. The former receives God's wrath for being an enemy of God's children and plundering the land; the latter receives God's restoration and redemption because they are God's children.

It will also become evident upon studying this chapter that God has one purpose and only one purpose for what He does. His purpose is to restore His holy name and to demonstrate His sovereign control over the nation, and then all will *know that He is the Lord.*

---

[121] Feinberg, 205.

EZEKIEL 36:1–15
THE PLACE PURIFIED

Verses 1–7

The enemies of Israel took the land as their own possession. Clearly, in Genesis 12, God's desire was to give that land to Abraham and all his descendants. God never intended for any other nation to own it or possess it or even control it. The *ancient heights* referred to is a reference to the promised land, the land of Israel. Israel's enemies challenged its boundaries, but God promises that Israel will possess and own that land.

The sins of Israel's enemies are laid out before us in this section. They surrounded the land and made it their own possession. They mocked and slandered God's people. They bragged that they were in full control and their intent was to swallow up God's people. This phrase literally means to "inhale eagerly" and is a picture of an animal snorting and sniffing out its prey. King David writes in Psalm 56:1–2: *Be merciful to me, O God, for man would swallow me up; fighting all day he oppresses me. My enemies would hound me all day, for there are many who fight against me, O Most High.*

As the Lord pronounces His judgment upon Israel's enemies, He is at the same time making this a promise to His people. He addresses the personified *mountains of Israel* as if to say to the land, I will avenge your desolation and plundering. In other words, because they have laid waste God's precious land, God will lay waste their land. God addresses the *mountains, the hills, the rivers, the valleys, the desolate wastes*, and *the cities that have been forsaken*. This is an all-inclusive speech that leaves no part of the land unmentioned.

What drives the Lord's anger is His jealousy. As previously mentioned, God is a jealous God. Only our Lord can seek revenge, and when He does it is always in a righteous way (compare Deuteronomy 32:35, 41; Psalm 94:1; Isaiah 1:24; Jeremiah 51:6; Nahum 1:2; and Hebrews 10:30). By stating that they *gave the land to themselves,* He indicates that they took the land without permission. Notice that the Lord calls the land *My land.* They took it with great enthusiasm and joy and with spitefulness to boot, and their sole purpose was to plunder and destroy. Thus, because of their sin, God will set them up as an example of shame to the other nations. The Lord, to solidify His position, raised His hand in an oath. Feinberg suggests that the Lord does this not because He is partial to Israel, but rather in order to vindicate His glory and His will, for He has condescended to link His purposes on earth with the people of Israel.[122] However, it should be noted that the Lord remains partial to Israel. Deuteronomy 7:7–8 states: *The LORD did not set His love on you* [Israel] *nor choose you because you were more in number than any other people, for you were the least of all peoples; but because the LORD loves you, and because He would keep the oath which He swore to your fathers, the LORD has brought you out with a mighty hand, and redeemed you from the house of bondage, from the hand of Pharaoh king of Egypt.* Even though this may not be His primary reason—because His glory is always the central reason for everything He does—His love for His people is the driving force for His anger (verse six). It is hard to imagine the Lord condescending to anyone, let alone the enemies of Israel, but all His purposes in the Old Testament from Genesis 12 and following are linked to His purposes for

---

[122] Feinberg, 206.

Israel. God has promised to always preserve a remnant and He will accomplish His will! He has sworn to that.

Verses 8–12

The promise of these verses is the future restoration of the land of Israel. God will increase and multiply the land and it shall be extremely productive. The Lord declares that He is for them. What a great promise of assurance! It is a reminder of what the apostle Paul told the church at Rome in Romans 8:31: *If God is for us, who can be against us?* The answer, of course, is no one. Thus, knowing that the Lord is for them should have brought great hope as well as excitement to the people.

He promises that they will be tilled and sown again. This speaks to the productivity and the fruitfulness of the land. The population will increase, housing will increase, and the destruction caused by the invading Babylonians will be restored.

Productivity will increase in childbearing, not only among the men, but also among the beasts of the field, which shall bear young and increase. The Lord promises to make the land, the people, and the times better than they were before the captivity. The implication is that the numbers within the population will be higher than before.

Speaking to the land, again in a personification-type speech, the Lord promises the land that it will be inhabited again by His people, that they will own it and it shall be their inheritance as originally intended. This once again proves that not only is our Lord truthful and trustworthy, He is the God of promises and is faithful to keep His promises. The Hebrew word for *bereave* is "shakol" and it means to abort or miscarry. The picture is of an aborted baby. An abortion was performed on the land of Israel by the Babylonians and she was left barren. God has promised that there will be a future day when He will undo the abortion of Israel.

APPLICATION

Not to belabor the point, but that day has not yet come. Even as this commentary is being written, there are threats against Israel from other Middle Eastern nations. The government of present-day Iran is reportedly developing nuclear weapons and has threatened to eliminate Israel by blowing it off the face of the earth. Although statistics show that currently more Jews live in the land than in previous history, they have not yet "arrived," and in fact, the land promised to Israel is more than they presently occupy. According to Unger, the term "land of Canaan" covers all Palestine west of the Jordan (Numbers 34:2–12). This territory was situated between the great ancient empires of the Tigris-Euphrates and Halys rivers on the side and the great Egyptian empire of the Nile on the other.[123]

As we will see in the next chapter, Israel is pictured as dead bones in a dry valley, but the day will come when God will revive the nation and it will be given its proper position among the other nations. That promise has not yet been totally fulfillment, but the day is coming: mark it, it will happen!

Study Question
1. Do you believe God still has a future for the nation of Israel? Why?

---

[123] *Unger's New Bible Dictionary* (1988).

Verses 13–15

These verses contain a final word from the Lord concerning Edom and the surrounding nations. They will be dealt with. They will be removed. No longer will they be given the liberty to reproach and devour the land of Israel. As indicated earlier, Israel will be restored to her rightful position throughout the land (compare Deuteronomy 28:13 and Zechariah 8:13, 20–23).

EZEKIEL 36:16–38
THE PEOPLE PURIFIED

Verses 16–21

It is not as if Israel is innocent in all of this. With all the Lord had promised Israel, and the blessings He heaped upon them, they still could not stay away from idolatry. They did their fair share of corrupting the land. Their sin is compared to the *uncleanness of a woman in her customary impurity*. Under the law, a woman was not allowed to enter the Temple until her days of purification were complete (compare Leviticus 15:19).

The bloodshed referred to by Israel could point not only to the bloodshed and violence they experienced, but also to the child sacrifices they took part in. We read in 2 Chronicles 28:3 that Ahaz, King of Judah, made molded images for Baal and even burned his children in the fire before the god Molech. This is only one of many examples throughout the Old Testament of this kind of atrocity. Because of this, the Lord judged them and scattered them throughout the territory.

It was the Lord's intent to have Israel to be an example to the other idolatrous nations and for them to be a witness for the greatness of Jehovah. Instead, Israel followed the pagan nations, worshipped the pagans' gods, and walked in their ways.

They profaned the name of the Lord among the nations—and for that they found themselves on the receiving end of God's wrath.

Verses 22–23

The purpose for the Lord's wrath upon Israel is not for their sake but in order to return the holy name of the Lord to its proper place. Israel profaned His name and He was going to have it restored. God's name is both great and holy and by partaking in the deeds of the nations, they degraded that name.

To do nothing would cause the surrounding pagan nations to think that the God of Israel was weak and useless. They would conclude that their gods were stronger and more powerful than Jehovah. Isaiah 48:11 states, *For My own sake, for My own sake, I will do it; for how should My name be profaned? And I will not give My glory to another.* The Lord promises to have His holy name separate from that of the other names so that the other nations will know He is God. The people had the responsibility to represent God properly to the rest of the world, and they failed.

APPLICATION

Believers today have the same responsibility. The apostle Paul makes a similar plea as from the Lord: *Now then, we are ambassadors for Christ, as though God were pleading through us: we implore you on Christ's behalf, be reconciled to God* (2 Corinthians 5:20). An ambassador is a representative and we are called to represent God in this present chaotic world. We have been commissioned to take the Gospel to all creatures (Mark 16:15). We, like Israel, must live holy and pure lives in order not to profane God's name. If believers show no difference in their walk from unbelievers, then what are unbelievers being asked to believe and follow? Why would someone want to decide to follow Christ if there is no difference between his life and the life of the ambassador? Messengers or ambassadors must give credibility to their message by the life that they live.

Study Questions
1. According to Romans 11:11, why did God turn to the Gentiles?
2. Are you living a life that causes the unsaved to be jealous of your relationship with Christ?

Verses 24–33
It becomes obvious that these events are still in the future. Even though the Jews are back in their land, they are still not loyal to the Lord and remain in their iniquities. The Lord first states that He would regather them and place them back into their land. Even though they did return after the Babylonian Captivity, there were still some who did not return and, as mentioned earlier, they still do not have control of the land the Lord originally gave to them.

The Lord further states that He will clean them by sprinkling *clean water upon them*. This is not to be confused with water baptism but is understood as the Mosaic rite of purification. Cleansing with water was a ceremonial cleansing from sin (compare Leviticus 15:21–22 and Numbers 19:17–19). The Lord mentions filthiness and idolatry as the two sins they would be cleansed from.

God promises to restore them, not only physically but also spiritually. To accomplish this, God will give them a new heart and remove the stony heart, this for the purpose of following Him. He would put His Spirit within them for the purpose of transforming them and empowering them to accomplish His will. This promise was first given in Ezekiel 11:19.

A stony heart is one that refuses to hear and obey the Word of the Lord. This heart will be replaced with a *heart of flesh*. It is the heart of flesh that can be responsive to God's voice and message if it seeks God wholeheartedly.

The language here is very similar to the language of Ezekiel 11. Its repetition here is for emphasis. It is God's desire that His people walk according to His laws and are obedient to his commands. When they do so, God is glorified. With God's Spirit indwelling them, they will be motivated to follow God and to obey His laws and statutes. This coming of the Spirit is not to be confused with the Spirit's coming at Pentecost. The Spirit's coming was for all believers, Jews and Gentiles alike, but this promise is unique to the Jews and is intended to be special only to them. Jeremiah called this new work of God in the lives of the Jews the *New Covenant* (Jeremiah 31:31, 33).

The physical blessing that follows this spiritual renewal is productivity of the land. Their grain will be multiplied and there will be no need to fear a famine. The fruit of their trees will increase, and the fields will yield a tremendous crop, again so that they will *never bear the reproach of a famine again.*

Upon seeing this increase in productivity, the people of God will be humbled. They will realize that they have sinned against a Holy God, loathe themselves for the abominable deeds they have committed against Him, and conclude that they do not deserve His good favor. This will be a true repentance, not one that is concerned merely with looking good to the other nations, but a repentance that will glorify God and result in a new walk (compare 2 Corinthians 7:8–12).

Verses 33–38
God continues his promises of restoration. God has promised to restore the people, giving them a new heart; He has promised to restore the land, causing it to be more productive; and now He promises to fill the cities and allow Israel once again to inhabit the land. Notice that this is all made possible because God allows it.

The purpose of this restoration, once again, is so the surrounding nations will know that it is the Lord who made all this possible. He is the one who rebuilt the cities and He is the one who reinhabited the cities.

The Lord will allow the house of Israel to inquire of Him. There was a day when the Lord refused to listen to His disobedient people (compare Ezekiel 14:3; 20:3), but now the Lord will be accessible for their turning to Him in genuine repentance and will grant their requests.[124] It is obvious that the Lord would not allow them access unless He would be willing to listen. What a blessing to be restored, not only to their land but also to their relationship with Jehovah God!

APPLICATION

Believers under grace have this same blessing. We read in 1 John 1 that when we sin—and we all do (compare Romans 3:23)—our fellowship with God is broken. The only way to restore that fellowship is confession (1 John 1:9). What a blessing and joy for us today to know that our God hears us and is willing and desirous to have that special relationship and to have that relationship maintained. But to know that when we

---

[124] Feinberg, 210.

sin, we can confess, and God will hear and forgive us and cleanse us from all unrighteousness is not only humbling but honoring. It is the Holy Spirit Who will guide us and make us responsive and receptive to God's truth (John 14:26; 16:8, 13).

OLD	NEW
Old Covenant	New Covenant
Placed upon stone	Placed upon the heart
Based on the Law	Based upon desire to love and serve God
Must be taught	Known by all
Legal relationship with God	Personal relationship with God

God said that if the people asked, He would come to their aid. We cannot expect His mercy, however, until we have sought a new heart through trusting Jesus Christ as personal Savior. As Jeremiah 31:31 is a new covenant God made with Israel, the application is clear for us today who believe.

Study Questions
1. If all our sins, past, present and future, are forgiven, then why is it necessary to continue to confess our sins?
2. Define the difference between confession and repentance.

Ezekiel 37:1–28

The Regathering of Israel

As we enter chapter 37, we find two metaphors that teach the reviving and reuniting of Israel (compare 37:11 and 37:21). Not only will the Lord restore Israel back to their land, but He will unite them under one king and they will no longer be a divided nation as they were before the captivity. We have in chapter 37 a fulfillment of Ezekiel 36:26–28. Before dealing with the individual metaphors, it is important to note the finality of the Lord's comments. He states that "they shall no longer" or that "they will never again," which speaks of finality and a conclusion to the future of Israel. This type of language indicates a "once-and-for-all" attitude from the Lord, which would indicate that the fulfillment of these promises has not yet been fully realized by Israel. They are still a divided nation, and they are not fully back in their land, the land the Lord had originally given them (compare Genesis 13:14–17).

EZEKIEL 37:1–14
METAPHOR #1: THE VALLEY OF DRY BONES

This section of Ezekiel has been used—poorly, I might add—to teach anatomy to children. An old traditional spiritual was written:

"Dem bones, dem bones, dem dry bones,"
"Dem bones, dem bones, dem dry bones,"
"Dem bones, dem bones, dem dry bones,"
"Oh, hear the word of the Lord."

Sadly, most remember this chapter of Ezekiel by this song and nothing else and miss the rich spiritual significance of what the Lord is telling Israel. Above anything else, great hope is found in this section, as it demonstrates the faithfulness of the Lord. According to Feinberg, the main aim of this vision was to counteract the despair and pessimism that had laid hold of the despondent nation.[125] Thomas comments that God comes with a word of great encouragement to cheer the hearts of his despondent people. When things are at their lowest ebb, God intervenes with promises of hope, blessing, and revival.[126]

Verses 1–10

The first question to be asked is: Why did God use dry bones as a reference to Israel? Dry bones represent death, and certainly Israel was spiritually dead during their years of captivity. They were far from the Lord and had fallen deep into idolatry.

Ezekiel was transported to a valley in verse 1. What he saw was an open valley, full of bones. They are described in verse 3 as very dry bones, bleached and baked under the hot sun, which as indicated earlier, symbolized the spiritual condition of the house of Israel. The question posed to Ezekiel—*Son of man, can these bones live?*—seems rather strange because dry bones obviously cannot live; in fact, their being so very dry means that they have been dead for quite some time. Ezekiel's answer, *O*

---

[125] Feinberg, 212.
[126] Thomas, 242.

Lord God, You know, is a powerful statement of Ezekiel's faith and understanding in the sovereignty of God.

What happens next is strange by anyone's understanding. The Lord tells Ezekiel to preach to these dry bones. What is even stranger is that Ezekiel obeys and does just as the Lord commands him. What an example this is to all teachers of the Word! We are to be sensitive to the leading of the Lord and no matter how strange or inappropriate a passage may seem, if it is what the Lord desires, we are to obey and not question.

Ezekiel was to preach to these bones that the Lord would cause breath to enter them, that they shall live, that the Lord will connect them with tendons and cover them with flesh. Then breath would come upon these reassembled bones and God would cause life to come into them once again. What a beautiful picture of the resurrection—and the concept of resurrection was not unfamiliar to those in this part of the country. The Egyptians believed that some of the deceased rose as stars and took their place in the heavens. In other parts of the ancient world, they believed in the calling-up of spirits of the dead or the awakening of the fertility gods of nature cycles. These gods died annually in connection with the cycle of agriculture, in which every winter they died and every spring they came back to life.

A resurrection would not have been unfamiliar to Ezekiel, or to the nation for that matter. Earlier, Elijah raised the widow's son (1 Kings 17); Elisha raised the Shunammite's son (2 Kings 4), and Daniel prophesied of the resurrection of Israel (Daniel 12). Although these examples are of individual resurrections, what is referred to in Ezekiel 37:7–10 is a national resurrection. God promises to revive and bring back to life the nation as a whole.

What a sight Ezekiel must have seen when as he was preaching to these dead bones. They started to rattle. They began to come together, bone to bone. The tendons connected them to each other, and the flesh covered them, but when this process was finished, there was still no life. Ezekiel is told to continue preaching but this time he is to speak to the very breath, and as Ezekiel obeys, breath comes into these bones (not on them). They came to life and stood on their feet and appeared to Ezekiel as a great and mighty army.

There should be no mistake at this point in understanding where this life came from. Even though it was Ezekiel who was preaching, it was clearly the Lord Who was doing the work. This was not some miracle of Ezekiel or the power of Ezekiel; rather, Ezekiel was the agent through whom the Lord chose to work. What a blessing and joy to know that the Lord uses us to change people's lives!

Breath is the Hebrew word "ruwach" and can be translated *wind* as the King James Version uses, or *breath* as the NKJV and New American Standard Bible use. It is the same word in verse 14, translated *spirit.* The two-stage process of bringing these bones to life is reminiscent of the creation of man (compare Genesis 2:7). It was not until God breathed into man the breath of life that he became a living creature. Psalm 119:25 states: *My soul clings to the dust; revive me according to Your word.* In John 6:63 Jesus states, *It is the Spirit who gives life; the flesh profits nothing. The words that I speak to you are spirit, and they are life.*

For long centuries Israel has been a dead nation, sleeping among the Gentiles. In the day of Jehovah's power, they will be brought out from their graves, gathered from the countries into which they have been dispersed, and appear as an exceeding great host; those in whose hearts faith is found entering into everlasting life, and those who refuse to believe the message of that day given over to shame and everlasting contempt.[127]

APPLICATION

What power and presence the Word of God has! The apostle Paul reminds us in Romans 10:17, *Faith comes by hearing and hearing by the Word of God.* It is the Word of God that gives life; apart from the Word, one dies and becomes useless to the Lord. It is the very word of God that brings life into these otherwise dead bodies.

Study Questions
1. How does one grow spiritually?
2. In what way does Hebrews 4:12 help us to understand the power of the Word of God?

Verses 11–14
The Lord leaves nothing to guesswork. He clearly explains to us that these bones represent the *whole house of Israel.* This was a nation in deep despair and depression and total despondency. What joy and exhilaration should have come to them when they heard the words of Ezekiel as he explained this vision. They are told that they will be brought up from their graves of unrighteousness and unfaithfulness and taken to new heights and a restored relationship with their Lord. In fulfillment of His promises, God states that He will put His spirit within them (compare Ezekiel 18:31), and they shall live and be restored back

---

[127] Ironside, 259.

into the land that He previously had promised to give them. It is the Lord's word and it is the Lord's power that will bring this to fulfillment.

EZEKIEL 37:15–28
METAPHOR #2: THE TWO STICKS

This next metaphor naturally follows the first, in that once life has been restored to the nation, they will now be restored to their land. This time, though, they will not be divided as before the captivity but united, one nation, living in the land that God has promised them from their beginning.

Verse 15:17
Here we find the Lord commanding Ezekiel to take two sticks and write names on each of them. One stick is to be labeled *For Judah and for the children of Israel, his companions* and the other stick is to be labeled, *For Joseph, the stick of Ephraim and for all the house of Israel, his companions.* These sticks are to be held in one hand and joined so that they become one. When these nations return to their land after the captivity, they will return as one nation, no longer divided as they have been since the days of Rehoboam.

Verses 18–28
The question of explanation will be asked: *Will you not show us what you mean by these?* This very question indicates that this was not some private conversation that the Lord was having with Ezekiel, but that the message was made known to all who were listening. The Lord's explanation is very simple: He will

take the two sticks and make them one. But who exactly is represented by these two sticks?

Several explanations have been given to identify them. They range from the ridiculous to the reasonable. Some suggest that the first stick, the stick of Judah, represents the Bible in its entirety and the other stick, the stick of Joseph, represents the Book of Mormon. Those of this view also suggest that this explains the Anglo-Israeli delusion of the ten lost tribes. This can be dismissed with no apology at all, as the prophets all recognized the northern tribes as still in existence and knew of no such error as "lost tribes."[128]

It is best, and most reasonable, to understand these two sticks as the sticks of the Southern Kingdom (Judah) and the Northern Kingdom (Ephraim). After King Solomon died, his son, Rehoboam, became the fourth king of Israel. It was under his reign that the kingdom split, around 931 BC: the Southern Kingdom became known as Judah and the Northern Kingdom was called Israel, or Ephraim, because it was Ephraim who was the strongest and most influential tribe and also because the first king of the Northern Kingdom was Jeroboam who was an Ephraimite (compare 1 Kings 11 and 12).

The promise of verses 21–23 is that the Lord will reunite these two nations, bring them together as one, and return them to their own land. He will make them one nation and one kingdom under one king. They shall never again be divided. The Lord promise continues, stating that they will never again be defiled with the idols of the land. He will deliver them and cleanse them, and they shall enjoy that unique and special

---

[128] Feinberg, 215.

relationship with Jehovah God as He had originally wanted and desired from their very inception.

The Lord continues to promise them that He will make His servant David king over them once again. This causes some an interpretive problem as to whether the Lord means a literal David or a symbolic David. Feinberg explains: "Apart from the fact that God would not design a culmination age with two supreme rulers on earth in a sort of coregency, a concept foreign to Old Testament prophecy and the repeated mention of the numeral "one" in connection with their final king, there is no inherent reason why David must rule again. There was no such implication in the original Davidic covenant of 2 Samuel 7."[129]

On the other hand, Dyer argues, "nothing in Ezekiel 34:23 demands that Ezekiel was not referring to the literal king David who will be resurrected to serve as Israel's righteous prince. David is referred to by name elsewhere in passages that look to the future restoration of Israel (compare Jeremiah 30:9; Ezekiel 37:24–25; Hosea 3:5). Also, Ezekiel indicated that David will be the prince of the restored people (Ezekiel. 34:24; 37:25)."[130]

Though both schools of thought are compelling in their own arguments, it is hard to miss that this prince of Israel will prepare for himself and the nation a bull for a sin offering (Ezekiel 45:22). It would make no sense—and be highly inappropriate—for Christ to offer a sin offering for Himself; therefore, it might be best to understand this king of verse 24 as the literal resurrected David. As difficult as that may seem, remember, our God is the God of resurrection and power and can

---

[129] Feinberg, 216.
[130] Dyer, 1295.

accomplish anything He desires (we did, after all, just see his "resurrection" of the dry bones).

We need to pause and remember that whether a literal resurrected David or a representative of the Davidic Throne—namely, Jesus Christ—is the reference here, we should not miss the point of this prophecy. God is in control and Jesus Christ is returning to establish His kingdom (compare Revelation 19), so ultimately Christ is in control and will rule with a rod of iron (Isaiah 11:4), whether through or with His servant David or alone. It will come to pass.

The result of such restoration and reign will be complete peace for the nation. Make no mistake: this will be the same land that was given to Abraham and Jacob, (Genesis 12, 26, and 35) and they shall dwell there, their children and their grandchildren. God will establish an everlasting covenant with them, and they shall live in peace (Jeremiah 31:31–34). Finally, the peace they have so longed and sought for will be theirs.

As we have seen with Israel when they left Egypt, God was pleased to dwell in a tabernacle among them, and so it will be when He restores them to their land. Once again, Israel will enjoy this special relationship that no other nation or people enjoy, and it will be this way for all eternity. The Lord will again be set up amid His people and He will be their God and they shall be His people. It is then they will understand that he is Jehovah God and set them apart from the other nations and they will never be destroyed again.

APPLICATION

This promise of dwelling with them is explained and amplified further in closing chapters of Ezekiel, but for now one would do well to notice the many terms of finality used. Notice how often eternity is mentioned. In verse 25, they shall dwell *forever*. Their occupation is to be *forever*, the kingship of David is *forever*, the covenant of peace will be *forever*, and the sanctuary will be *forever*. These events have not happened yet and once again, if the literal meaning makes sense, then seek no other interpretation. To accept this as symbolic or as an allegory of something else is just wrong. Forever means forever, and we will not see the culmination of these events until the return of Christ when He comes to establish His kingdom once and for all. The Israelites residing in Palestine today are not the fulfillment of this prophecy. Rather, it will be fulfilled when God regathers believing Israelites to the land and Christ returns (compare Matthew 24:30–31).

Study Questions
1. Do you believe God has a future plan for Israel?
2. Do you believe the church today has inherited the future promises of Israel?

Ezekiel 38:1–39:29

The Northern Invasion

Chapters 38 and 39 constitute one prophecy. Much has been written as to the meaning of this prophecy. When this prophecy takes place and exactly who the players are has caused more than a little debate. With the ever-changing political world, commentators have written and rewritten explanations as to the exact meaning of these two chapters.

The different views as to the timing of this prophecy include: a) sometime during the end of the church age, b) sometime during the seven-year tribulation period, c) upon the return of Christ after the tribulation period, or d) at the end of the thousand-year reign of Christ known as the Millennial Kingdom.

Without question, the prophecy involves an invasion from the north. Many believe that this northern invasion is Russia invading the Middle East, specifically Israel. Dyer points to several explanations as to why this could be Russia: 1) Some of the countries mentioned here were in what is now Russia; 2) the armies do come from the north; 3) Ezekiel speaks of a coalition of nations, many of which are aligned with Russia today.[131]

Some would disagree. James F. Matheny has written a little booklet entitled, *Is There a Russian Connection?* and his conclusion is that Russia is not a player. "[D]oes the Bible still

---

[131] Dyer, 1300.

teach in Ezekiel 38 and 39 a Russian invasion of Israel? Many claims that it does. Some even believe that a Russian attack on Israel will be the preliminary battle in the Armageddon campaign. Our purpose in this study is to provide solid biblical evidence that Ezekiel 38 and 39 do not predict a Russian invasion of Israel and that the truth of the passage in Ezekiel demands no connection with the present nation of Russian whatsoever."[132] I will attempt to hammer out some of these arguments in the rest of this chapter.

EZEKIEL 38:1–23
GOG'S INVASION

In chapter 37, Ezekiel revealed how Israel (God's people) would be restored to their land from many parts of the world. Once Israel became strong, a confederacy of nations from the north would attack, led by Gog (compare Revelation 20:8). Their purpose would be to destroy God's people.

Verses 1–3
Five names are referenced in this section: *Gog, Magog, Rosh, Meshech,* and *Tubal.* Ezekiel is told to set his face against them in the sense that he is now to turn his attention to this northern confederacy and prophesy against them. The problem posed in this verse is the exact identity of those called by these five names (see earlier comments).

With Ezekiel being told to prophesy against *him*, singular, it would seem logical to understand all these names as referring to one person and one nation. Verse 2 reads: *Son of man, set your*

---

[132] James F. Matheny, *Is There a Russian Connection?* (Enid, OK: Jay & Associates, 1987), 9.

face against Gog, of the land of Magog, the prince of Rosh, Meshech, and Tubal, and prophesy against him. This reading seems to clarify that a person by the name of *Gog*, from the land of *Magog*, who is called the prince of *Rosh, Meshech, and Tubal* is the one being addressed. Verse 3 would seem to support this view. Pentecost argues that *Rosh* is the name given to the leader of this confederacy and his land is called *Magog*, which is composed of Rosh, Meshech, and Tubal.[133]

Many believe that Rosh, Meshech, and Tubal are a reference to Russia in that *Rosh* sounds like Russia, *Meshech* has reference to Moscow, and *Tubal* would have reference to Tobolsk. It should be noted that these simplistic equivalencies are based only on the names' slight similarity to modern ears. At the time Ezekiel received this word from the Lord, he had specific geographic locations in mind, so this should be the starting point as to identifying who these are nations and hordes are. Ezekiel had historical places in mind, not the modern locations and entities that we now know.

Some suggest that the name *Gog* should be associated with Gyges, who was a Lydian king associated with the land of Gugu, but this is not possible as his reign was before the time of Ezekiel. The *Gog* referenced in these verses is the leader of the land of *Magog* and *Magog* is not found in any reference outside the Bible. Feinberg notes that Jerome stated the Jews of his day held that *Magog* was a general designation for the numerous Scythian tribes.[134] Genesis 10:2 states: *The sons of Japheth were Gomer, Magog, Madai, Javan, Tubal, Meshech, and Tiras.* These were all known enemies of God's people.

---

[133] J. Dwight Pentecost, *Things to Come* (Grand Rapids, MI: Zondervan, 1964), 327.
[134] Feinberg, 220.

Concerning *Rosh*, the question should be asked, "is this word intended to be a proper noun, meaning the country of Rosh, or should it be understood as an adjective, meaning "head prince" or "chief"? MacArthur points out that the better reading of this phrase is "the chief prince of Meshech and Tubal." His reasoning includes the fact that more than 600 times in the Old Testament, this word is used as an adjective; the most ancient versions took it to mean "chief" and in all places other than chapters 38 and 39 where both *Meshech* and *Tubal* are mentioned, *Rosh* is not listed as a third person.[135] It would be difficult to dogmatically conclude that *Rosh* must be Russia. Many writers have connected the name *Rosh* with the Russians, but this is not generally accepted today. In fact, the Greeks included all these names under the nations of the north.[136] *Meshech* and *Tubal* were identified previously in Genesis 10:2 and are associated with Phrygia and Cappadocia. They dwelt in the area known as Magog.

Verse 4
This planned invasion of these nations is clearly an instrument of the Lord. We have seen that in times past God used other pagan nations to judge and chasten Israel, and this is no different. God clearly is orchestrating the events and using these northern nations to attack Israel.

The phrase *put hooks into your jaws* implies is that this is not a voluntary invasion by the northerners. They seem to be unwilling, but they nevertheless will be diverted from their original purpose. When Gog decides to attack, they will appear as a well-organized and well-armed army. They will be

---

[135] MacArthur, 1206.
[136] Feinberg, 220.

excellently equipped with horses and horsemen, with splendid armor and skillful swordsmen, and will arrive in great numbers.

Verses 5–6
Gog's allies would come from the mountainous area southeast of the Black Sea and southwest of the Caspian Sea (central Turkey), as well as from the area that is present-day Iran, Sudan, Egypt, and possibly the countries that made up the former Soviet Union. *Gomer* should be associated with Armenia and the *house of Togarmah* with present-day Turkey. This coalition of nations will come together for the purpose of annihilating Israel from the face of the earth.

Verses 7–9
Now the question must be asked as to when all this will take place. Once again, there are many opinions and diverse conclusions (refer to the positions discussed earlier in of this chapter). Many say that the battle Ezekiel described will occur at the end of human history, but there are many differences between the events described here and those in Revelation 20. Regardless of when this battle will occur, the message is clear: God will deliver His people and no enemy can withstand the powerful mighty arm of the Lord. It should be noted that no past historical event has yet matched this prophecy, which argues that it refers to a yet-future date.

The similarities between Revelation 20:7–9 and this text include the mention of *Gog* and *Magog*, but that is hardly enough to conclude that both texts speak of the same event. First, as Dyer points out, the results of these wars do not coincide.[137] The

---

[137] Dyer, 1300.

dead in Ezekiel 39:12–13 are buried, but Revelation explains the next event as the resurrection of the unsaved dead. Why take seven months to bury the dead if they are to be soon resurrected? In Ezekiel 39:9, Israel will make a seven-year fire using the weapons of the enemy as fuel; whereas in Revelation 21:1–4 the very next event will be the ushering-in of eternity with the new heaven and new earth.

The results of the battles seem to be different as well. In Ezekiel, the battle seems to be used of the Lord to draw Israel to Himself and set them apart from the other nations after their captivity; in Revelation, Israel would have just finished a thousand years of faithful service and reign with Christ on the earth.

It seems more likely that Ezekiel's prophecy speaks of the battle that will usher in the Millennium Kingdom, or (to put it more succinctly) to end the seven years of tribulation on the earth (compare Revelation 19:17–21).

The invaders are told to prepare themselves for battle in verse 7. Interesting that the Lord would speak to the enemy of His people and command them to prepare for battle. They are told this battle would be yet *many days*, in fact in the *latter years*, which would give even more support for a future date, namely the end of the tribulation period. They are to invade like a coming storm, *covering the land like a cloud* and leaving nothing unoccupied. The implication at least is that Israel will be ill prepared, as she will be dwelling in safety and not expecting the coming invasion.

Verses 10–13

The purpose of this invasion is stated and simply put: it is to devour the land and rob it of its riches. The enemy will seize the opportunity and invade a nation that will be caught totally off guard. Israel will be living in peace; having just returned from captivity, they will not have rebuilt their walls or gates. They have a false sense of security. They have had time to acquire possessions such as livestock and such. They will be like a lonely innocent lamb with the preying wolf close behind and ready to pounce. But suddenly, as if from nowhere, they will be attacked, caught off guard, and occupied by the enemy.

Some have written of the similarities between this passage and the passage of Daniel 9:27. Israel will be experiencing a false peace when, after the rapture of the church (compare 1 Thessalonians 4:15–17), the then-known ruler, known to many as the Antichrist, will sign a peace accord with Israel. This will initiate the beginning of the seventh week of Daniel. At this time, Israel will be living in peace being protected by this "big brother." Daniel tells us that in the middle of this seventh week, the Antichrist will break this peace treaty (compare Matthew 24:15–22). This is known as the *abomination of desolation* and will mark the beginning of the great and terrible day of the Lord.

Verses 14–16

These verses contain repetitive statements from the early part of this chapter. The focus is upon the complete invasion of Israel's land while they are living in a false sense of security. The *latter days* are mentioned again, emphasizing the yet-future date of these events. God will use Gog, a pagan nation, to glorify His name. This is not the first time we have seen this—compare

Nebuchadnezzar in the book of Daniel—and certainly will not be the last. By dealing with Israel as He does, and by using Gog to accomplish His purpose, God will again show the world that He is holy and sovereign.

Verse 17

Earlier prophets have spoken of these events as well. The wording of Kind David in Psalm 18 is like that of this passage. Although as difficult as it may be to point to a prophecy concerning these specific events, especially concerning Gog, many did write concerning the judgment of Israel and her destruction: compare Jeremiah 3–6; Joel 3; Daniel 2:44–45; and Zephaniah 1:14; 3:8.

Verses 18–22

After seeing how the Lord raised Gog and used him to invade, plunder, and devastate Israel, we now see the Lord's vengeance against Gog and his army. One of the great mysteries, at least to this author, is that the Lord raises nations to enact His judgments on Israel and clearly the hand of the Lord is directing them—and then, when all is accomplished, the Lord judges them for their attack on and control of Israel. We have seen that the Lord hardened the heart of Pharaoh to accomplish His purpose with Israel during the Exodus, and thereafter He judges him and his nation for their treatment of the Jews (compare Exodus 14).

Paul explains in Romans 9:14–21: *What shall we say then? Is there unrighteousness with God? Certainly not! For He says to Moses, 'I will have mercy on whomever I will have mercy, and I will have compassion on whomever I will have compassion.' So, then it is not of him who wills, nor of him who runs, but of God who shows mercy. For the Scripture says to the Pharaoh, 'For this very purpose I have raised you up, that I may show My power in you, and that My name may be declared in all the earth.' Therefore, He has mercy on whom He wills, and whom He wills He hardens. You will say to me then, 'Why does He still find fault? For who has resisted His will?' But indeed, O man, who are you to reply against God? Will the thing formed say to him who formed it, 'Why have you made me like this?' Does not the potter have power over the clay, from the same lump to make one vessel for honor and another for dishonor?*

The wording of this remaining section of chapter 38 is very similar to that of the judgments described in Revelation during the tribulation period. When the armies of Gog reach their destination and begin their attack, the Lord will revolt against them and show His fury. Because of His righteous jealousy, He will come to the aid of Israel and cause an earthquake to stop the invading army. All living beings, including those in the sea, the air, and on land will tremble at the mighty work of the Lord. There will be chaos and brother will turn against brother. Mountains will be replaced; walls will fall, and God will rain hail and brimstone upon them with great hailstones. There will be pestilence, bloodshed, and floods. These events are eerily like those of the sixth seal (compare Revelation 6:14); the second trumpet (compare Revelation 8:8); and the seventh bowl judgment (compare Revelation 16:17ff).

Verse 23

The closing verse of this chapter summarizes God's intent. By opposing the invasion of Gog, and by coming to the rescue of Israel, God will magnify Himself and set Himself apart as the Holy God that He is. Because of God's actions, the nations will know that He is God and all nations will be humbled. God is going to be glorified no matter what He does. God is going to make himself known, even in judgment, and get honor to Himself. God is jealous of His name. If God is zealous to maintain His honor, then so should we be.[138]

Thomas continues by quoting Ryle: "'A zealous man in religion,' wrote J. C. Ryle, 'is pre-eminently a man of one thing. It is not enough to say that he is earnest, hearty, uncompromising, thorough-going, whole-hearted, fervent in spirit. He only sees one thing, he cares for one thing, he lives for one thing, he is swallowed up in one thing; and that one thing is to please God.'"[139] To which this author adds: Amen!

EZEKIEL 39:1–29
GOD'S PURPOSE IN THE INVASION

Verses 39:1–8
What is initially striking in this section is that twice the Lord states: *They shall know that I am the Lord.* After redirecting Gog and causing them to revolt and fight against Israel, God will come against them solely for the purpose of putting Himself on display and revealing His character to the nations.

God's displeasure with Gog continues in this chapter and is repeated for the sake of emphasis (compare Ezekiel 38:18, 21). God will strike them at the mountains of Israel. What is obviously the major weakness of Gog as he comes to fight against Israel is that he relies on his own strength and numbers and upon the weakness of Israel and totally forgets the one element that will destroy him and his armies: he fails to take the God of Israel into account. God will remove their weapons from their

---

[138] Thomas, 259.
[139] Thomas, 259.

hands and the once-mighty army will become lunch for the birds of the air and the beasts of the field. This judgment will not be confined to the destruction of the army of Gog alone, but according to verse 6 will also extend to the land of Gog, and to all the heathen nations that are dwelling in apparent security. God will send fire upon them, which implies total destruction and annihilation.

The events of this destruction are like events that take place during the Tribulation period. As noted earlier, during the Tribulation period there will be earthquakes and hailstorms (compare Ezekiel 38:19, 22); there will also be a feast of the birds of the air as they clean the earth of dead corpses (compare Revelation 19:17–18).

Some have a problem with this assessment because Ezekiel speaks of weapons such as bows and arrows, and it seems inconceivable that armies of the Tribulation would use such antiquated equipment. This is easily explained, as Ezekiel would have had no clue as to the recent developments of weaponry and is only using terms he is familiar with. Regardless as to whether these two events are the same, it is important not to miss the real point: God is sovereign and in control and He will be victorious. Gog will be destroyed, and he and his armies will no longer be able to blaspheme God's holy name.

Verses 9–16

Another purpose we find for this invasion is that God desires to place His people in a conspicuous position and honor them (compare verse 13). This will be accomplished as Israel spends seven years burning the enemy's weapons and seven months burying the enemy's dead soldiers.

After the defeat of Gog, Israel will take their weapons; their *shields and bucklers*, their *bows and arrows*, their *javelins and spears,* and will make a *fire of them* that will burn for *seven years.* There will be no need to cut down trees, as there will be plenty of fuel from these weapons to make this fire hot for its intended period. With much irony, the once-mighty nation of Gog, which came to defeat and plunder Israel, will themselves be defeated, plundered, and pillaged by the very nation they intended to defeat. What an amazing turnaround of events. It is not good to underestimate the power of God (compare 1 Peter 5:6).

After the battle, it will be Israel's responsibility to bury the dead. Eastern cultures bury their dead within a day. Previously we saw that the birds of the air and the beasts of the field will devour these corpses, so one wonders if Israel will be burying just the bones. This burial will be of such massive nature that the travel routes will be blocked by the graves. Imagine it taking seven months to bury these bodies. That is a lot of bodies! Gog will be given a burial place in Israel, as the men of Israel employed those travelers to help in their "search and burial" operation. These graves will serve as a constant reminder to Israel of the strength and power of their God and the protection of His right hand.

The procedure was for anyone traveling through the land to set up a marker if they discovered bones, and then the buriers would come along later to bury the remains. The place of burial is called *The Valley of Hamon Gog* or "The Multitude of Gog" with the name of the city itself called *Hamonah* or simply "Multitude." One cannot help but remember the carnage and destruction caused by the terrorists who attacked the United States on September 11, 2001. For months, in fact, years, workers were finding bones at the site of the twin towers in New York City. It is hard to imagine that after only seven months Israel would have buried all the dead of Gog, but because of God's intervention, it will be made possible. God will use a search party, better understood as travelers, to help find the remaining bones.

Dyer comments that the valley where Gog's army will be buried is "on the east side of the Dead Sea (NIV marg.) in what is today Jordan. The phrase 'those who travel east' could be taken as a proper name. It might refer to the 'mountains of Abarim' east of the Dead Sea that Israel traverses on her way to the Promised Land, compare Numbers 33:48. If so, Gog's burial will be in the Valley of Abarim just across the Dead Sea from Israel proper in the land of Moab. Yet the burial will be in Israel because Israel controlled that area during some periods of her history, compare 2 Samuel 8:2; Psalm 60:8." He further notes that the "way of the travelers" could be translated "Abarim."[140]

Rooker suggests that the Valley of Abarim is the same as the Jezreel Valley. Additionally, he notes that this valley was a vital strategic link on the route from Egypt to Damascus in biblical times. Rooker equates this valley with the valley where the great battle of the Tribulation period known as Armageddon will be located (compare Revelation 16:13–16).[141]

Verses 17–29

The third and final reason given in this chapter for God's purpose of the invasion is to educate the nations of the earth. This section begins with an instruction to the birds of the air and the beasts of the field to go forth and devour the flesh of the

---

[140] Dyer, 1302.
[141] Rooker, 290.

corpses. This is not a second meal for these animals, but a further explanation of Ezekiel 39:4.

There are striking similarities between this text and Revelation 19:17–18. In Revelation, it is called *great supper of God*. However, Feinberg is quick to point out that although the time factor is explicit in Ezekiel and Revelation, there is no ground for equating the *Gog* of Ezekiel with any individual or group mentioned by John in Revelation. The concept of the Lord's sacrifice was already found in Isaiah 34:6; Jeremiah 46:10; and Zephaniah 1:7–8.[142]

The feast is called a *sacrificial meal* as well as the Lord's Table. The imagery used compares the slain men to *rams, lambs, goats,* and *bulls.* Again, the irony of the text is obvious, as it is usually men who slaughter these animals and eat them, not the reverse.

The reference to *Bashan* (compare Ezekiel 27:6), according to the *International Standard Bible Encyclopedia*, often occurs with the article—"the Bashan,"—to describe the kingdom of Og, the most northerly part of the land east of the Jordan. It stretched from the border of Gilead in the south to the slopes of Hermen in the north.[143] The picture given to us in verses 17–20 portrays a vivid figure of carnage, God's judgment, and irreversible destruction.

The lesson these nations, the Gentiles, were to learn is that it is the God of Israel who is orchestrating all these events, and nothing happens without His knowledge and control. They will witness firsthand God's hand of judgment. They will be taught that God's people went into captivity because of their sins

---

[142] Feinberg, 231.
[143] International Standard Bible Encyclopedia Electronic Database.

and unfaithfulness to Jehovah. God dealt with them according to their sins and He hid His face from them.

The Gentiles will also learn that it was Jehovah who returned Israel to her land, and that He showed His mercy upon the whole nation because of His holy jealousy and His desire to have His name honored. Once Israel returns, she will once again honor the Lord and worship Him and return to the God that loves them. If the people of God could discern the working of God among the nations, then it is equally true that the nations of earth could learn the character and will of God from His relationships with His chosen people. The visitation of the Lord upon the rebellious nations will first have significance for Israel. Contrariwise, the nations will then realize that Israel suffered captivity and defeat not because of any inherent weakness in God, but because of their sinful ways which He punished in this manner.[144]

This section ends with the full return of Israel to the land the Lord has given them, which occurs after the defeat of Gog. Again, words of finality are used by our Lord: *left none of them captive any longer* and *I will not hide my face from them anymore.* As Ironside comments, "This seems to prove definitely that the events we have been considering as set forth in these two chapters, will take place during the time of the Great tribulation and before the manifestation of the Lord Jesus Christ as King of kings and Lord of lords."[145]

---

[144] Feinberg, 231.
[145] Ironside, 276.

APPLICATION

The Lord promises to pour out His Spirit on the house of Israel. Joel 2:28 states: *And it shall come to pass afterward that I will pour out My Spirit on all flesh.* This verse is quoted by the apostle Peter at Pentecost in Acts 2:17, which would indicate a yet-future date (compare Zechariah 12:10). The ultimate result of this great battle is the restoration of the nation of Israel as they repent and turn back to God. This will be fulfilled once and for all in the Millennial Kingdom.

Dr. John Walvoord gives us an appropriate conclusion to these two chapters in his book entitled, *Prophecy: 14 Essential Keys to Understanding the Final Drama:*

> Inherent in all the prophecies concerning possessing the Land is the promise that Israel will be restored as a nation—spiritually, politically, and territorially. Just as the nation of Israel will possess the Land forever, so they will constitute a nation forever, and Christ will reign over them. Many passages in the Old Testament confirm this. Isaiah 2:1–5 describes Jerusalem as the center of the divine government with Christ ruling the world from the throne of David. Isaiah 11 speaks of the righteousness of this kingdom; verses 1–16 picture God's righteous judgment as well as the peace and tranquility which will characterize the kingdom. Psalm 72 describes the universality of His rule, and other Old Testament passages confirm these prophecies. Although whether a certain generation would inhabit the land

depended on their obedience, God's ultimate plan to restore Israel is clear. The fulfillment of this promise is just as sure as those describing Christ's Second Coming."[146]

---

[146] John F. Walvoord, *Prophecy: 14 Essential Keys to Understanding the Final Drama* (Nashville, TN: Thomas Nelson, 1993), 79–80.

Ezekiel 40:1–43:27

The Millennial Temple

The final nine chapters of the book of Ezekiel have been the most divisive of the whole book. More disagreement among Bible scholars as to the exact meaning of these chapters exists than regarding any others. Those who agree with a literal translation generally fall in the camp calling themselves "premillennialists," as opposed to those who choose to allegorize its meaning and call themselves "amillennialists."

Charles C. Ryrie helps us to understand the difference between these two camps. He states that in general the premillennialists hold to a literal interpretation of the Scriptures. "Premillennialists believe that the promises made to Abraham and David are unconditional and have had or will have a literal fulfillment. In no sense have these promises made to Israel been abrogated or fulfilled by the Church, which is a distinct body in this age having promises and a destiny different from Israel's."[147]

At the close of this age, premillennialists believe that Christ will return for His Church, and then a period of seven years will follow which is called the Tribulation period, which is what Daniel spoke of in Daniel 9 in reference to the seventieth week. The end of the Tribulation period will be marked by the

---

[147] Charles C. Ryrie, *The Basis of the Premillennial Faith* (Neptune, NJ: Loizeaux Brothers, 1953), 12.

second coming of the Lord, in which He will crush all unrighteousness, cast Satan into the bottomless pit, and establish His kingdom on earth for a thousand years—hence the term *millennium*. It is to this time period that the last nine chapters of Ezekiel refer concerning the Millennial Temple.

In contrast, an amillennialist is one who believes the teaching that "only the visible coming of Christ to this earth which the Church is to expect will be for judgment and will be followed by the final state. It is anti-chiliastic or a-millennial, because it rejects the doctrine that there are to be two resurrections with an interval of a thousand years between them."[148]

Amillennialism teaches that the church and Israel are not distinct; in fact, the church is the kingdom and is reigning now, or at least should be. All the promises to Abraham and David apply to the church and are to be received by the church. Therefore, to deal with the thousand years spoken of in Revelation 20, they hold that this number, the number of perfection or completion, is a symbolic number that refers to the complete period between the first advent of Christ, his incarnation, and the second advent of Christ in Revelation 19.

Renald Showers has written an excellent book in which he deals with this very subject, comparing both camps. (There are more than these two camps, but for the sake of this book, only the two most prominent views are discussed: premillennialism and amillennialism). Showers contrasts both views and shows the remarkable difference. This author recommends his book with much enthusiasm for future study.[149]

---

[148] Ryrie, 14.
[149] Renald E. Showers, *There Really Is a Difference!* (Bellmawr, N.J.: The Friends of Israel Gospel Ministry, 1990).

"To read the last nine chapters of Ezekiel in their literal force is to learn that God has glorious plans in view for Israel and through them for all the earth. But such predictions of blessing never carry with them the assurance that there will be blessing for individuals anywhere apart from personal response in faith to the invitation of the Saviour."[150]

Verses 40:1–5

We have seen, in Ezekiel 37:26–27, that God has already promised to build a new tabernacle among His people. Some suggest that Ezekiel was predicting the rebuilding of Solomon's Temple after the return from captivity. This can be rejected because the Temple built upon return did not follow the specifications given by Ezekiel.

Before proceeding with an analysis of this chapter, I would like to stress the specificity of God's instructions. Anyone who would conclude that our God is not a God of details has not read this section or the book of Leviticus, among others. God desires things to be done His way and His way only, which includes everything in our relationship to Him. We cannot choose to do things our own way in our own manner without violating that which God intended. This includes our prayers, our worship, and the whole of our service. God is a God of specificity and He desires that we do things His way!

Chapter 40 opens with a date. This vision comes in the *twenty-fifth year* of captivity, at the *beginning of the year*, on the *tenth day of the month*, in the *fourteenth year after the city* (Jerusalem) *was captured.* This would put the date somewhere

---

[150] Feinberg, 239.

around 573 BC. In this vision, the Lord takes the hand of Ezekiel and transports him to the city of Jerusalem.

The Lord takes Ezekiel and sets him on a *very high mountain*. We do not know exactly which mountain. Some suggestions are Mount Scopus, which is the northern extension of the Mount of Olives, but this is highly unlikely, as the Temple will be built in an area north of the city.[151] Others suggest that this is Mount Zion, but really no conclusions can be made with certainty. Thomas suggests that because Jerusalem was located on a relatively low mountain, and Ezekiel was taken to a high mountain, this could be a reference to the New Jerusalem of Revelation 21.[152]

Upon arrival on this mountain top, Ezekiel is met by his own personal tour guide, described as a man with the *appearance of bronze* who stood at the *gateway* of the Temple. This man is not identified by Ezekiel, but some suggest with certainty that he is the Angel of the Lord, otherwise known as the preincarnate Christ. He is referred to as Lord in Ezekiel 44:5. Keil and Delitzsch's opinion is that in Ezekiel 44:2 and 44:5, it is not the man who is speaking, but rather that the prophet is there addressed directly by the apparition of God (Ezekiel 43:2ff). This, however, is proven untenable by the simple fact that the speaker (Ezekiel 44) admonishes the prophet in verse 5 to attend, to see, and to hear, in the same words as the man in verse 4 of the chapter before us. These place the identity of the two beyond the reach of doubt.[153]

---

[151] John Schmitt and Charles Laney, *Messiah's Coming Temple* (Grand Rapids, MI: Kregel, 1997), 77.
[152] Thomas, 267–268.
[153] *Keil and Delitzsch Commentary.*

This man had in his hand two measuring devices. Because Ezekiel is going to be told to measure and his measurements would consist of various lengths, the two devices were necessary. A *line of flax* was used to measure longer distances and the *rod* was used for shorter distances. Ezekiel is told to carefully look upon everything and study it. The sole reason for bringing him to this point and showing him these things was that he might declare them to the house of Israel.

The temple was surrounded by a wall and a measurement was taken of the width and height of that wall. The *rod* was *six cubits long*, each being a *cubit and a handbreadth*, and the *width* was measured to be *one rod* and the *height to be one rod*.

The exact length of the cubit is not known, as there seems to have been a double standard between the Hebrews and the Egyptians, and because we have no undisputed example of the cubit remaining to the present time. The Babylonians also had a double standard, the so-called royal cubit and the ordinary one. Because it was the royal cubit that made its way to Western culture, most agree that the cubit referred to here by Ezekiel is the royal cubit, which was approximately twenty-one inches in length.

Taking these dimensions into consideration, both the width and the height of the wall surrounding the temple would be ten and a half feet. This wall encloses the temple area itself, which measures 500 cubits by 500 cubits, about 750 feet by 750 feet, which would fit almost three football fields end to end.[154]

---

[154] Schmitt and Laney, 83.

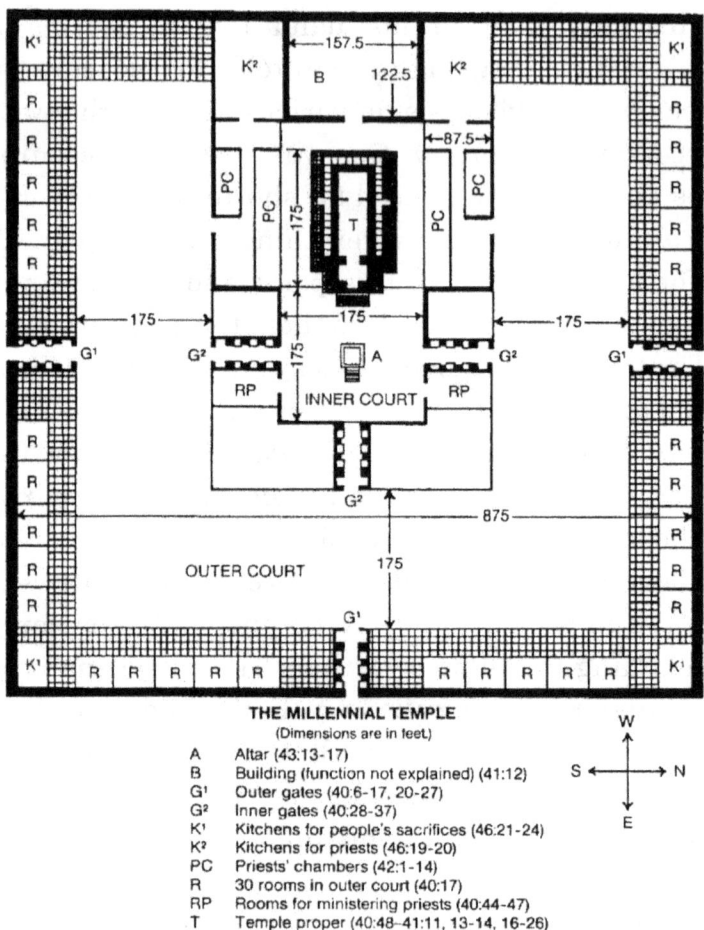

Figure 1: The Temple[155]

---

[155] Adapted from Charles Dyer, "Commentary on Ezekiel" in *The Bible Knowledge Commentary* (Wheaton: Victor Books, 1986).

Verses 40:6–11

Next, we have a description of the eastern gateway of the temple (see Figure 2). This *gateway* carries great significance because it serves as the basis for describing all the other gates. Having gone up the *stairs* at the gateway, Ezekiel measures the *thresholds of the gateway*. They both measure one rod each, which again would be equivalent to ten and half feet. The area of the *gate chambers*, three on each side and each separated by a wall, was ten and a half feet by ten and a half feet and the distance between the *gate chambers* measured five cubits or approximately eight and three-quarter feet. The *vestibule* of the inside and the outside gate measured one rod or ten and a half feet. The width of the gate itself was ten cubits or seventeen and a half feet and the length of this gate was thirteen cubits or twenty-two and three-quarter feet.

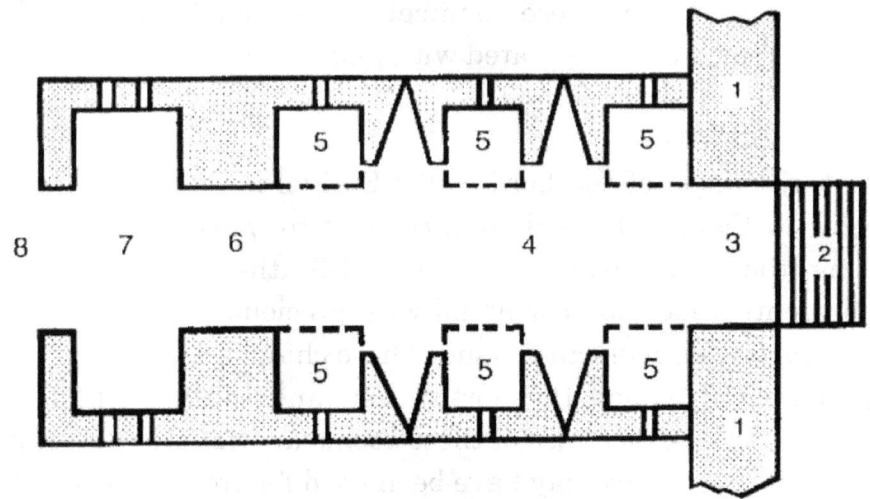

Figure 2: Eastern Gateway[156]

---

[156] Adapted from John Taylor, *Ezekiel: An Introduction and Commentary* (London, UK: Tyndale Press, 1969).

Verses 40:12–16

Next, Ezekiel goes into a detailed description of the *gate chambers*. The space on either side of the *gate chambers* was one cubit (twenty-one inches) and the *gate chambers* themselves measured six by six cubits (ten and a half by ten and a half feet) square. From one door of the chambers across the gate to the other door of the chamber, described as from roof to roof, measured twenty-five cubits (forty-three and three-quarter feet). The *gateposts* measured sixty cubits (105 feet) high. From the front end of the *entrance gate* to the front of the *vestibule* at the other end measured fifty cubits (eighty-seven and a half feet).

Each *gate chamber* had windows on the inside of the gateway all around, and likewise in the vestibules, which were probably similar to the narrow windows in the towers of ancient castles.[157] These windows were all around on the inside and would suggest that these chambers were completely enclosed. The gateposts were decorated with palm trees.

Verses 40:17–19

Next, the angel of the Lord walks Ezekiel into the *outer court* (refer to Figure 3) which was covered by *pavement* that ran along the outer wall. In Esther 1:6, the term *pavement* represents a mosaic floor inlaid with precious stones. There he saw *thirty chambers* all around. These chambers were probably spaced evenly along the north, east, and south walls of the temple.[158] The exact uses of these rooms are not stipulated, but some speculate they may have been used for storage or possibly meeting rooms for the purpose of celebrating the feasts. The distance from the *front of the lower gateway* (east gate) to the

---

[157] Schmitt and Laney, 85.
[158] Dyer, 1304.

inner court exterior (to the threshold of the gate leading to the inner court) was one hundred cubits (175 feet).

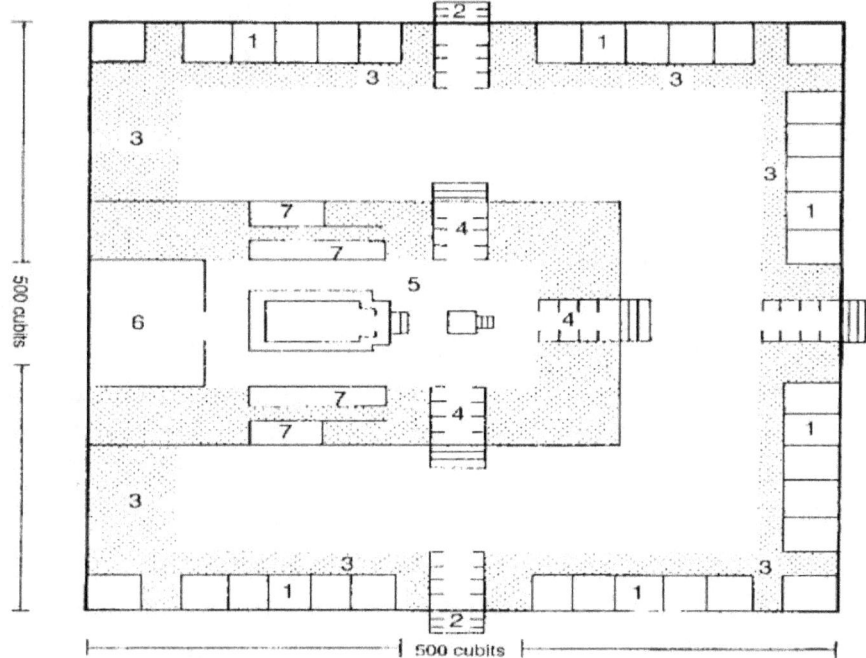

Figure 3: Outer Court[159]

Verses 40:20–27
The northern and southern gateways explained in these verses are very similar in size and description to the *eastern gateway* of verses 6–16. The numbers seven, twenty-five, fifty, and one hundred are frequently used.

---

[159] Adapted from John Taylor, *Ezekiel: An Introduction and Commentary* (London, UK: Tyndale Press, 1969).

Verses 40:28–37

In many ways, the *inner court* gates were like the outer gates. In fact, some suggest they were a mirror image. The inside of the *outer gate* is the outside of the *inner court gate*. No wall is mentioned, probably because the inner court was surrounded by the three gateways on the north, east, and south.

Verses 40:38–43

Clearly, sacrifices were to be offered in this temple. If this is indeed the Millennial Temple, as we have suggested, then this question must be posed: "Why, after Christ's death, are sacrifices being offered?" Those who oppose the millennial view suggest that this would contradict the truths of the book of Hebrews.

Feinberg offers this explanation: "Hebrews is not speaking primarily nor specifically of the millennial era. Also, the sacrifices here will have no more redemptive efficacy now than they did before Calvary. Again, nothing and no sacrifice, before or after the work of Christ on the cross, [can] invalidate or render unnecessary that glorious work which we shall praise throughout the eternal ages."[160] Just as the Lord's Supper serves as a memorial of the death, burial, and resurrection of Christ for the church age, sacrifices will serve as a memorial for the millennial dwellers.

The specificity of these verses makes it hard to allegorize. If the literal sense makes sense, then seek no other sense. They were to cleanse their sacrifices by the *gateposts of the gateway*. The *vestibule* contains eight tables, two on each side for the purpose of slaying the animal for the *burnt, sin, and trespass*

---

[160] Feinberg, 243.

offerings. There were four other tables made from *hewn stone*, one and a half cubit long and wide (a little larger than two and a half feet square), and one cubit (twenty inches) high. The purpose of these four tables was to hold the instruments used for slaughter. These tables contained *hooks* on the inside that were a *handbreadth wide* for the purpose of hanging the sacrifice on the table.

Verses 40:44–46
We are told of the participants in the sacrificial rites. Outside the inner gate were chambers used by the singers (refer to Figure 2). There was one facing south at the side of the northern gateway and the other facing north at the side of the southern gateway. These singers are identified as priests who will occupy the chamber that faces south. The chamber that faces north is to be used by the priests who have charge of the altar. These priests will be descendants of Zadok, who is from the sons of Levi. They are the ones permitted to approach the Lord to minister. Feinberg is correct to point out that the use of these proper names adds credibility to the historical and literal understanding of this text.[161]

Zadok is first mentioned in 2 Samuel 8:17 serving as a priest under the reign of King David and in fact was the only one who remained faithful to David his entire life. What an honor to serve the King of Kings during this time. Some have suggested that these priests were chosen because of Zadok's original faithfulness to David and as a reward, were granted the privilege of serving.

---

[161] Feinberg, 243.

Verses 40:47–49

The inner court was a square surrounding a square temple. Its measurement was *one hundred cubits long* and *one hundred cubits wide* (175 feet square). *The altar was in front of the temple.* The *doorpost of the vestibule* measured five cubits on each side (eight and three-quarter feet high) and the width of the gateway was three cubits on either side (five and one-quarter feet). The length of the vestibule was twenty cubits (thirty-five feet) and the width was eleven cubits (nineteen and a quarter feet). There were *steps* with *pillars* on either side.

Many have compared the structure described here with Solomon's Temple as found in 1 Kings 6–7. Some continue to allegorize these details. One writer observes that if this plan were to be implemented, it would have had to supply more particulars. It is not clear what this writer meant, and equally unclear how many more details we would need. It is my opinion that we have so many details in this description (and chapter 41 is no exception) that it is a stretch to allegorize this structure and regard it only as a symbol of something else. Again, if the literal sense makes sense, then seek no other sense.

Verses 41:1–4

Entering the *sanctuary*, the *doorposts* were measured. They were six cubits (ten and a half feet) wide on one side and six cubits (ten and a half feet) wide on the other side. This was also the width of the tabernacle.

The *entryway* into the sanctuary was ten cubits (seventeen and a half feet) wide with side walls five cubits (eight and three-quarters feet) high on either side. The length of the entryway was forty cubits (seventy feet) and its width was twenty cubits (thirty-five feet).

It is interesting that the angel next goes further inside to the inner sanctuary, leaving Ezekiel on the outside. Some have suggested that in keeping with the requirements of the law, Ezekiel, being a priest, was allowed into the outer sanctuary but not into the most holy place (compare Hebrews 9:6–7). "Holiness becomes God's dwelling place, and it is constantly emphasized throughout the Old and New Testament."[162]

As the angel goes inside, he measures the *doorposts* to the entry of the inner sanctuary. They were two cubits (three and a half feet), with the entrance being six cubits (ten and a half feet) high and seven cubits (twelve and a quarter feet) wide.

The inner sanctuary itself measured twenty cubits (thirty-five feet) long and twenty cubits (thirty-five feet) wide. The angel called this room the *Most Holy Place*. The mention of a holy place indicates the same two divisions in this temple as we have seen in previous temples. We read in Exodus 26:31–33, *You shall make a veil woven of blue, purple, and scarlet thread, and fine woven linen. It shall be woven with an artistic design of cherubim. You shall hang it upon the four pillars of acacia wood overlaid with gold. Their hooks shall be gold, upon four sockets of silver. And you shall hang the veil from the clasps. Then you shall bring the ark of the Testimony in there, behind the veil. The veil shall be a divider for you between the holy place and the Most Holy.*

It should be noted, as Schmitt and Laney point out, that there is no mention of a veil here in Ezekiel. While this is true, there is a clear reference to two rooms, one being called *The Most Holy Place*. "This does not necessarily mean that the veil is missing, but it is unlikely that Ezekiel would omit some

---

[162] Feinberg., 245.

reference to it if the veil were there. Second, there is no ark of the covenant. We suggest that these missing items are representations of the Messiah (compare Romans 3:25; Hebrews 10:20; 1 John 2:2). Since the future temple will be blessed by the physical presence of the Messiah, there will be no need for such physical representations of His person."[163]

Verses 5–11

The wall of this sanctuary measured six cubits (ten and a half feet) and around this wall were three levels with a series of thirty chambers, called *side chambers,* on each level, a total of ninety chambers in all (Figure 4). These chambers rested on *ledges* attached to the wall, but the chambers themselves were not attached to the wall. Moving up, at each story the chambers become wider and the ledges serve as stairs (compare 1 Kings 6:8). Only three walls contained these chambers—the north, the south, and the west—because the east side served as the entrance to the Temple.

The dimension of each chamber was four cubits (seven feet) square. The foundation was a full rod or six cubits (ten and a half feet) high. The thickness of the *outer wall* of the chamber was five cubits (eight and three-quarter feet). There was twenty cubits (thirty-five feet) between the outer wall of the tabernacle and the wall of these chambers. This space is called a *terrace* (compare verse 9), and it was five cubits (eight and three-quarter feet) wide all around. The doors of these chambers opened into the terrace area.

We should note, before leaving the discussion of these chambers, that no exact purpose has been given for them. Some

---

[163] Schmitt and Laney, 93.

have speculated that they would be used for the storage of Temple equipment and the people's tithes and offerings; others suggest that they will be used to house the priests.

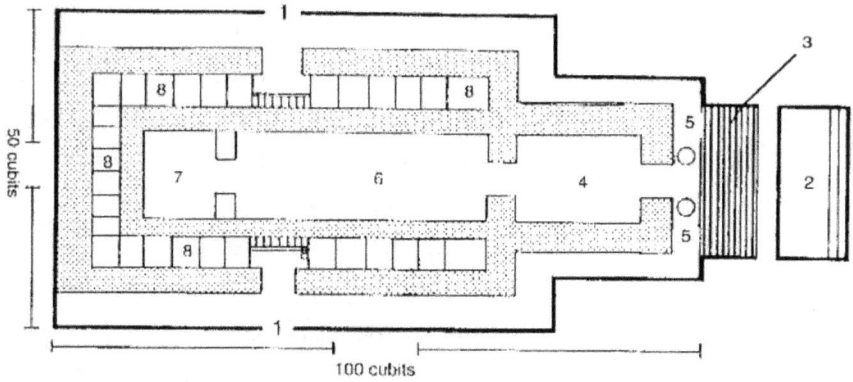

Figure 4: Chambers[164]

Verse 41:12
Next, there is mention of a building that is detached and separated from the other structures. Again, no purpose is stated for this building. It was located on the western end of the temple and was seventy cubits (122½ feet) wide and ninety cubits (157½ feet) long, with its walls being five cubits (eight and three-quarter feet) thick. Some relate this building to the *parvarim* of 2 Kings 23:11, where horses were formerly kept that was held to be sacred to the sun god (see also 1 Chronicles 26:18).[165] Schmitt and Laney suggest that the separate place is a storage area for those things that have somehow become ritually unclean. Since

---

[164] Adapted from John Taylor, *Ezekiel: An Introduction and Commentary* (London, UK: Tyndale Press, 1969).
[165] Feinberg, 246.

they have become unholy, they must be separated from those things that are holy.[166]

Verses 41:13–16a
The temple itself measured one hundred cubits (175 feet) long. The *separating courtyard*, including the building and its walls, was one hundred cubits (175 feet) long. The width of the *eastern face of the temple*, which included the *separating courtyard* as well, was one hundred cubits (175 feet). The length of the building facing the *separating courtyard* with its *galleries* on either side, including the *inner temple* and the *porches of the court,* measured one hundred cubits (175 feet).

These dimensions are somewhat hard to comprehend, but anyway you choose to look at it, this is one massive structure. The entire structure covered a space of 5,000 cubits square (compare Ezekiel 40:24–27).

Verses 41:16b–26
As Pentecost points out, it is noteworthy that in all of Ezekiel's detailed description, there is no mention of an ark, or mercy seat, or veil, or cherubim above the mercy seat, or tables of stone. The only article of furniture mentioned is the table or altar of wood, which would be a reference to the table of showbread, that which speaks of communion with God.[167]

This should not be too difficult to understand considering the prophecy of Jeremiah 3:16–17: *Then it shall come to pass, when you are multiplied and increased in the land in those days, says the LORD, that they will say no more, 'The ark of the covenant of the LORD.' It shall not come to mind, nor shall they*

---

[166] Schmitt and Laney, 98.
[167] Pentecost, 515.

remember it, nor shall they visit it, nor shall it be made anymore. At that time Jerusalem shall be called The Throne of the LORD, and all the nations shall be gathered to it, to the name of the LORD, to Jerusalem. No more shall they follow the dictates of their evil hearts.

The righteous will indeed flourish in the kingdom of Christ, for He will rule with a rod of iron and there will be no unrighteousness upon the earth at this time. He will cast out all who do iniquity and offend. There will be no room for rebellion in the Millennium Kingdom.

Included in the interior were wood-paneled galleries all around the three stories from the ground to the windows, the windows themselves being covered. These galleries had carvings which included *cherub* with a *palm tree* between each one. Each *cherub* had *two faces;* one face was that of a *man* and the other that of a *lion.* Each one faced its own *palm tree.* The *cherubs* and *palm trees* covered the walls from top to bottom.

These are not the first cherubs we have seen in Ezekiel (compare chapters 1 and 10). Cherubs throughout Scriptures seem to fulfill the role of protectors. They were placed at the entrance of the Garden of Eden in Genesis 3 to guard the way to the tree of life (Genesis 3:24). They also served as the protectors of the throne, serving as a throne-chariot (compare Ezekiel 1 and 10). Feinberg suggests that the palm trees are related to or signify righteousness and victory.[168]

Also included in this description was an *altar* made of wood. It was three cubits (five and a quarter feet) high and two cubits (three and a half feet) long. The angel gives Ezekiel the name of this altar: *the table that is before the Lord.* Because the

---

[168] Feinberg, 246.

dimensions are closer to that of the altar of incense, many conclude that this altar is the same, as opposed to the table of showbread (compare Exodus 30:1–2).

The *doors* described are like the doors described in 1 Kings 6:31–35. There were *two doors* each for the temple and the sanctuary. Each door had *two panels* that folded. These *doors* had carvings of *cherubim and palm trees,* like the walls. At the front of the *vestibule*, on the outside, was a *wooden canopy* which was carved with *palm trees* and had *beveled window frames.*

Verses 42:1–14

The description in chapter 42 is complex. There are many details describing even more chambers, but the purposes of these chambers are clearly stated (compare 42:13). Whether these chambers are the same as those in Ezekiel 40:44–46 is debatable. Some have questioned why there is so much detail and why Ezekiel is getting so "bogged down" in the minutiae. Here again is another example of the complexity of our Lord and how He is a God of details and exactness. If our Lord is so concerned with and exacting about the temple construction, it stands to reason that He is equally (if not more) concerned about His children and their relationship with Him.

The next movement we see by this angel and Ezekiel is their going to the *outer court* and into the chamber of the inner court which was opposite the building toward the north. The length of this chamber is one hundred cubits (175 feet) and the width is fifty cubits (eighty-seven and a half feet).

Ezekiel continues by describing *gallery* against *gallery* that consists of *three stories.* The structure of these galleries was such that the upper level was narrower than the lower level. We are told that the *inner court* around these *galleries* was twenty cubits (thirty-five feet) and that they were *opposite the pavement of the outer court* (compare Ezekiel 40:17–18). The walkway in front was ten cubits (seventeen and a half feet wide) and one cubit (one and three-quarter feet) long and the *doors faced north*.

Schmitt and Laney suggest that the mention of galleries makes the description of these chambers problematic. They state that this is the only place in Scriptures where this Hebrew word is mentioned. "The Hebrew word *a'tiyq* is an architectural term that refers to an offset ledge or terrace."[169] Given this, they conclude that the building must look very similar to a stair-step structure with skylights. Pillars support the open area around the skylights except for the third floor. Because this floor is the narrowest, the span does not need supporting pillars.[170]

There was also a *wall* that ran *outside and parallel to these chambers*. It was located toward the front in the direction of the outer court and its length was fifty cubits (eighty-seven and a half feet). The suggestion is that this wall served as a screen wall to screen the windows as the priests changed their garments.

The length of the chambers facing the outer court was fifty cubits (eighty-seven and a half feet), whereas that which faced the temple itself was one hundred cubits (175 feet) long. There was an entrance on the east side into the lower chamber for those entering from the outer court.

Next, we have a description of chambers that were toward the wall, opposite the *building* and *separating courtyard*. These chambers have the same dimensions as those mentioned

---

[169] Schmitt and Laney, 99.
[170] Schmitt and Laney, 99.

previously. They were as long and as wide as the others and their entrances were according to the plans of the others.

The purpose of these chambers is revealed in verses 13 and 14. The chambers served two purposes: 1) it was where the priests were to eat the *most holy offerings* and 2) where the priests were to *lay the most holy offerings:* the *grain offering* (compare Numbers 28), the *sin offering* (compare Leviticus 4:1–5:13), and the *trespass offering* (compare Leviticus 5:14–26). There were certain sacrifices that the priests were allowed (better understood as commanded) to eat.

Leviticus 2:1–3: *When anyone offers a grain offering to the LORD, his offering shall be of fine flour. And he shall pour oil on it and put frankincense on it. He shall bring it to Aaron's sons, the priests, one of whom shall take from it his handful of fine flour and oil with all the frankincense. And the priest shall burn it as a memorial on the altar, an offering made by fire, a sweet aroma to the Lord. The rest of the grain offering shall be Aaron's and his sons'. It is most holy of the offerings to the LORD made by fire.*

Leviticus 10:12–15: *And Moses spoke to Aaron, and to Eleazar and Ithamar, his sons who were left: 'Take the grain offering that remains of the offerings made by fire to the LORD and eat it without leaven beside the altar; for it is most holy. You shall eat it in a holy place because it is your due and your sons' due, of the sacrifices made by fire to the LORD; for so I have been commanded. The breast of the wave offering and the thigh of the heave offering you shall eat in a clean place, you, your sons, and your daughters with you; for they are your due and your sons' due, which are given from the sacrifices of peace offerings of the children of Israel. The thigh of the heave offering and the breast of the wave offering they shall bring with the offerings of fat made by fire, to offer as a wave offering before the LORD. And it shall be yours and your sons with you, by a statute forever, as the LORD has commanded.'*

We are also told that the chambers were to serve as storage for the priestly garments. They were to change from their holy garments before entering the outer court to greet the people.

It is quite fascinating to notice the similarities between the laws of the Levitical system and those that will be required in the Millennial Temple. This provides yet another argument that Israel and the church are not the same and will be forever distinct from each other.

Verses 42:15–20

After measuring everything there was to be measured in the inner temple, the angel then escorts Ezekiel out through the east gate and measures the exterior of the temple itself. The angel has measured the height and thickness of the outside wall, the outer court, and the inner court. Now he is going to measure the extent of all the temple buildings outside. This will prove to be a massive structure that will require the typography of Jerusalem to change. The entire area was much too large for Mount Moriah which was the place where Solomon's and Zerubbabel's Temples stood.

Zechariah 14:10 states: *All the land shall be turned into a plain from Geba to Rimmon south of Jerusalem. Jerusalem shall be raised up and inhabited in her place from Benjamin's Gate to the place of the First Gate and the Corner Gate, and from the Tower of Hananel to the king's winepresses.* Given this prophecy from Zechariah, which includes the same time period that Ezekiel is referencing, we can now understand the events of the Tribulation. The judgments of the Tribulation period will include major earthquakes in which mountains will be moved or removed and the typography of the Middle East will be drastically altered. It is possible to see how this Temple will be built and an area large enough to house it will be formed.

The outer dimensions of the temple create a square measuring 500 rods or 3,000 cubits (5,250 feet), which is thirty feet short of a square mile on each side. It should be noted that some tend to alter the numbers of this text. Dyer, in his commentary, using the New International Version (1978 edition) of the Bible, determines the measurements of this temple to be 500 cubits square (a total area of 562,500 square feet), which he states is enough for more than thirteen football fields.[171]

In the end, any scholar at the time will determine the criteria of which dimension to use. In either case, the fact remains that this is a massive structure and things are going to have to change for it to be placed around Mt. Moriah, which in turn, supports Zechariah 14:10.

The wall, which served to separate the *holy areas* from the *common* or profane, measured 500 cubits (750 feet) long and 500 cubits (750 feet) wide. It was intended to protect the sacred from the unsacred.

APPLICATION

John clearly explains, in 1 John 1, that sin separates the believer from God. It causes fellowship to be broken, and confession is the only means to restore that fellowship. Here, the wall of separation gives us that symbolism: its purpose is to maintain

---

[171] Dyer, 1308.

that separation so that fellowship is never broken, because God can never be worshipped or have fellowship with those who are unlike His holy character and nature.

Peter explains that God has placed His divine nature within the believer (compare 2 Peter 1:4), and a believer should maintain that fellowship through confession (compare 1 John 1:9). What an awesome thought that holiness and purity and separation will be maintained throughout the Millennial Kingdom!

Study Question
1. What are the implications of a believer possessing the divine nature of God?

Verse 43:1–9
If chapter 10 of Ezekiel is the most heart-wrenching and grievous chapter of this book, then chapter 43 is the most glorious and joyful chapter. In chapter 10 we have the glory of God departing the temple. In chapter 43, we have the return of God's glory. It has been almost twenty years between the visions of the departing and returning and one cannot imagine the emotions that Ezekiel must have experienced.

After spending three chapters giving complete details of the description of this temple, one can only guess at what Ezekiel might have been thinking. He knew that the glory had departed, and why have a temple if God's glory is not going to reside there? But at the proper time, His glory returns, and all is well. When God chooses to restore His people, He not only places them back in their land but also returns to them a visible presence of His being.

Another point to be made before moving on to the details of this chapter is that some use this to prove that these events are still in the future, in that the glory of God is never mentioned in connection with the temple that Zerubbabel built after the return from exile. This is a rather weak argument, as it is hard to argue from what is not in the text.

Ezekiel is now led to the east gate in which he beholds the glory of the Lord coming from the east. This is the very gate by which the Lord left (compare Ezekiel 10:19).

How does one describe the glory of God? Ezekiel did so by describing the voice he heard which sounded like that of *many waters,* which speaks of power and authority. Compare John's description of the vision he saw of the Son of Man, Jesus Christ, in Revelation 1:15b.

Ezekiel connects this vision with previous visions he has seen, which keeps this book intact and unified (compare Ezekiel chapters 1 and 10). In the first vision, the Lord was coming to destroy the city; in this vision; the Lord is coming to a restored city to reside there once again. Once again, the Spirit of the Lord transports Ezekiel into the *inner court* where he witnessed the *glory of the Lord filling the Temple.* Sin drove the Lord away, and it is holiness that brings Him back.

Next, Ezekiel hears a voice. This voice assures Ezekiel that the place he is standing is the throne of the Lord, *the place of the soles of My feet,* and the place where He will dwell amid His people forever. No more shall they—an all-encompassing term that includes their kings—blaspheme God's holy name, and no more shall idolatry infiltrate the land.

No more shall they defile God's house with their prostitution and worthless idols of their kings, and no more shall high places be constructed. Twice the Lord mentions the *carcasses of the kings,* which could be a reference to the practice of burying their kings near the Temple (compare 2 Kings 14:20; 21:18; 23:30). They had defiled the Lord's holy name by their *abominations* and God consumed them with His anger. That is all past and God has restored them to their place of honor and promises to never leave them again.

Verses 43:10–12

The real purpose behind this vision, which began back in chapter 40, is given. Ezekiel was to describe the temple to the people of Israel so that they may be ashamed of their sins. When they hear of this temple and its massive beauty and hear that the Lord will return His glory to it, then they will repent and be ashamed. The shame will come when they realize all that was lost because of their sins.

Ezekiel is told to give them the complete understanding of all he has seen, which includes the design of the temple and its arrangement, *its exits and its entrances, its entire design and all its ordinances, all its forms and all its laws.* The understanding is that not only were they to know what this temple should look like, but they were to understand how they were to behave and function within this temple.

Ezekiel is commanded to write it down so they would have a permanent record and possibly read it on a regular basis to serve as a constant reminder. There was to be no mistake, the *law of the temple* was sure: *The whole area surrounding the mountaintop is most holy.* It does not take a rocket scientist to see that this has yet to happen. We are awaiting these events to be fulfilled in future days, and that time would be the advent of the Millennial Kingdom.

Verses 43:13–17

Next, Ezekiel is told the measurements of the *altar* for the sacrifices (see Figure 5). They are given in cubits. In a parenthetical thought, we are told that a cubit here is a cubit and a handbreadth, which would be equivalent to the royal cubit.[172] The dimensions are somewhat smaller than that of Solomon's altar.

The base was one cubit (twenty-one inches) high and one cubit (twenty-one inches) wide and had a *rim around its edge of one span.* Depending on the determination of the size of a cubit, a span is about half a cubit (approximately ten and a half inches).

The *altar* was in three levels. From the *base on the ground* to the first *ledge* was two cubits (three and a half feet) high and its ledge was one cubit (twenty-one inches) wide. From the first ledge to the second ledge was four cubits (seven feet) with the width of the ledge being one cubit (twenty-one inches).

From the second level to the top level or the *altar hearth* was four cubits (feet) high. This would make the total height of this altar ten cubits (seventeen and a half feet) tall. *The hearth* had *four horns*, one on each corner, which *extended upward. The hearth* itself measured twelve cubits (twenty-one feet) by twelve cubits (twenty-one feet), which would form a twenty-one-foot square. Its *ledge* was fourteen cubits (twenty-four and a half feet) long and fourteen cubits (twenty-four and a half feet) wide, with a *rim* of half a cubit (ten and a half inches) around it. Its *base* was one cubit (twenty-one inches) all around.

The top of this altar was accessible by *steps* that *faced towards the east.* This means as the priests ascend these stairs, they would be facing west. In Ezekiel 8:15–16, Ezekiel describes

---

[172] See commentary on verses 40:1–5.

what our Lord calls an abomination: twenty-five men with their backs toward the temple and their faces toward the east. We are told they were worshiping the sun toward the east. By having the altar stairs situated thus, the priests would always face west in their ministering, which would eliminate the temptation to repeat the past errors.

The very presence of this altar causes problems for some, especially those who would call themselves nondispensationalist. Feinberg points out that one of the chief reasons for this confusion is the abandonment of the literal interpretation of prophecy, in which he states must be adhered to in keeping with the grammatical and historical approach to the Scriptures.[173]

To best correct this faulty view, one needs a correct understanding of the function of the Old Testament sacrifices. They were never meant to be efficacious and were never intended to remove the penalty of sin. The author of Hebrews makes that perfectly clear in Hebrews 10:4. Therefore, we cannot assume that the presence of an altar here is for the purpose of removing sin. This altar has been called *Ariel*, which means *"lion of God"* and is a reference to the lion from the tribe of Judah (compare Genesis 49:9; Revelation 5:5). This would be none other than Jesus Christ. This altar, then, would represent the sacrifice of Jesus Christ.

Make no mistake: this is not the golden altar of incense for prayer and intercession, as some try to explain it. This is clearly the altar of sacrifice, but that should not pose a problem. As stated earlier in this commentary, these sacrifices were meant as memorials, much as the Lord's Supper is meant for a memorial today (compare 1 Corinthians 11:23–26).

---

[173] Feinberg, p. 254.

Feinberg makes the excellent observation that not all the people of the Millennial Kingdom will have experienced their resurrected bodies. Some will enter the kingdom directly from the Tribulation period without experiencing either death or resurrection. [174] Thus, it is easy to see the need for a remembrance of the death, burial, and resurrection of Jesus Christ as a constant reminder of the atoning work of Christ.

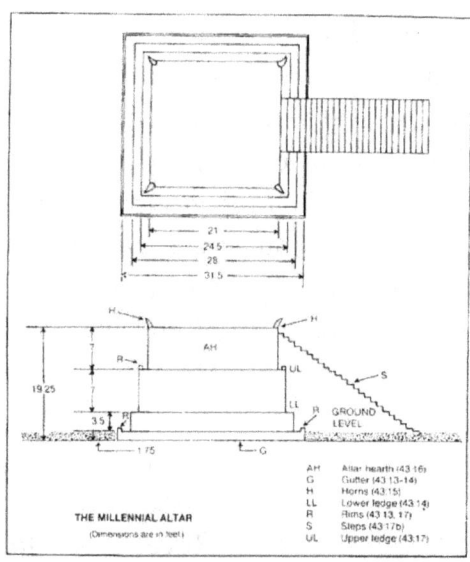

Figure 5: The Altar[175]

Verses 43:18–27
What is next explained to Ezekiel is a seven-day ritual of separating this altar apart from everything else so it might be used to offer burnt offerings and peace offerings. The Lord tells Ezekiel that *these are the ordinances for the altar* upon

---

[174] Feinberg, p. 254.
[175] Adapted from Charles Dyer, "Commentary on Ezekiel" in *The Bible Knowledge Commentary* (Wheaton: Victor Books, 1985).

completion of its construction. This altar will be used for *burnt offerings* and for *sprinkling blood on it.* The ministers of this consecration service will be priests who are descendants of Levi and of the *seed of Zadok* (compare Ezekiel 40:46). These services will be similar to those commanded to Moses (compare Exodus 40:10) and Solomon (compare 2 Chronicles 7:8–9) when they were told to sanctify the house of the Lord.

On day one, they are to take the blood of a young bull used as a *sin offering* and sprinkle its blood on the *four horns of the altar, on the four corners of the ledge and on the rim around it.* By so doing, they will have cleansed the altar by making atonement for it. This same *bull* is to be taken *outside the sanctuary* and burned in its *appointed place.*

On day two, the altar is be cleansed in similar fashion as day one, but this time they are to use a *kid of the goats without blemish,* as well as a *ram from the flock*, it too being *without blemish.* As these animals are being offered, the priests are to *throw salt* on the sacrifice and then offer it up as a *burnt offering to the Lord.*

Leviticus 2:13 states: *and every offering of your grain offering you shall season with salt; you shall not allow the salt of the covenant of your God to be lacking from your grain offering. With all your offerings you shall offer salt.* Eating bread with salt is a common event at every Orthodox Jewish meal today. The salt was added to purify the sacrifice. Salt was relatively indestructible in ancient times and therefore was a useful means of reminding that a covenant is eternal. The addition of salt was possibly the Lord signifying that He would not forsake His promise to forgive and dwell with them forever.

This ritual of cleansing the altar was to continue for *seven days,* repeating the actions of the first and second days through this period. When these days are over, on the *eighth day* and every day thereafter, the priests can then offer on this altar a *burnt offering* and a *peace offering* to the Lord and because of this consecrating week, the Lord promises to accept them and their offerings. What a great future Israel has in store for themselves, especially to those who remain faithful until the end.

Ezekiel 44:1–46:24

Worship in the Millennial Temple

After spending a great deal of time describing the Millennial Temple (figure 1), Ezekiel now describes the way worship will be conducted. One thing becomes abundantly clear in these chapters: worship will change and will be conducted in an honest manner (compare Ezekiel 45:9–10). A glance back at chapters 8 and 9 of Ezekiel will show just how corrupt things had become. Purity will return to worship, for the people are reminded of past practices, and the Lord is perfectly clear that those days are gone!

Chapter 44 is an explanation of the regulations concerning three specific groups: the prince, the gentiles, and the priests. Chapter 45 explains the distribution of the land for the Lord's use, as well as commercial and worship regulations for the prince, and chapter 46 continues with more worship regulations for the prince and ends with instructions for preparation of the offerings.

Verses 44:1–3
Ezekiel is brought back to the outer gate of the sanctuary. It was the east gate, but it was shut. The Lord explains why this gate is shut and why it is to remain shut. This is the gate through which the glory of God entered the temple; therefore, it has become sacred, and no man shall enter it.

The only exception to this exclusion is *the prince.* He may sit in the gate for the purpose of eating bread before the Lord. He is to enter by way of the *vestibule of the gateway* and is to go out the same way. This prince will have special privileges that no one else will enjoy. He is in a sense, the Messiah's representative.[176] But who is he?

Some would say this is a fulfillment of Zechariah 2:10: *"Sing and rejoice, O daughter of Zion! For behold, I am coming, and I will dwell in your midst," says the LORD.* Although the Lord will fulfill this promise and no doubt will return to the earth to establish His throne (compare Revelation 19:11–16), it is highly unlikely that the prince and Christ are one and the same. Ezekiel 45:22 speaks of the prince preparing an offering for himself, and this is inconceivable of Christ.

Ezekiel 34:24 has already identified this prince as God's servant David (see comments about chapter 34) but according to Feinberg, this poses some problems. "Though not possible, such identification with David is not probable in view of the broad context of prophecy concerning the kingdom."[177] Some believe that King David will be resurrected and thus that the reference to the prince is to be taken literally. They suggest that David himself will come and serve as the Messiah's representative.[178]

In the end, it may not be so important to understand who this prince is as it is to understand what this prince does. "It must be obvious that such a person, with such an important ministry, is unique to the millennial age and has no counterpart in the Levitical order and thus represents a major change in that

---

[176] Feinberg, 258.
[177] Feinberg, 258.
[178] Dyer, 1309.

coming age."[179] He will have the special privilege of sitting at the very gate the Lord used, will perform religious acts before the Lord, and will have particular access to the Temple. John MacArthur sums it up best: "The designation 'prince' is used at least fourteen times in chapters forty-four through forty-seven. He is not the Lord Jesus Christ, but someone distinct from Him (cf. 'eat bread before the Lord'); he has sins for which he offers sacrifice (45:22), and father's sons (46:16–18). He cannot enter by the East gate which the Lord used but can come in and go out by the gate's vestibule and eat bread by the gateway. He cannot perform priestly duties (45:19) as Messiah will (cf. Ps. 110:4; Zech. 6:12–13), and he must worship the Lord (46:2). Most likely 'the prince' is one who is neither a priest nor the king, but rather one who administrates the kingdom, representing the King (the Lord Jesus Christ) on one hand, and also the princes (14:8,9) who individually lead the 12 tribes. Possibly, he will be a descendant of David."[180]

Verses 44:4–9
As Ezekiel is brought to the *north gate,* he observes the *front of the temple* which is filled with the glory of the Lord. His response was to fall on his face and worship. The Lord then speaks concerning the ordinances and laws of the temple, beginning first with a direction of who is to be admitted and how. Ezekiel is told to *mark well* or to take notice of everything. He is to accomplish this by visual as well as audio means. He is to register everything he sees and hears so fully that he will be able to relay this information to the children of Israel in minute and exacting detail.

---

[179] Pentecost, 524.
[180] MacArthur, 1216.

This regulation concerning the Gentiles begins with an indictment of the Jews. The Lord calls the house of Israel *the rebellious*. They were rebellious specifically in that they allowed *foreigners*, the *uncircumcised*, to enter and defile God's house and the Lord refers to this as an *abomination*. Interestingly, the Lord refers to *Us*, which may be a reference to the Trinity. In other words, we—the Father, Son and Holy Spirit—will have no more of these abominations; enough is enough! This new Millennial Temple will not be defiled as the temple had been in the past. They even broke God's covenant in the sacrifices they offered.

This is not a ban against allowing foreigners to present an offering to the Lord. This was allowed under the law (compare Leviticus 17:8–12; Numbers 15:14). Rather, it is a restriction against foreigners officiating at the ceremonies.

Israel did not protect God's *holy things*, in that they had allowed anyone they chose to attend to that responsibility. God's final edict is extremely clear: *no foreigner, uncircumcised in heart or uncircumcised in flesh shall enter My* [God's] *sanctuary, including any foreigner who is among the children of Israel.* In the past, Israel was only interested in fulfilling her own desires regardless of what the Lord had commanded. If something served her purpose and met with her approval, she did not seem to bother with what the Lord's desires were.

Verses 44:10–14
Here the Lord singles out those of the priestly line who caused Israel to fall into sin before the captivity. They *went astray*, they followed *their idols,* and they will be held responsible for their actions. Having said that, God demonstrates His mercy in that they will have the privilege of serving in God's house, although

they will be refused the privilege of offering up sacrifices. Their services will include *gatekeepers of the house*; they will be allowed to *slay the burnt offerings* and will have some part in ministering to the people. This is different from the Mosaic Law, under which the worshipper had to kill his own sacrificial animal.

They will be refused the duty of the higher services of the priesthood, which include services in the holy place. Their duties will be limited to the outer court. They will in some regard be looked upon as inferior to the other priests. In so doing, they shall bear their shame and blame for the abominations which they have committed.

Verses 44:15–31

The remainder of this chapter deals with the priest from the line of Levi, descendants of *Zadok*. These were the ones who were faithful even while the rest of the nation fell into idolatry, and they did not go astray from the Lord (compare Ezekiel 40:46). It is the Zadokites who will have the special privilege of offering sacrifices before the Lord. They will be allowed to enter the holy place, minister at the altar of burnt offerings, and be in charge of all the sacrifices.

Zadok was the son of Ahitub from the line of Eleazar (compare 2 Samuel 8:17; 1 Chronicles 6:7–8). He was faithful to David during the rebellion of Absalom (compare 2 Samuel 15), and anointed Solomon as king after Adonijah's failed attempt to take over the throne (compare 1 Kings 1). It was the priests from this line who remained faithful to the Lord and kept themselves free from idolatry. Because of their faithfulness, the Lord will reward them during the Millennial Kingdom and grant them special services.

These priests, the Zadokites, while undertaking their priestly functions, will wear regulated *garments* designed especially for them. No *wool* is to be worn, as wool is hot and causes perspiration that is considered unclean. To avoid this perspiration, they are to wear *turbans on their heads* and *trousers on their bodies* made of *linen*. They are never to wear their holy garments in the presence of the people. These *garments* are to be kept in the *holy chambers*.

These priests are not to have their *heads* shaven, nor is their *hair* to be worn long, which is a sign of mourning (compare Leviticus 10:6; 21:5, 10). They are to be neatly trimmed. They shall not *drink wine* before entering the *inner court* (compare Leviticus 10:9). Although the purpose of this regulation is not clear, it should be noted that there have been times when joyful worship and exultation before the Lord were confused with drunkenness (compare Acts 2:13, 15). They are allowed to marry, but only *virgins who are descendants of the house of Israel*. They cannot marry a *widow*, unless she is a *widow of a priest*, nor can they marry a divorced woman (compare Leviticus 21:14).

They are to teach the people the difference between right and wrong, *holy and unholy* and *clean and unclean,* and some of this will be accomplished by the lifestyle they lead before the people. They will serve as *judges* and make judgments according to God's Word. They themselves are always to obey God's commandments and remain holy and follow the standards of the Lord. Not doing so will negate any teaching of holiness they give. They are to sanctify the *Sabbaths*.

A priest shall not approach a *dead person* for in so doing he will *defile* himself. Death is viewed in Scripture as Levitical defiling. The only exception is that for family: *father, mother, son, daughter, brother,* or *unmarried sister*. Everyone else is unapproachable. Even after attending to these relatives' dead bodies, he still must take *seven days* to *cleanse* himself and then *offer his sin offering in the inner court.*

This answers the question: "Will there be death in the millennial age?" We have concluded that this is a millennial setting and that these regulations are for the millennial priest, so the answer to this question would have to be yes. While there will be longevity of life during the Millennium, death will exist. Isaiah 65:20 states: *No more shall an infant from there live but a few days, nor an old man who has not fulfilled his days; for the child shall die one hundred years old, but the sinner being one hundred years old shall be accursed.*

The Zadokites shall not receive an inheritance. Their portion and their possession will be found in Jehovah. Their needs shall be supplied from the offerings of the people. In the next chapter, we see that they are given a portion of the land, that which immediately surrounds the temple (compare Ezekiel 45:1–5). They will receive the *best of the first fruits of any kind and from every sacrifice.* The people will be blessed as they graciously give the priests the *first of their ground meal.* The only dietary restriction mentioned here is that the priest is not to eat anything that *died naturally* or was *killed by other beasts* (compare Leviticus 17:15; 22:8; Deuteronomy 14:21).

APPLICATION

The care specified for these priests is like the teaching found in the New Testament concerning the ministers of the Gospel. 1 Corinthians 9:14 states, *Even so the Lord has commanded that those who preach the gospel should live from the gospel* and 1 Timothy 5:17–18 states, *Let the elders who rule well be counted worthy of double honor, especially those who labor in the word and doctrine. For the Scripture says, 'You shall not muzzle an ox while it treads out the grain,' and, 'The laborer is worthy of his wages.'*

As was the case under the law, so it will be in the Millennial Kingdom: the Zadokites will be cared for solely by the Lord (compare Deuteronomy 18:15). When this order is followed, it results in blessings, spiritual and otherwise. There is no greater joy than realizing that the Lord loves and cares for His children, and these priests will be no exception.

Study Questions
1. Name some promises found in the Bible regarding God's care for His children.
2. What factors should be considered in determining if an elder is worthy of double honor?

Verses 45:1–8
In this section we have the land divided out for the priests and the people (see Figure 6). Thomas makes an excellent point concerning the excitement these exiles should have experienced when they heard that the land was going to be divided and they were to get a portion for their inheritance.[181] This promise of distributing the land back to the people is a fulfillment of the covenant God made way back with Abraham, when He originally called them out of the land of the Chaldeans (compare Genesis 12:1–3).

---

[181] Thomas, 284.

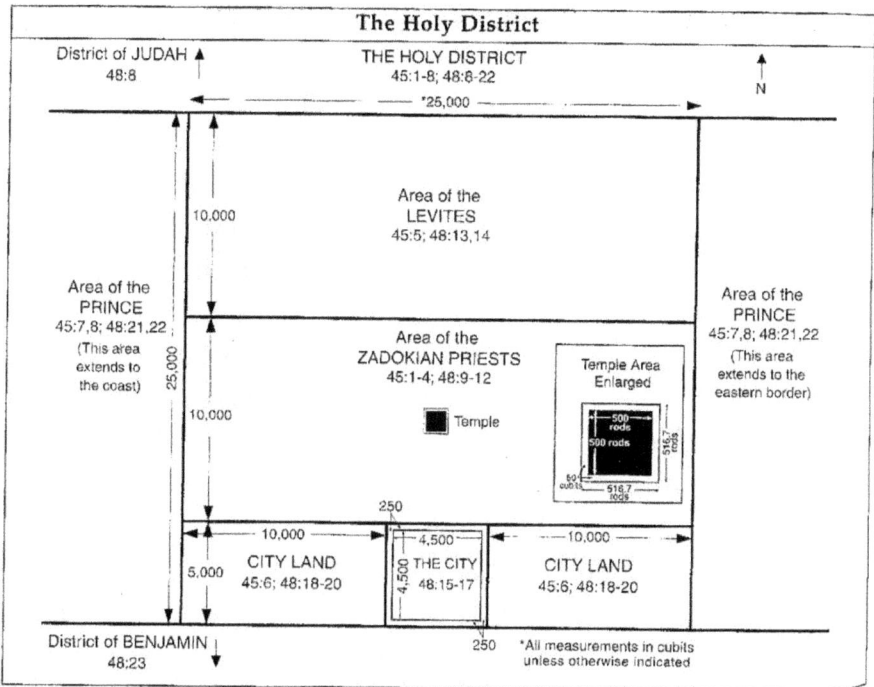

Figure 6: The Holy District[182]

First, there was to be the setting apart of a section of land called the Holy District. The land itself will cover a territory of about eight miles square (compare Ezekiel 48:8), with a section of this land to be dedicated for the Lord, intended to be holy throughout its territory all around. It measured *twenty-five thousand cubits* (eight and one-third miles) long and *ten thousand cubits* (three and one-third miles) wide.

Within this plot of land, there was to be a section *five hundred rods* (approximately nine-tenths of a mile) square with an *open space* around it measuring *fifty cubits* (eighty-seven and

---

[182] Adapted from the *MacArthur Study Bible* (Nashville, TN: Word Bibles, 1997).

one-half feet). This section was to be set apart for the house of God.

This land, the Holy District, is to *belong to the priests* and will house their dwelling places as well as the sanctuary of the Lord. The entire area of *twenty-five cubits by ten thousand cubits* will belong to the *Levites* who are responsible for serving in the Temple. These Levites will possess *twenty chambers* as well.

Next, a portion of land, which was to border the Holy District, is divided out for the *whole house of Israel*. It measures *five thousand cubits* (one and seven-tenths miles) wide by *twenty-five thousand cubits* (eight and one-thirds miles) long. This will be the city of Jerusalem itself. The prince was to have a portion on either side of the Holy District.

As noted in Figure 1, the Temple portion will be the central focus of this area. It was this way in times past and it will be no different during the Millennial Kingdom. The holy area, that which contains the sanctuary, will be in a sense protected by the sectors around it. The priests' area will be on the east and west sides, the Levites will be on the north, and the city will be on the south, thus having all sides of the sanctuary covered and protected. Later, as set out in chapter 48, the remaining portions of the land will be divided among the twelve tribes of Israel.

Another cause of rejoicing for Israel is that the prince will *no longer oppress the people.* This is taken to mean that the rulers of the land shall not take away the land possessed by the people. In the past, the kings would often confiscate the people's property and, if necessary, use violence to do so (compare 1 Kings 21). Earlier, before the exile, the Law was specific as to ownership and Israel was expected to adhere to its demands (compare Numbers 36:7–9). In the Millennial Kingdom, no one will be deprived of his rightful possession given by the Lord.

Verses 45:9–12
Feinberg suggests that Ezekiel now reverts to the present and addresses the princes of Israel in his day, those living during the sixth century BC. He comments that verses 9–12 are Ezekiel addressing his contemporaries.[183] However, we do not see any evidence within the context that this is happening. It is best to understand that Ezekiel is continuing to address the conditions of the millennium and gives commercial regulations for the prince. We know that there will be sin during this time, although no outward rebellion (compare Isaiah 11). When Satan is released after the millennium from the bottomless pit, he will come to the earth and gather an army whose number is as the sand of the sea (compare Revelation 20:7–9). Where will this army come from? From those who are living during the millennium, which only indicates that although there will be no outward display of sin, an inward sinful attitude will still exist that will come alive upon the return of Satan to the earth.

The princes of the earth are told to *remove violence and plundering*, to *execute justice and righteousness* and to *stop dispossessing the people*. Most of this is in reference to their commercial dealings as it pertains to false measures and weights. They are told to have *honest scales*, an *honest ephah* and an *honest bath*. An *ephah* was a dry measurement equivalent to about one bushel. The *bath* corresponds to the *ephah* in liquid measure and both are the standard for measuring grain and similar articles, since they are classed with

---

[183] Feinberg, 264.

balances and weights (compare Leviticus 19:36 and Amos 8:5) in the injunctions regarding just dealing in trade. In Zechariah 5:6–10 the word *ephah* is used for the measuring utensil itself.[184]

Each of these, the *ephah* and the *bath,* made up one-tenth of a *homer* each. A *homer* was approximately seven and a half bushels or sixty gallons, depending on the article to be measured. The Hebrew word for *homer* is like the Hebrew word for donkey, and thus a *homer* is sometimes referred to as a "donkey load."

According to Feinberg, verse 12 poses a problem for some commentators. He suggests that most commentators believe that the text of this verse has been corrupted, and therefore they have adopted the rendering of the Greek as "And the five shekels shall be five, and the ten shekels shall be ten, and fifty shekels shall be your maneh."[185] This seems to be at best a conjecture and has little evidence to support it, so I consider is best to stick to the text as it is translated from the Hebrew.

What is mentioned of the *shekel* in verse 12 is that it is equivalent to twenty *gerahs.* The term *gerah* means grain or kernel and was the smallest unit of measure used by Israel. A shekel weighed a little less than eleven and one-half grams (about two-fifths of an ounce). The *mina* is equivalent to sixty shekels (*twenty plus twenty-five plus fifteen*) which would make it equal to twenty-four ounces or one and one-half pounds.

Verses 45:13–17

Having defined for them the exact measurements, the Lord now requires them to use these measurements in their offerings. No longer shall the Lord be shortchanged in His worship! They will

---

[184] International Standard Bible Encyclopedia Electronic Database.
[185] Feinberg, 264.

stick to the accurate measurements given them and thus present their offerings.

According to verse 16, the material for the prince's offerings will be given to him from the people in Israel. From these materials, he is to make a *sin offering*, a *burnt offering*, a *grain offering*, and a *peace offering*, the last of which was usually accompanied by a *drink offering* at every appointed feast (that is, the new moon and the Sabbaths), and at all the appointed seasons of the house of Israel. The previously mentioned measurements were to be used.

His offering consisted of *one-sixth of an ephah of wheat* that was to be taken from a *homer* and *one-sixth of an ephah of barley*, also taken from a *homer*. One percent of the *oil* was to be offered or *one tenth of a bath*. This *oil* was to be taken from one *kor*, which is equivalent to *ten baths* or one *homer*. From every flock that contained *two hundred lambs*, the prince was to give *one lamb*.

Verses 45:18–20

These verses lay out the appointed feast of the New Year. On the first day of the first month, a *young bull without blemish* shall be offered for the purpose of *cleansing the sanctuary*. This is to be done by taking some of the blood and smearing the *doorposts of the temple, the four corners of the ledge of the altar and the gateposts of the gate of the inner court*. The same is to be done on the *seventh day of the first month* for those who have *sinned in ignorance*. This will provide atonement or cleansing for the temple (compare Leviticus 4:1–3). Some believe that this feast will replace the Day of Atonement (compare Leviticus 23:26–32).

The feast of *Passover* will be celebrated on the *fourteenth day of the first month*. This feast lasts for *seven days*, during which time only *unleavened bread* will be eaten. It is specifically mentioned that in that day it is the *prince* who will prepare a sin offering for himself, which strongly supports the argument that this prince is not Christ. The sin offering included *seven bulls, seven rams without blemish,* and a *kid of the goats,* all to be offered once on each day of the feast. The *grain offering* will consist of *one ephah* mixed with *one hin of oil* for each bull and for each ram. The last feast of the year to be celebrated was the Feast of Tabernacles (compare Leviticus 23:33–34), a seven-day celebration beginning on the *fifteenth day* of the *seventh month.*

Keep in mind that this period is still the Millennium Kingdom. We have discussed earlier how this poses a problem for some. It should be noted that in the discussion concerning these feasts there is one feast that is omitted: The Feast of Pentecost. This further supports the millennial view, as the Feast of Pentecost is connected to Acts 2, when the Holy Spirit came and the church age was born. The Feast of Pentecost also signifies the uniting of Gentile and Jew.

APPLICATION

Paul states in Galatians 3:28–29: *There is neither Jew nor Greek, there is neither slave nor free, there is neither male nor female; for you are all one in Christ Jesus. And if you are Christ's, then you are Abraham's seed, and heirs according to the promise.* Having made his point that we are all one in faith (verse 27), Paul establishes the fact that everyone, whether Jew or Gentile, will be declared righteous because of faith in the shed blood of Jesus Christ and thus a new entity—the new man—will be created (compare Ephesians 2:15).

This uniting of the two will not be the order of the day in the Millennium Kingdom. It will be preeminently the age in which Israel, long the tail of the nations, will assume her promised place as leader and head of the nations.[186] In truth, the millennium age will be a time when Israel, God's chosen people, will once again enjoy the limelight and lasting fellowship with God.

At this time, the Gentiles will be blessed as the bride of Christ and reap the blessings and glories of this kingdom as well. But make no mistake: there will be a distinction between Israel and the church throughout all eternity. The covenant made with Abraham in Genesis 12:1–3, and repeated in Genesis 15:18–21, 17:1–21, 26:2–5, and 28:10–17, is called an everlasting covenant (compare Psalm 105:7–11); Ezekiel gives us the details of how this will be fulfilled once and for all. Everlasting means everlasting!

How many times does our Lord have to state this fact before we believe? It is with Israel that He will find His delight. Taking nothing away from the church, it is Israel whom God first chose, and Paul states that the Gentiles were grafted in for the purpose of making the Jews jealous so that they would repent and return to the Lord. Romans 11:11–12: *I say then, have they [Jews] stumbled that they should fall? Certainly not! But through their fall, to provoke them to jealousy, salvation has come to the Gentiles. Now if their fall is riches for the world, and their failure riches for the Gentiles, how much more their fullness!*

Yes, Israel was restored to her land after the captivity, but not completely. This final and complete restoration will not

---

[186] Feinberg, 266.

be realized until the Millennium when the Lord, the King of Kings and Lord of Lords, returns to establish His throne on the seat of David. Is there any question as to why we would not cry out with the apostle John, *"Amen, even so, come, Lord Jesus!"* (Revelation 22:20b)?

Study Questions
1. Define "unconditional covenant."
2. How does Genesis 15 support an unconditional covenant?

Verses 46:1–3
What is interesting about these regulations is that the going into and the going out from the sanctuary seem to be just as important as the actual act of offering up the sacrifice. Everything regarding these sacrifices is to be done a specific way. This truly demonstrates that our God is a God of details and exactness.

In this section, three specific offerings are mentioned: the *burnt offering*, the *peace offering*, and the *grain offering*. An explanation of these different offerings would be useful at this point. The *International Standard Biblical Encyclopedia* explains: "The term (*burnt offering*) applies to beast or fowl when entirely consumed upon the altar, the hide of the beast being taken by the priest. This was perhaps the most solemn of the sacrifices, and symbolized worship in the full sense, that is, adoration, devotion, dedication, supplication, and at times expiation."[187] The *peace offering* was a "sacrifice of friendship expressing or promoting peaceful relations with the Deity, and almost invariably accompanied by a meal or feast, an occasion of

---

[187] International Standard Bible Encyclopedia Electronic Database.

great joy."[188] The *grain offering* was usually performed in conjunction with burnt or peace offerings (never with sin or trespass offerings) or by itself. The meaning often ascribed to these offerings is that of a "symbol of the spiritual food that Israel strove after as the fruit of its spiritual labor, or those good works in which true sanctification must necessarily embody itself."[189]

The *east gate* of the inner court was to remain closed during the work week. The work week consisted of six days. This gate shall be opened on the Sabbath and on the day of the new moon. This is also to be the gate by which the prince enters, and when he does, he is to stand by the gatepost. There he is to prepare his burnt offering and his peace offering before the Lord. This is all to be done at the *threshold of the gate.* When he is finished, he is to exit through the same gate, but the gate is to remain open until evening. The people also shall worship at the entrance to this gate and again, only on the *Sabbath and the New Moons.*

Verses 46:4–8
Ezekiel gives the details of the *burnt offering* and the *grain offering* that this prince is to make. The Sabbath Day offering consists of a *burnt offering* of *six lambs* and *a ram*. By now it should be understood that these animals are to be without blemish. The *grain offering* for the Sabbath Day would consist of *one ephah* for the *ram* and for the *lambs*; this would be left to the discretion of the prince, although for every *ephah* he was to include a *hin of oil*. It should be noted that the offering required

---

[188] International Standard Bible Encyclopedia Electronic Database.
[189] *Unger's New Bible Dictionary.*

here for the Sabbath Day is considerably more than that for the Old Testament Sabbath Day offering (compare Numbers 28:9).

For the *New Moon* offering, he shall offer a *young bull without blemish* as well as *six lambs* and *a ram.* Israel's calendar was based upon the lunar cycle, so the new moon had much significance and the feasts were determined in relation to the phases of the moon. Along with the lambs and the ram, he was to offer a *grain offering* of *one ephah for the young bull, an ephah for the ram,* and again, as *much as he wants for the lambs,* as long as he included a *hin of oil for every ephah.* Upon completion of these offerings, the prince is to exit the *vestibule of the gateway* the same way he came in.

Verse 46:9–11
Ezekiel now explains the entrance and exit of the people. There were two gates they could enter, the north and the south, but whichever gate they entered, they were to exit through the opposite gate; they were not to return by way of the gate through which they entered. Many agree that because of the vast number of people (estimates range to more than 200,000) these regulations had to be put into place to prevent congestion and confusion. Our God is a God of order and not confusion (compare 1 Corinthians 14:33, 40.

The prince is to be present in their midst. What a time of joy this will be for the people of Israel! Not only will they be able to worship again, but *the prince* will also be there among them as an example. He thus sets a godly example of worship by his presence.

Verse 46:12
Freewill offerings by the prince are to be spontaneous and voluntary; upon doing so, the east gate will be opened for him, and after his offering is complete, he is to exit, and the east gate is to be shut. Notice that this is the one time the regulation of verse 46:1 (about departing through a different gate) is to be suspended.

Verses 46:13–15
These verses describe the morning sacrifice. This offering, which consists of one lamb, is to be performed daily. A *grain offering* is to be included: a *sixth of an ephah* and *a third of a hin of oil* for the purpose of *moistening the fine flour*. This *grain offering* was to be uninterrupted and offered daily every morning. Daniel 11:31 declares that the removal or nonperformance of this daily morning sacrifice is equivalent to defiling the sanctuary, and is called the *abomination of desolation*.

Numbers 28:3–4 mentions two offerings, one in the morning and the other in the evening. Ezekiel makes no mention of an evening offering, which leads some to believe that it has been omitted in the Millennial Kingdom. Dyer comments that this omission could be explained by the fact that Ezekiel is only giving the highlights of the sacrificial system and by listing the morning sacrifice, readers may assume that the evening is included as well.[190] However, with the amount and specificity of the details given in this text, such an assumption seems unwarranted; it is best to conclude that an evening sacrifice will not be a part of this sacrificial system.

---

[190] Dyer, 1312.

Verses 46:16–18

Instructions are given concerning the inheritance of the prince. The indication is that this *inheritance* refers to land. He may give a gift to his sons, but his sons are not to give it away to anyone else. This gift is to remain in the possession of the son.

In contrast, if the prince gives an inheritance to any of his servants, this servant is only permitted to keep it until the *year of liberty*, after which time he is to return it to the prince. This is probably a reference to the year of Jubilee, when ownership of property reverted back to the original owner. Leviticus 25:33 states, *And if a man purchases a house from the Levites, then the house that was sold in the city of his possession shall be released in the Jubilee; for the houses in the cities of the Levites are their possession among the children of Israel.*

What some do not recognize from this text is that the prince will undoubtedly be married, as he will have sons. This is another text that should prove this prince is not Jesus Christ, as some have surmised. The prince's sons can keep their inheritance and will not have to return it as do the servants. This assures that the land will stay in the possession of the family.

The prince is given a stern warning as well not to take any of the people's inheritance or property. If he gives an inheritance to his sons, it is to come from his own land and no one else's. This ensures that God's people will no longer live under the threat of being thrown off their land and scattered throughout the country (compare Ezekiel 45:8).

Verses 46:19–20

Ezekiel is next taken to the *chambers* where the offerings are prepared, that is, the kitchens. The kitchens are on the extreme west end of the priest's chambers. Many agree that it was probably not the priests themselves who prepared these offerings, but their servants (compare Ezekiel 46:24). These servants were to be careful not to prepare the offering in public so as not to cause any of the people to be sanctified and so interrupt their daily routine.

Verses 46:21–24

Next, Ezekiel is taken to the *outer court* where he passed by the *four corners* of the courtyard. There he noticed that a separate court was in every corner of the *outer court.* These separate courts measured *forty cubits* (seventy feet) long and *thirty cubits* (fifty-two and a half feet) wide and all four corners were the same size. These separate courts contained the *kitchens*; refer to the diagram in Figure 3.

These courts were surrounded by a *row of building stones* and a *cooking hearth* was made, *under the rows of stones.* Feinberg points out that the phrase *under the rows* means close to the ground, as opposed to the stories above.[191]

APPLICATION

In the last seven chapters we have been given specific details concerning the Millennial Temple which include the dimensions, the offerings, and the people. What specificity! The descriptions include not only requirements but also restrictions, which only proves that our God desires things done His way and in His time. With all these details, it is hard to conclude that this is all symbolic. God is not finished with the Jews: the personal close

---

[191] Feinberg, 270.

fellowship which He so desired in the Old Testament will finally be realized during the millennium.

Study Questions

1. Since God is a God of specificity, would the same apply to the worship service today?

2. What activities would God require in the worship service today?

3. What activities would God reject in the worship service today?

Ezekiel 47:1–12

Waters of the Millennial Temple

These verses constitute another passage in Ezekiel that some scholars prefer to take symbolically. Ezekiel speaks of a river that is flowing from the temple, which contains life-giving water. Nothing in the passage suggests anything other than a literal river. It should not be that hard to accept. Originally, in the Garden of Eden, when God first created man, there were rivers. Genesis 2:10–14 states: *Now a river went out of Eden to water the garden, and from there it parted and became four riverheads. The name of the first is Pishon; it is the one which skirts the whole land of Havilah, where there is gold. And the gold of that land is good. Bdellium and the onyx stone are there. The name of the second river is Gihon; it is the one which goes around the whole land of Cush. The name of the third river is Hiddekel; it is the one which goes toward the east of Assyria. The fourth river is the Euphrates.*

Few would understand this passage to be merely symbolic, so it is hard to understand why these same scholars want to see the river in the Millennial Kingdom as a symbol. As stated earlier, this is a literal river and nothing in the text suggests otherwise.

Verses 1–2

Ezekiel observes *water* coming out of the temple from under the *threshold*. This *water* was flowing east or out of the *front of the temple* (the front of the temple was on the east side), on the south end. To observe this water, Ezekiel was escorted out the *north gate*, brought *around the outside* along the north side of the temple to the east gate. There he saw the *water running out on the right side*.

When compared to Zechariah 14:8 and Joel 3:18, one can see a similar description of this river, and these two prophets are speaking of the same time period as Ezekiel. In fact, it is Zechariah who calls this river the *living waters*. If this passage in Ezekiel teaches anything, it reveals that all this will be a result of the working of God's power; it is miraculous.[192]

Verses 3–6
Ezekiel's escort now begins to measure the depth of the waters; to underscore its reality, Ezekiel is taken into the water. In the previous verses, Ezekiel tells us this river was just a trickle (literal rendering of *running out* in verse 2) but the further along they get, it becomes an out-and-out *river*.

To measure the depth of this water, the angel takes Ezekiel along the river in one-*thousand-cubit* (1,750 feet) increments. The first stop found the waters only *ankle* deep; at the second stop, the water was up to his *knees*; at the third stop, the waters were up to his *waist*; and finally, at the last stop, the waters could not be crossed, and they were over Ezekiel's head. All in all, from the start where the depth was only ankle deep to where one would have to swim to cross, the total distance was 4,000 cubits (7,000 feet). At this point, Ezekiel is returned to the bank of the river.

---

[192] Feinberg, 271.

Verses 7–12

We are told that along the *banks* of this river are many *trees*. It flows toward the *eastern region, goes down into the valley* or the *Arabah*. The Arabah is the Jordan Valley. Traveling through this valley, it eventually ends up in the *sea,* which is the Dead Sea. When it reaches the Dead Sea, that sea's *waters will be healed.*

Currently nothing can live in the Dead Sea, for it is six times saltier than the ocean. During the period Ezekiel was shown, however, when any living things come in contact with these waters, they will be revived and *healed;* thus they are called "living" waters. There will be *very great multitude of fish* in these waters. Everything that moves, *wherever the rivers go,* will live.

Through the miraculous power of God, the Dead Sea will become a vital spot for trade and sport for fishermen. They will spread their nets from *En Gedi,* located about the middle of the west shore of the Dead Sea to *En Eglaim. En Eglaim* may be the spot where the Dead Sea scrolls were located; if this is correct, these two locations represent the extreme ends of the sea. In other words, from one end to the other, fishermen will cast their nets and they will catch the same kind of fish that come from the Mediterranean Sea.

This river will continue to have its *swamps and marshes.* They *will not be healed* but will be overcome by the *salt* of the sea. Why are we given this information? Salt is essential for the economy and life of Israel and even now, we see God providing for all of Israel's needs. Salt was also valuable for the sacrifices. The Talmud mentions that salt from the Dead Sea was preferred above all other kinds because it was reported to hasten the burning of sacrifices, as well as to minimize the unpleasant odors of burning flesh.[193]

---

[193] Feinberg, 273.

Ezekiel 47:13–48:35

The Land of the Millennial Temple

This begins the final section of the book of Ezekiel. The borders are mentioned in the remaining verses of chapter 47. Chapter 48 gives us the division of the land among the tribes and finally, this vision comes to an end with a description of the gates of the city. This will take us full circle from where we began.

We have God's reminder of His promise to give this land to Israel and, because our God cannot lie (compare Titus 1:2), He will keep that promise. This is a promise to Israel and not to the church. Even though Israel's blessings in the land depended upon her obedience, ownership was never intended to be conditional. Her right to possess the land was never revoked.

Verses 47:13–17
The land is to be divided *among the twelve tribes of Israel,* with *two portions* given to *Joseph* in keeping with the promise of Jacob to Joseph in Genesis 48:5–6. The land was to be divided *equally with one another,* that is, evenly among the twelve tribes. God swore by an *oath,* the gesture of the raised hand, and He is a God of promise and is faithful to keep His word. The borders are like those promised to Israel during the time of Moses (compare Numbers 34:1–12).

Not all the places mentioned here are familiar to geographers today. Verses 15–17 give us the northern border. *Hethlon* is unknown and appears to be the name of a road. Some suggest it is located somewhere in southern Lebanon. *Hamath* is equally difficult to locate, but some suggest this to be identified with the city of the same name located on the Orontes River in modern Syria. *Zedad* should probably be identified with the town of Sedad, located about twenty-five miles north of Damascus. *Berothah and Sibraim,* located between the border of *Damascus and Hamath,* are unknown locations. *Hamath* is located north of *Damascus. Hazar Hatticon* and *Hazar Enan,* possibly one and the same place, is located on the *border of Hauran,* a district east of the Sea of Galilee north of the Yarmuk River. It is a popular opinion among some that *Hauran* is an important desert oasis northeast of Damascus. So, the northern border of this land will stretch east from the Mediterranean Sea, north of the modern city of Tripoli, and will include what was then the northern border of Syria.[194]

Verse 47:18

Moving in a clockwise direction, Ezekiel now explains the *east side* of the territory. This boundary runs between *Hauran and Damascus* and between *Gilead and the land of Israel* and follows the *Jordan River* south to the eastern side of the Dead Sea.

Verse 47:19

Next, we have the description of the southern boundary. This runs from *Tamar* to the *waters of Meribah by Kadesh* (possibly Kadesh-Barnea [compare Numbers 20:3–14]; 34:4), along the *brook* to the Mediterranean Sea. The exact location of *Tamar* is unknown, but many agree that it is southwest of the Dead Sea.

---

[194] Dyer, 1315.

Verse 47:20

Ezekiel finishes his description of the boundaries by looking at the western border. This begins at the *southern boundary* and runs north along the *Great Sea* until one reaches the *point opposite Hamath.*

Verses 47:21–23

These verses serve as a prelude to chapter 48 in that, now that the boundaries have been set and delineated, the land is to be divided. What is interesting in this distribution of land is that the stranger will not be forgotten. Leviticus 19:33–34 states: *And if a stranger dwell with you in your land, you shall not mistreat him. The stranger who dwells among you shall be to you as one born among you, and you shall love him as yourself; for you were strangers in the land of Egypt: I am the LORD your God.* This law will not be forgotten when the land is distributed. God's mercy will be evident even now, for they will be considered native born.

APPLICATION

These final verses of chapter 47 should bring great joy to the Gentiles. Many have asked, "But what about the Gentiles during the Millennial Kingdom?" It is here that we find the answer to that question. Gentiles should consider themselves the strangers; for believing Gentiles, God will not forget but give them an inheritance of this land as well. Although the Millennial Age will be a time dedicated to the Jew, it will be a time when the Gentile will be blessed as well.

Study Questions
1. Have you ever broken a promise?
2. Have you ever felt that God has abandoned you and broken His promises?

Verses 48:1–7
As of the last chapter of the book of Ezekiel, Israel has come full circle: from Genesis 12, when God first called Abraham and promised him a land flowing with milk and honey; to now, when Israel in the Millennial Kingdom is having that same land divided out among them (more specifically, among the twelve tribes). Once again, it is hard to spiritualize this text or interpret it as merely symbolic, because the twelve specific tribes are mentioned.

To understand this distribution of land, it would be best to view the land as upper, middle, and lower sections. Verses 1–7 give details of the upper (northern) section, which will be divided among seven tribes. *Dan* will be in the far north, along the *border of Damascus*. Continuing south, bordering *Dan* will be *Asher;* bordering *Asher* will be *Naphtali;* bordering *Naphtali* will be *Manasseh;* bordering *Manasseh* will be *Ephraim;* bordering *Ephraim* will be *Reuben;* and bordering *Reuben* will be *Judah*.

Verses 48:8–12
The middle section is described as an area *set apart unto the Lord;* the measurements given are *twenty-five thousand cubits* square (approximately eight and one-third miles square) (compare Ezekiel 45:1–8). It begins at the southern border of Judah's allotment and continues south to the northern border of Benjamin's allotment. These two tribes will have the distinct

privilege of bordering the holy district because they were the ones who remained faithful to the Davidic throne. This section or district is referred to by the New King James version as *a district of land* but according to Schmitt and Laney, the Hebrew word used literally means "a contribution or an offering."[195] Perhaps the King James Version more correctly captures the meaning of this word in translating it as *offering.*

Of this middle section, *the priests* shall have a district *twenty-five thousand cubits* (eight and one-third miles) long by *ten thousand cubits* (three and one-third miles) wide. It is within this section that the *sanctuary* will be placed, in the middle. Again, we are told that *the priests* who are descendants of *Zadok* (compare Ezekiel 40:46) will be set apart to officiate because *they did not go astray, as the Levites went astray.*

Verses 48:13–14
Opposite the border of these priests will be the land of the *Levites*. They will be given an area equal to that of Zadokites. The Levites are not permitted *to sell or exchange* any part of this land because it will be deemed holy by the Lord.

Verse 48:15–20
Another section to the south of the holy district, a width of *five thousand cubits* (one and two-thirds miles) is to be designated for general use, that is, *dwellings and common land,* and *the city* (Jerusalem) is to be placed *in the center.* The measurement of the city will be *four thousand five hundred cubits* (one and one-half miles) on each side. The city will be surrounded by common land measuring *two hundred and fifty cubits* (437½ feet) on each

---

[195] Schmitt and Laney, 126.

side. The remaining land—that which borders the holy district and measures *ten thousand cubits* (three and one-third miles) to the west and east—will be used for farmland to supply *food for the workers and the city*.

Verses 48:21–22

The outer areas, which are adjacent to the tribal portions and extend to the east and to the west, shall be set apart for *the prince*. This section is located on either side of the priest's section. The western section belonging to *the prince* will extend west to the Mediterranean Sea and the eastern section will extend to the far eastern border. According to Feinberg, this section for the prince is strategically positioned in order to administer governmental affairs committed to him by the ruling king.[196]

Verses 48:23–29

These verses set out the land allotment for the remaining tribes. First, continuing south of the holy district, we find *Benjamin*. Bordering *Benjamin* is *Simeon;* bordering *Simeon* will be *Issachar;* bordering *Issachar* will be *Zebulun;* and finally, bordering *Zebulun* will be *Gad*. For the sake of clarity, it should be noted that the tribe of Levi was not to inherit any land, as they were to serve and live on the land allotted to them in the holy district. As for Joseph, his allotment was divided between his two sons, Ephraim and Manasseh.

APPLICATION

What organization! What uniformity! Our God is a God of order. This allocation will make for a great arrangement so that the

---

[196] Feinberg, 278.

Millennial Kingdom will have order instead of chaos and the administration of the kingdom will be uniform and just. It is easy to understand how the Tribulation saints, just before the administration of the bowl judgments, can sing the song of Moses: *Great and marvelous are Your works, Lord God Almighty! Just and true are Your ways, O King of the saints! Who shall not fear You, O Lord, and glorify Your name? For You alone are holy. For all nations shall come and worship before You, For Your judgments have been manifested* (Revelation 15:3–4).

Study Questions
1. Can you name other passages in the Bible which demonstrate that God is a God of order?
2. Read 1 Corinthians 14:33. With reference to spiritual gifts, how does this passage demonstrate the truth that God is a God of order?

Verses 48:30–35
The last vision that Ezekiel is privileged to see is the description of the *gates*. These *gates* are referred to as *exits*; there are three on each side, twelve in all. Ezekiel is told that the *gates* shall bear the name of each tribe.

The three gates on the north side will be called *Reuben, Judah,* and *Levi*. The three gates on the east side will be called *Joseph, Benjamin,* and *Dan*. The three gates on the south side will be called *Simeon, Issachar,* and *Zebulun*. Finally, the three gates on the west side will be called *Gad, Asher,* and *Naphtali*. Some scholars conclude that because Levi was given a gate,

Ephraim and Manasseh were combined under the name *Joseph*.[197]

APPLICATION

The book of Ezekiel ends by renaming the city of Jerusalem. Its new name will be *THE LORD IS THERE* (48:35). Thus, this great book ends with God dwelling among His people. We have seen in this study that the glory departs the temple (compare Ezekiel 8–11), but finally His glory will return and will dwell in the temple, in the very center of the nation of Israel. With this conclusion, God has fulfilled all His promises to His people and we can agree with the apostle Paul that our God cannot lie (compare Titus 1:2).

"With this final note, all of the unconditional promises which God has made to Israel in the Abrahamic Covenant, compare Genesis 12; the Priestly Covenant, compare Numbers 25; the Davidic Covenant, compare 2 Samuel 7; and the New Covenant, compare Jeremiah 31, have been fulfilled. So, this final verse provides the consummation of Israel's history—the returned presence of God!"[198]

Study Questions
1. Define the contents and meaning of each of the covenants listed above.
2. List all the covenants found in the Bible and distinguish which ones were conditional and which ones were unconditional.

---

[197] Dyer, 1316.
[198] MacArthur, 1224.

Bibliography

Allen, Leslie C. "Ezekiel 20–48." In *Word Biblical Commentary*, David Hubbard and Glenn Barker, general eds., vol. 29. Waco, TX: Word Books, 1990.

Biblesoft's New Exhaustive Strong's Numbers and Concordance with Expanded Greek-Hebrew Dictionary. Biblesoft, Inc. and International Bible Translators, Inc., 1994, 2003.

Block, Daniel I. *The Book of Ezekiel, Chapters 1–24.* Grand Rapids, MI: Eerdmans, 1994.

Brownlee, William H. "Ezekiel 1–19." In *Word Biblical Commentary*, David Hubbard and Glenn Barker, general eds. Waco, TX: Word Books, 1986.

Dyer, Charles H. "Ezekiel." In *The Bible Knowledge Commentary*, John Walvoord and Roy B. Zuck, general eds. Wheaton: Victor Books, 1986.

Feinberg, Charles Lee. *The Prophecy of Ezekiel, The Glory of the Lord.* Chicago: Moody Press, 1969.

Gingrich, Roy. *The Book of Ezekiel.* Memphis, TN: Riverside Printing, 2005.

International Standard Bible Encyclopedia Electronic Database. Biblesoft, 1996.

Ironside, H. A. *Ezekiel the Prophet.* Neptune, NJ: Loizeaux Brothers, 1949.

Keil and Delitzsch Commentary on the Old Testament. New updated edition [electronic database]. Peabody, MA: Hendrickson Publishers, 1996. http://www.biblesoft.com.

MacArthur, John. *The MacArthur Study Bible.* Nashville, TN: Word Bibles, 1997.

Matheny, James F. *Is There a Russian Connection?* Enid, OK: Jay & Associates, 1987.

McGee, J. Vernon. *Ezekiel* (Thru the Bible Commentary Series). Nashville, TN: Thomas Nelson, 1991.

Nelson's Illustrated Bible Dictionary. Nashville, TN: Thomas Nelson, 1986.

Pentecost, J. Dwight. *Things to Come.* Grand Rapids, MI: Zondervan, 1964.

Rooker, Mark. Ezekiel. In *Holman Old Testament Commentary,* Max Anders, general ed. Nashville, TN: Broadman & Holman, 2005.

Ryrie, Charles C. *The Basis of the Premillennial Faith.* Neptune, NJ: Loizeaux Brothers, 1953.

Schmitt, John, and Charles Laney. *Messiah's Coming Temple.* Grand Rapids, MI: Kregel, 1997.

Showers, Renald E. *There Really Is a Difference!* Bellmawr, N.J.: The Friends of Israel Gospel Ministry, 1990.

Strong, James. *Strong's Exhaustive Concordance.* Nashville, TN: Crusade Bible Publishers.

Thiessen, Henry Clarence. *Lectures in Systematic Theology.* Grand Rapids, MI: Eerdmans, 1979.

Thomas, Derek. *God Strengthens.* Darlington, England: Evangelical Press, 1993.

Unger's New Bible Dictionary. Originally published by Moody Press of Chicago, IL, 1988.

Vine's Expository Dictionary of Biblical Words. Nashville, TN: Thomas Nelson, 1985.

Walvoord, John F. *Prophecy: 14 Essential Keys to Understanding the Final Drama.* Nashville, TN: Thomas Nelson, 1993.

www.ingramcontent.com/pod-product-compliance
Lightning Source LLC
Chambersburg PA
CBHW070606170426
43200CB00012B/2599